JUNGLE JACK

JUNGLE JACK
My Wild Life

JACK HANNA

with AMY PARKER

Thomas Nelson
Since 1798

NASHVILLE   DALLAS   MEXICO CITY   RIO DE JANEIRO   BEIJING

Published in Nashville, Tennessee, by Thomas Nelson. Thomas Nelson is a registered trademark of Thomas Nelson, Inc.

Managing Editor: Heather Skelton
Page Design: Mandi Cofer

Thomas Nelson, Inc., titles may be purchased in bulk for educational, business, fundraising, or sales promotional use. For information, please e-mail SpecialMarkets@ThomasNelson.com.

Cataloging-in-Publication Data is on file with the Library of Congress.

Printed in the United States of America

08 09 10 11 QW 6 5 4 3 2 1

To some amazing women who have known no boundaries
in their lifelong contributions to the animal world:

In honor of Betty White,
a longtime friend with unbelievable character and generosity.
If everyone in the world were like Betty White,
no animal—domestic or wild—would endure needless suffering.

In memory of Claire Wilson,
a dear friend taken far too soon from her family, friends,
and four-legged buddies left here on earth.
Her infectious love for the outdoors and all that inhabit it has forever changed
the landscape of the animal world in Montana and beyond.

With infinite gratitude to Suzi Hanna,
my wife and partner in this endeavor to make a small dent
in the lives of animals and people around the world.
And to my three wonderful daughters, Kathaleen, Suzanne, and Julie.
Without all of you, this book, these adventures, and Jack Hanna would not exist.

Contents

CONTENTS

There Is No Zoo

Crazy things just seem to happen when I'm around. Sometimes I ask for it; sometimes I'm an innocent bystander. Sometimes it's funny, and sometimes it's not—at least not while it's happening. For instance, in 1978, at the age of thirty-one, I was flying into Columbus, Ohio, for an interview for the position of director at what I understood to be the local zoo. And before I even landed, there was an air traffic controller trying to tell me that Columbus did not have a zoo.

I didn't even have enough money back then to buy an airplane ticket, so I had asked my good friend Stan Brock, costar of TV's *Wild Kingdom,* to fly me up from Knoxville for the zoo interview—I'd pay for the gas. Stan is a hardy Englishman, an adventurer who will fly anywhere. Only a year earlier, we had flown two jaguars down to the Amazon for release into the wild—but more on that later.

So here we were, zipping over central Ohio on a perfect, clear spring day. Inside my new sport coat, I had my little letter from the trustees, my future employers. I learned later that they weren't sure I even owned a coat and tie. They knew I was from Tennessee, so they probably thought I didn't own shoes or socks either. From pictures, all they had ever seen me in were safari clothes, which are—to this day—about all I ever wear.

Forty miles from Columbus, Stan asked if I'd like to see the zoo from the air. I said that would be neat. He called the tower and said something British like, "I say, chap, could we vector over and have a look at your zoo from the air?"

The voice from the tower returned and requested a "repeat." Stan explained that he had a passenger visiting the zoo who wanted to see it from above. This time the controller came back saying he had no idea what Stan was talking about, that Columbus didn't have a zoo.

Stan looked over at me and said, "Jack, old boy, what have you done this time?" We'd done some pretty crazy things over the past few years. "Is this Columbus, Ohio, you want, or perhaps Columbus, Georgia?"

I said, "Stan, it's Columbus, Ohio—here, look at the stationery."

He told the controller that we had a letterhead that said Columbus Zoo, Riverside Drive, Columbus, Ohio. I yelled into the receiver that I knew it was north of downtown. About five minutes later, the controller was back: "Yes, we understand there is a zoo—up on the river. Just follow the river north of town."

We followed the river—luckily the right one, because there were two—and spotted the big dam, which was our landmark. I saw the zoo, and I thought, *It's gorgeous*, and it was, from the air. It was bigger than anything I'd ever worked with; the buildings looked neatly laid out, surrounded everywhere by trees and woods; and there was all that water—very few zoos are on water.

We circled it a few times, then headed back to the airport. I kept looking back at the zoo until I couldn't see it anymore. Did the place really need a new director? Was this the promised land?

After we landed and parked the plane, I went out to the front of the airport to get us a cab. We climbed into the back—I was still riding high from seeing the zoo—and the cabbie asked us where we wanted to go.

"Columbus Zoo!" I sang out.

The cabbie turned around with one of those don't-mess-with-me expressions, and for the second time in an hour, I was told Columbus didn't have a zoo. He wasn't very polite, and I really didn't know what to do. I wasn't particularly thrilled with the lack of community interest going on around here, but at least *I* knew that there was a zoo, and we were darn well going to get there.

I shoved my letter at him over the front seat. He looked at it, unimpressed, and pointed out that the address was way to the north, which I knew already, and that he'd have to radio for a price on the fare. Now I'm thinking, *Uh-oh, big bucks.* Stan just smiled and shook his head.

After over twenty miles of weaving our way up there, I finally saw first-hand that Columbus did indeed have a zoo . . . well, sort of. I hadn't really had an idea of what the place would look like, and I didn't expect a grand physical plant along the lines of the Bronx or San Diego zoos, but I certainly didn't expect what I saw either—especially not after the bird's-eye view.

The entrance, with its chain-link fence, looked like something from an old mental institution or prison. In front, there was a big mud hole—it was supposed to be a lake someday. And up close, the buildings looked pretty run-down, though I could tell right away that all they really needed was some fresh paint and a little stucco here and there.

What really struck me, especially on such a beautiful, sunny day, was that this zoo wasn't very crowded, to say the least. I also noticed right then that there wasn't much warmth around the employees, neither among themselves nor toward the visitors. The animals that I saw seemed to be in sound, healthy shape, even if their environments were pretty substandard. Aside from the pachyderm area, which had just been completed, there were no natural habitats. Most of the animals were still contained by bars and fences.

Probably the biggest problem here was that the zoo was in the process of being booted out of the AAZPA (American Association of Zoological Parks and Aquariums). That's like a college team getting kicked out of the NCAA. You can still play, but who will take you seriously?

In spite of it all, something about the place quickly swung my mood back up. Standing there looking at this 142 acres in partial disrepair, I had no idea, really, what the future would bring. I didn't even know if I'd get hired. But with all this land, all this space, there was so much potential everywhere—so much to work with. I knew immediately what the zoo needed and how I could fit in. I wanted to put this place on the map. I wanted every cabbie and air traffic controller in the state of Ohio to know about the Columbus Zoo—and how to get there. Still, at that moment, there was no way you could've convinced me that I would one day be traveling the world taping my own television series, meeting world leaders, sitting at a desk across from David Letterman, or, most of all, that I was standing on the grounds of a zoo that would become one of the largest, most innovative, history-making zoos in the United States.

"We had sixty-four applications and narrowed them down to five interviews. Jack stood out far and above the other candidates."

—BLAINE SICKLES, FORMER PRESIDENT OF THE ZOO BOARD
AND MEMBER OF ZOO DIRECTOR SEARCH COMMITTEE

But all of this and so much more would come with the job. I did know a few things about promotions and public relations, about community needs, about animals. I also knew that, for most of my life, animals and my love for them had carried me through.

CHAPTER 1

Down on the Farm

Bu-Ja-Su, the farm in Tennessee where my family moved when I was five years old, was the kind of place every kid dreams about—streams, woods, horses, everything. My father bought the land after having a successful career in real estate, and he named it after my brother and sister, Bush and Sue, and me. It was so rural and isolated out there that it made the Knoxville subdivision we'd just come from seem like the inner city. It was here that I first became fascinated by little furry creatures.

We rode our horses up and down Ebenezer Road, a hilly rural route where we were the only inhabitants other than the chickens, goats, rabbits, pigs—you name it. Today it's a major highway. Bu-Ja-Su wasn't a working farm, but it sure was an animal farm—at least it grew to be one after I got going.

Our farm in Knoxville, Tennessee, called Bu-Ja-Su, was where I spent my childhood days, playing in the creek and discovering the abundant surrounding wildlife. (Jack Hanna)

One of the first things I remember from Bu-Ja-Su was hand-milking a cow. There was an old mill up the road, one of the last of the old grain-grinding mills, run by a Swede named Ott Andersen. Ott had seven cows, and he taught me how to milk them, a technique

My older brother, Bush, age four, and me, age one. (Jack Hanna)

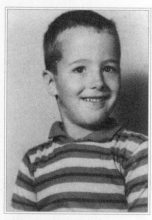

A few years later in elementary school. (Jack Hanna)

that would come in handy about thirty years later, when I'd demonstrate it by squirting David Letterman from a goat's udder on national TV.

Bush and I named those cows, and I loved them all—Kismo, Babyface, and especially Streetwalker. We called her Streetwalker because she was always busting out and walking down the road. Today, zoo directors take clear-cut positions on whether or not to name their animals—it falls under anthropomorphization, a long word and a sensitive subject in the zoo world that, simply put, means humanizing nonhumans. But kids will always want to name animals, and in that respect, I guess I'm still a kid. Besides, didn't God tell Adam, the first man ever created, to name all the animals? I believe naming animals is just a tendency long-ingrained in human nature.

Every afternoon I would go to Ott's and watch his mother make cottage cheese in little sacks out on the front porch. As for Ott, we could smell his moonshine still up in the woods, but we were smart enough to keep quiet about it. Ott sold his booze to the local farmers, but my dad wouldn't drink the stuff. He preferred the Kentucky bourbon that was brought in at night once a month. It was just like in the movies—so much so, in fact, that they filmed a movie about moonshine, *Thunder Road*, right in front of our farm on Kingston Pike.

My first two pets were a couple of collies that were right out of Lassie. Lance and Vandy were big, beautiful outdoor dogs who went everywhere with me. One day I went along with my dad to take the dogs to the vet in

Knoxville. I'll never forget that day, because it was then that I met one of the most influential people in my life, Dr. Warren Roberts.

I was fascinated by every aspect of Dr. Roberts's work. I couldn't wait for his visits to the farm to treat our horses. Knowing also that he was the veterinarian for the Knoxville Zoo made him seem as big-time to me as Mickey Mantle was to other kids.

At first I'd just go up there and hang around the Knoxville Animal Clinic and watch Dr. Roberts at work. I was probably more of a nuisance than anything else. Then one day, sometime during the summer when I was eleven, my dad went to Dr. Roberts and told him that I'd like to work for him. As a favor to my father, the vet said, "Okay, let's see how he likes it."

That first summer was for no pay, but that didn't bother me a bit. Dr. Roberts started me right off with cleaning cages. I'm talking crap—cleaning, scraping, and hosing the cages of over forty dogs and cats. Maybe I'm crazy, but I didn't mind it at all. Doing that kind of work, you really get to know if you like animals. If you can somehow enjoy cleaning out their cages, then you know you genuinely love animals.

As I progressed, Dr. Roberts let me do more and more. He let me stand in on a dog spaying. He was impressed with the fact that I wasn't too squeamish and didn't complain about cleaning poop. Soon I was riding along in his station wagon to all the farms and was feeling pretty important. One day up at a farm, Dr. Roberts handed me some rubber gloves, then told me to put them on and "reach up into that cow and hook those chains around the calf's legs." I quickly learned not to eat my lunch before we went pulling calves, but there was no greater feeling than that of helping a creature come into the world.

I didn't earn a dime that whole summer, but work is work. My dad never questioned the nights I would come back from Dr. Roberts's office at ten o'clock. There was no lunch hour; I would take ten or fifteen minutes to inhale the sandwich my mother had made me, then go back to working my little butt off. I'd polish doorknobs if there was nothing else to do.

The next summer I asked if I could come back, and Dr. Roberts said that was fine. I was paid something like ten dollars every two weeks. If I couldn't find a ride, I'd take a bus or hitchhike the seventeen miles. I never missed a day of work.

Gradually, Dr. Roberts was giving me more and more responsibility. By the time I was thirteen, I was opening the business for him every day, cleaning, feeding, and watering the animals before he got there. While doing this, I learned the value of taking care of animals. Like children, they need to be watched twenty-four hours a day, at least when they're at the vet's, or as I would later find out, when they're at the zoo or in your hotel room. I took pride in that responsibility, especially when Dr. Roberts would ask for my opinion, like, "Jack, how do you think the Smiths' dog we operated on last week is doing?"

Probably one of the reasons Dr. Roberts liked having me around, in addition to the help, was that I kept him laughing. I always saw potential for humor in animals. I loved them, and I was always telling stories about them—some of them I just made up.

The most thrilling days of all with Dr. Roberts were our visits to the Knoxville Zoo. That wasn't until my second and third summers there, and it opened up a whole new world to me. Sometimes we dropped by the zoo just for my benefit, even if there weren't any appointments for Dr. Roberts.

The star attraction of the Knoxville Zoo was Ol' Diamond, the largest African bull elephant in captivity. I was totally in awe of this animal—to me he looked like some sort of prehistoric monster. He had come to the zoo from Ringling Brothers, who had given him up when he became uncontrollable. Since then, he had injured many keepers by using his trunk as a battering ram. Everyone was afraid of him.

One visit I'll never forget was when Ol' Diamond needed treatment for a broken tusk. In the center of his corral made from railroad irons was a huge old oak stump on which the elephant would spend hours sharpening his tusks. One day Diamond got one caught in a crevice and couldn't pull it loose. He did manage to break it off, but it eventually became infected and needed treatment.

Treating male elephants is difficult because they're so aggressive, and it's even more so when they're ailing. Dr. Roberts tried to get closer to have a look—outside the bars, of course—and Ol' Diamond let him have it with a spray of spit blown through his trunk. From a safe distance, Dr. Roberts decided to hit him back with some antibiotic spray out of a three-gallon container. That tusk infection cleared up, but Diamond would eventually die many years later from a foot infection that could not be properly treated without risk to life and limb. Today, in the zoo world, if an elephant were to develop a foot infection, it would be relatively easy to treat, thanks to improvements in veterinary care.

That incident, among others, opened my eyes to the care and caution required to deal with wild animals, especially those—such as elephants—that are intelligent and can be friendly, but are also powerful and potentially dangerous. I didn't know it at the time, but on a larger scale, working with Dr. Roberts was laying the groundwork for some sort of animal-related career.

All the time that I was working at Dr. Roberts's, I was also building up my little menagerie out at Bu-Ja-Su. With my brother, Bush, and my sister, Sue, we had pigs, goats, horses, rabbits, birds—just about anything we could handle that moved. I even had a big pet groundhog that we stuffed when he died. I'd go down to the creek and catch huge fish, then put them in the little ponds we had. Sometimes I kept them in the toilet bowl temporarily before transferring them. Of course, my mother wasn't thrilled about that.

Looking back now, I realize how very important those first experiences with animals were for me as a kid. I'm very much a proponent of children having pets because of all of the invaluable life lessons to be learned through the course of caring for an animal. Constant care, unconditional love, and the inevitable loss of our animal friends are all gentle introductions to those parallel experiences we'll have with humans.

Fortunately, my parents were usually quite tolerant of all my animal whims. My father had grown up in rural, backwoods Arkansas, so he understood. My mother, being from a good northern, city family in St. Paul, Minnesota, just shook her head most of the time. But with my rabbit collection, I pushed them both too far. It started out innocently enough with three females and two males, but, well, rabbits will be rabbits. I was fascinated with the little fur balls and was intent on seeing them multiply as quickly as possible. I built forty rabbit hutches with runs and back doors, a whole intricate setup. I cleaned up after them all the time and loved it. My dad kept after me to give some away to friends or pet shops . . . or to his friends, who would eat them, but I wouldn't go for that.

Finally, when my rabbit family grew to over a hundred, he'd had enough. One day he told me he was going to have Lloyd, a man who worked on the farm, "dispose" of them. Well, no way was I going to let Lloyd kill my rabbits. So that night I went out and let every last one of my friends loose. Boy, was my dad hot the next morning when he learned of the great rabbit exodus. And for three or four years after that, you would see little white-and-brown rabbits crossing Ebenezer Road.

When I was fourteen, I received the Christmas gift I'd wanted for over a year: two miniature donkeys. They were about the size of large sheepdogs. I had been crazy about these things ever since I had read about them in some magazine, and I had been lobbying hard for them. They were beautiful, from Sicily, with a little donkey cart and brand-new harnesses. It was the best Christmas present I had ever gotten.

Those donkeys bred, and of course, before long, I was collecting them

When I was fourteen, I received the best Christmas gift ever: these two Sicilian donkeys with a cart. (Jack Hanna)

too. I bought two more, and all of a sudden I saw myself in the donkey business. It wasn't quite what my parents had in mind.

As for school, it would have been nice to say that my grades were so bad because I never spent enough time with my homework, but the truth was, I did work hard. I just wasn't very gifted when it came to books and studying. When I was fifteen, my grades weren't improving so my father decided to send me away to Kiski, a boarding school in Saltsburg, Pennsylvania. Of course, Kiski had to let me in first.

I was leaving Webb, a private day school that didn't want me back. And I was headed to Kiski, a school not too excited about getting me. In fact, the admissions office had already decided not to take me. "He just doesn't have it," they had said. Still, my father took me to meet Mr. Jack Pidgeon, the Kiski headmaster.

I gave it my best shot: "Mr. Pidgeon, I've gotta go to your school. I've gotta go to your school." I assured him I could make it. Even though I was just a teenage boy up against a tough football coach and headmaster, I was relentless. Something I said must have worked, because in the end, he decided that if any boy wanted to go to Kiski as badly as I did, they had to let him in. I am eternally grateful for Mr. Pidgeon's decision, because he has been one of the most influential role models in my life. There is no way to put a price on what he taught me.

"If you really love something, and if you're going to pursue it,
pursue it with your whole heart and soul, and you'll get there.
That's what Jack taught me."

—JACK PIDGEON, FORMER KISKI HEADMASTER

Of course, I could not leave the meeting without asking Mr. Pidgeon if I could bring my donkeys to school too. My father about went through the

The values instilled by Mr. Pidgeon, the headmaster at Kiski, have remained with me throughout my entire life. (OLMA Photography)

ceiling. Luckily, Mr. Pidgeon thought it was kind of funny. He told us that I could come, but that the donkeys would have to stay at home.

While at Kiski, I missed my wildlife, though I did try to work animals into school life in one way or another. I started a pig-greasing contest that turned into a big fundraiser. People seemed to be happy to donate in order to watch the participants running and falling in mud and pig muck trying to catch the slippery little guy. We were the Kiski Cougars, so I had also begun the process of obtaining a cougar for a mascot. But when I found out they weren't going to let us keep it, I dropped that. I continued to have trouble with my studies, but I worked harder than ever. Fortunately, they had "effort" grades, and I did receive the proverbial "*A*'s for effort."

One subject I did find to my liking was speech, and it's probably the most important subject I ever had. I've given thousands of speeches over the years, but I'll never forget my first speech back at Webb. The subject was—surprise—rabbits, and I brought five or six of them with me as props. That's one thing I learned back then, and I've stuck to it ever since: always bring an animal along to any speaking appearance.

Anyway, here I was in front of the whole student body, two hundred boys, and I was showing them how to hold a rabbit. I picked up the rabbit behind the neck, and it peed and crapped all over my arm, just like what happens on TV these days. Even though I was embarrassed at first, I quickly caught on to the value of a few laughs while speaking in public. I guess that's where it all started.

After graduating from Kiski, I was somehow admitted to Muskingum, a small liberal arts college in New Concord, Ohio. I say "somehow" because my

SAT scores were terrible. I talked my way into that school too, and I knew enough this time *not* to ask if I could bring along a donkey. I just brought it without asking. The donkey stayed behind the fraternity house until the authorities found out. Then I had to move it to a farm outside of town—which cost me thirty dollars

Suzi and Doc the donkey at the homecoming parade in New Concord, Ohio, where Muskingum College is located. (Jack Hanna)

a month. The donkey eventually became the school mascot and helped me meet the girl of my life, Suzi Egli.

Across the row from me in French class sat this pretty girl I always wanted to talk to. One day she had missed a button on her blouse, and being well-endowed, this caught the attention of some football players, who started laughing at her. I wouldn't have minded looking myself, but the laughter bothered me. So I leaned over and told her that her "stomach" was showing.

With my clumsy Coke-bottle glasses, baggy pants, and white socks, I wasn't much of a ladies' man. But Suzi, the cutest girl in French class and captain of the cheerleading squad, somehow thought I was funny, and when she heard about my donkey, she knew I was a real character. I kept her going with my stories about my donkeys, and we became fast friends. Later that year we danced once, and it just took off from there.

"The reason why I fell in love with Jack was because he is a genuine guy with a big heart. Of course the southern accent was charming with his marvelous nonsensical humor. For better or worse, he has always been my best friend."

—Suzi Egli Hanna, Wife

Suzi and I had connected from the beginning. She somehow understood—and maybe even appreciated—all the animal craziness and has
supported me through it from day one. The first year after we met, she took
me to Long Island to go fishing for flounder with her father, who was a minister and school principal from Wayne, New Jersey. On the way back, we
stopped at a Long Island duck farm. I looked out over all those cute little
penned-in ducks and asked Mr. Egli, "These are pet ducks, right?"

"No," he said, "these ducks are to eat."

I decided right then that three of them were going to be pets. I picked
out three choice little ones, bought them, and told Suzi and her father that I
was taking them back to Muskingum. Suzi's mom, Dorothy, thought this was
a great idea because of the fond memories she had of her pet ducks.

"You're not really going to take those back to college, are you?" Mr. Egli
asked me.

"Oh yes, he is," giggled Suzi. We named them Aquaduck, Viaduck, and
Ovaduck, and I took care of them all through college, starting out in my
dorm room. When Suzi and I became engaged our junior year, we left those
ducks in the college lake, where they enjoyed swimming for years to come.

Much to the dismay of our parents, who thought it was too soon, we got
married during senior year, which was one of the best decisions of my life.
On December 20, 1968, Suzi and I exchanged vows and danced to "Born
Free." Little did we know that song represented so much of what the future
held in store for us. Even our honeymoon was spent at Lion Country Safari
and Busch Gardens in Florida.

To our surprise, on our honeymoon Suzi became pregnant with our first
daughter, Kathaleen, who was born nine months and nine days later. As a
physical education major, Suzi was five months pregnant in a leotard, doing
her gymnastics routine for her final exam. During her last semester at college,
I brought home a baby goat as an Easter present. When I gave it to her, I
excitedly explained, "I'm bringing you a 'kid' to practice on." Lucky for me,
Suzi enjoyed my wacky sense of humor and adored this baby goat.

Just before our marriage in December, Dr. Bill Miller, president of

Suzi and I were married on December 20, 1968, at Brown Chapel on the
Muskingum College campus. (Jack Hanna)

Muskingum, called me into his office. I was scheduled to graduate a semester
early, the week before our wedding. When I entered his office, Dr. Miller was
looking over a form on career choices that I'd filled out months earlier. "It
says here that you want to be a zookeeper," he said, looking at me with his
head askew.

"That's right, sir."

"I didn't know anybody ever wanted to be a zookeeper. This college is
almost a hundred and fifty years old. I've been here thirty-seven years, and as
far as I can recall, no one's ever put down 'zookeeper.' You're sure about this?"

"Positive."

"Well, good luck with it."

I had no idea then how much I would need it.

CHAPTER 2

Hanna's Ark—A Growing Menagerie

After finishing college, Suzi and I moved back to Knoxville, where I began to collect a variety of exotic animals. Maybe I was making up for lost time, but I had always known that, once I was old enough, I could and would have all the pets or wild critters I wanted. I went full steam ahead with this idea, and it just about ruined us.

My father gave us a cottage on the farm to live in for several months, and the area was perfect for my grandiose plans. Suzi was always a great sport about it; in fact, her enthusiasm often matched mine. Some people spend money on clothes, jewelry, cars, what have you; our thing was animals—even if we didn't have the money. Ever heard of buying an elephant on credit?

Like so many newlyweds just out of college, we had a rough first year. A number of odd jobs and small-time business ventures just never worked out. If they didn't involve animals, my heart just wasn't in it.

During those very hot and humid August days, Suzi—who was eight months pregnant with Kathaleen—and I bounced around in a truck with no air-conditioning, delivering tons of soap samples door to door. After Suzi was attacked by a large dog, it was time to move on to a new job.

Next I bought a chainsaw and put an ad in the paper selling firewood. The first tree I cut down fell through somebody's greenhouse and caused two thousand dollars worth of damage. I tried to mow yards but ran over a man's vegetable garden and overturned my dad's shiny red tractor. I invested in an all-terrain-vehicle scheme in which I had to buy the first one, a demo model. I could not earn a dime until I sold one, which I never did. During a demonstration next to a shopping mall, I proved that it wasn't actually suited for all terrains when it overturned on a hill, resulting in a broken arm and a mess of stitches to my passenger. After being fortunate enough not to get sued, I quit that business while I was ahead.

At one point that year, I planned to turn Bu-Ja-Su into a zoo. An architect drew up the blueprints, and I even had a name: West Knoxville Zoo. In the beginning, I would just add animals I could afford; later I would expand. That was the plan, anyway. My father was terrifically supportive. He even pleaded my case before the county commissioners, but zoning was denied. I still think it was a good idea. It could have been a great place for both people and animals.

Meanwhile, our zoo at home included lions, llamas, deer, elk, a bear, a South American spotted leopard cat, an ocelot, chimpanzees, a spider monkey, a mynah bird, macaws, parrots, goats, a horse and pony, dogs, a cat, and other assorted critters. Some were in the house, and some were outside in the yard. It seems like I was always building new pens and enclosures, putting up more fencing. It was helter-skelter, but it was a lot of fun.

Most of my animals were purchased fairly cheaply through mail-order catalogues—a fairly common practice then, but something you would never do today. In the 1960s, you could order and have delivered to your home almost any kind of animal, no matter how endangered or dangerous. You could buy pet raccoons, possibly carrying rabies, for thirty-five dollars; ocelots, which today are endangered, for ninety-five dollars; bears; mountain lions; timber wolves; deadly copperheads; and water moccasin snakes. How about a golden eagle for seventy-five dollars? Most zoos today would have difficulty even finding a golden eagle to put on exhibit. No questions were ever asked; it was a cash business. And at the time, I had my mind set, and I knew they were coming to a good home, so I never thought twice about it. Fortunately, most of the animals available back then are protected today.

My main animal dealer was a man named Bill Chase down in Miami, who obtained his animals from the wild or from breeders. He was an old-timer who sold to zoos and pet shops, as well as to private individuals. I learned a lot about animals from him. There were very few regulations then, but he always went to great lengths to ensure that his animals were in good health. Today there are international laws that regulate the trade of exotic animals, but back then all a dealer needed was to place an order and wait.

The first animal I ever ordered from Chase was an African pygmy goat. I had hoped to start breeding them and earn some much-needed income from the investment. I drove out to the Knoxville airport to pick it up with Suzi, and we brought the crate back home to open in front of my father. When he saw it, he was less excited than we were. He asked me what I paid for it. "Well, the airfare was three hundred dollars," I told him, "but the goat only cost seventy-five."

"What?" my dad exploded. "You paid three hundred seventy-five dollars for a damn goat?" He couldn't believe it.

"Yeah, but this is a pygmy goat from Africa," I explained. "I'm going to make a lot of money with this goat."

"Looks like a regular goat to me," he said, and just walked away. And, of course, I never made a penny with that goat.

Appropriately enough, my string of odd jobs ended with a six-week stint in a brand-new pet shop. The owner was a Mr. Rasmussen, a nice German man, who had absolutely no business sense at all. Mine wasn't much better, but I did help him start up his business in time for Christmas 1970. At the same time, I learned everything I could about pet shops: where to order the dogs, cats, fish, who all the wholesalers were, where to get all the paraphernalia. One

Kathaleen with our donkey that soaked up all of the attention he got in our petting zoo at Pet Kingdom. (Jack Hanna)

day I came home and told Suzi I was going to borrow some money and open up my own pet store.

The timing of this venture, Pet Kingdom, worked out perfectly, since my brother was in the process of buying an old motel and had some space to spare. I never could have done it without my father and my brother. It was one of those great, inspired efforts: "Hey, let's build a pet store." And we did.

I'll never forget the excitement of opening day. We had about forty fish tanks, loads of boarding kennels for dogs and cats, and, of course, some exotic animals, which were not for sale. Everything was meticulously clean; all the animals were healthy. I even had a little petting zoo out back with baby llamas, miniature donkeys, goats, ducks, and other furry creatures.

One terrifying moment with Pet Kingdom started with a phone call in the middle of a wintry night while we were living on my parents' farm. "Your store's on fire!" a voice said from the other end of the line. Half-asleep, I threw on my glasses and jumped into Suzi's VW bug, a graduation present. The store was about twelve miles away, and, man, I was flying down those snow-covered roads. All of a sudden, I was spinning, and in the next split second, the car was wrapped around a tree. Amazingly, I wasn't hurt, but now I had just totaled our car, and my pet store was still burning.

When I finally got there, the scene was almost comical. There were parrots in the cab of the fire engine, talking to each other, nibbling on the seats of the fire truck. There were puppies, hamsters, lizards—everything was everywhere. It was a fiasco, but every animal was saved, and the store was salvageable. Suzi's car, on the other hand, was a different story. All in all, we considered ourselves lucky; it could have been much worse.

Despite the setback from the fire, Pet Kingdom was successful right off the bat, and it probably caused me to get a little carried away with my private zoo back at the farm. The only time in my life that I ever remember my dad flat-out saying no to one of my plans was when I tried to buy an elephant. That's right, an elephant. Ever since my days with Dr. Roberts, I loved elephants—working with them, reading about them, even cleaning up after them. What I should have considered, however, was checking with my dad before buying one—especially since it was going to live on his property.

In the winter of 1971, Suzi and I had gone down to Florida to visit my parents, who were vacationing there. I took a side trip over to Chase's in Miami and found the cutest little Indian bull elephant. I say "little"; it weighed about three hundred pounds and was still being bottle-fed. Anyway, I put a five-hundred-dollar deposit on the elephant—his name was Crumb—who cost two thousand dollars total. Then Suzi and I went back to the farm in Knoxville (my parents were still out of town) and, with my brother, I began fixing up a cattle barn into an elephant house. We put in heating, a concrete floor, big pilings, drains—the works.

When my dad came home, he immediately exclaimed, "What the hell is going on in the barn?"

"I bought a baby elephant," I told him. I was actually quite excited about telling him, even if I didn't know how he'd react.

"How much did you pay for him?" he asked.

"Two thousand dollars. Actually only five hundred dollars on deposit," I told him.

"You just lost five hundred dollars," he said. And that was that.

Looking back on it, not buying that elephant was one of the better things that's ever happened to me. I wish I had been so lucky with Daisy, our lioness.

By the time our second daughter, Suzanne, was born, we had built our dream house, surrounded by animals, named Hanna's Ark. This was another family effort, aided by a seventy-two-year-old man named Mr. Ball. Only four of us built the entire house with rough wood inside and out. Unfortunately, lifting the heavy wooden beams caused me to rupture a disk in my back, resulting in my first back surgery.

Some things didn't work as they should in our new home. Our friend, Lee Cohn, was visiting us from Arizona and showed up wearing a white, lightweight suit in the middle of the winter. The weather was miserable, cold and muddy. When I drove up the driveway, the car became stuck. I asked Lee to push the rear of the car while I steered, and he stood behind the back wheels as mud spattered him and that white suit from head to toe. I'm sure that was the last time he wore that suit! Then, after he went into our home to use the toilet, he came out frustrated, saying, "Your toilet bowl is frozen!"

Yet, not long after we moved in, the backyard began to look like a little African plain. There was one large enclosure with trees, rocks, a pool, and lots of little pens. Suzi and I would sit

Our dream home, Hanna's Ark, in Knoxville, was constantly surrounded by lions, Indian water buffalo, llamas, chimpanzees, a spider monkey—our own little animal sanctuary. (Jack Hanna)

out on the back porch and watch the zoo animals graze. Many of these had been given to us by the overcrowded Knoxville Zoo, and some were mixed in with Pet Kingdom animals. It was nuts around our house—organized chaos, if you will. What I couldn't sell of puppies, ducks, kittens, chickens—whatever—I'd bring home. Before you knew it, we were collecting our own eggs for breakfast. Inside the house, we were constantly entertained by Jocamo the spider monkey, Joe the mynah bird, and the parrots.

One afternoon Joanne Benton, Suzi's tennis partner, brought her daughter, Laura, to see the animals. As Joanne drove up in her brand-new Cadillac, Jocamo was frolicking around outside. He proceeded to greet our visitors by jumping through the car window and urinating all over Joanne's lap and the plush interior. Suzi was absolutely mortified and apologized profusely. Weeks later, Joanne graciously told her, "Suzi, that is the best cocktail story I've *ever* had to tell!"

One evening, in the middle of the night, Suzi was walking down the stairs in her nightgown when she heard, "What a delight! What a delight!" Thinking she was hearing a stranger in the house, she screamed frantically, which sent my heart rate through the roof. We were both relieved to learn it was just Joe, the mynah bird, being cordial.

Kathaleen, at that time, found her share of trouble around the house too. Once she fell on the raw wooden deck and became covered with over a hundred splinters. That same year, at the age of three, she somehow found some matches we had tucked away in a drawer and caught the rug on fire—just inches away from some puppy-training newspaper and the rough-side lumber walls. When Suzi heard Kathaleen say the word, "Burn," a red light went off in her head and she ran to the rescue and stomped the flames with her go-go boots, which then became embellished with the burnt strands of shag carpet. It did leave a large, charred area in the rug, but at least we didn't lose the house!

Another day, Suzi spotted tiny black spots on our young baby, Suzanne. The miniscule dots looked like they were moving, and we could not figure out what they were! Her crib was tucked in the corner of our master bedroom, and under the roof on the outside was a bird's nest. Apparently bird mites had infested the nest, and they had crawled through under the eaves onto Suzanne! Absolutely mortified, we immediately moved her crib.

One time Suzi left the front door open when a repairman came to fix the dishwasher. The chickens just paraded into the family room and made themselves at home. When he saw the chickens flapping around, he shook his head in disbelief and said, "This is the first time I've seen chickens as guests and not dinner!"

Out in the yard, we had some hoof-stock from the zoo, one being an Indian water buffalo that we had befriended by hand-feeding him watermelon. When he would lie down, our two baby goats would climb on top of him, as if he were a rock, staying balanced on his back as he stood up. What a comical sight it was to see those goats riding on the buffalo's back as he browsed the pasture.

Those are the same two goats that once climbed onto our low-hanging roof and peed and pooped all over it right next to the guest bedroom window. For the longest time, we couldn't figure out where that horrible smell originated, which explained why our guests never wanted to visit more than once.

Once Hector, our wild goat, got loose and ended up in some wealthy lady's elegant living room on the farm next door. With a friend helping us, we had to go lasso him out to greener pastures. At Easter, I sold loads of baby chicks, telling the parents that they could bring them back to me when they grew too big. They all came back, and I wound up with chickens running around everywhere at home. If I couldn't sell a puppy within a few weeks, I'd bring him home. Suzi was inundated with work but was very enthusiastic about her role as an animal keeper. Serving as a mother to both animals and children alike, she didn't want to get rid of anything. Kathaleen played with the lion cubs in her crib, while Joe the mynah bird went around screaming, "Aw, sh**!"—a phrase taught to him by his previous hippie owners.

Suzi's attitude was always positive, even if my shenanigans were sometimes a bit much. While she was nursing Suzanne one day, I was across the family room bottle-feeding a baby chimpanzee that was very sick at the time. I didn't know if the chimp would come around with the formula, and I suddenly had a strange idea. Before I could open my mouth, Suzi had read my mind.

"No way, Jack," she said.

"What?" I asked, kind of sheepishly.

"I know what you're thinking, and you can forget about it."

So much for that experiment. She told me later that she might have tried giving breast milk to a sick primate if we'd been in the middle of Africa or something. But her main fear right then was that I'd tell the whole world. She was probably right.

Still, our favorite animals were the lion cubs we raised. The first one we ordered through Chase arrived at the airport in what we thought was too large a crate for an eight-week-old cub. It was winter, the case was covered up, and we couldn't really see inside. So we brought it home, into the kitchen. When we pried open the crate, we heard a roar inside, and this forty-pound animal jumped out and up onto the kitchen counter. This thing was at least five months old, and I wasn't about to play around on the floor with it. Carefully, we packed it back up and returned it.

Eventually we had six baby lions behind the house. It was constant work

Suzi and Kathaleen with one of Daisy's lion cubs we raised as another member of the family. (Jack Hanna)

finding enough meat to feed them. Mostly I would find dying livestock at nearby farms. And in return, those cubs gave us a rewarding learning experience and so much joy.

Daisy was the first lion cub we owned and our most precious, beloved animal. She was a beautiful cat. Her temperament was that of a wild animal, but she also related to people. It wasn't long after we'd bought her from Chase that she became like a member of the family, staying with us at home, both inside and outside, riding in the car everywhere we went.

When Daisy grew to her full size and weighed three hundred pounds, I had to keep her outdoors. Our relationship was similar to that of Elsa and Joy Adamson in *Born Free*. I'd go into her pen every day and talk to her softly and she would vocalize—we totally bonded. There just was no way I could

Daisy even had her very own lion's den under our house! (Jack Hanna)

ever imagine that one day, in one sudden moment, she would all but destroy two families and break our hearts.

On that terrible day, a woman brought her three-year-old son to the shop. Once Pet Kingdom became established, it was common for parents to bring their kids around, not necessarily to buy anything, but just to look at the animals. the lady asked if it was possible to take her son to see my collection of animals back at the house, about eight miles away. I was busy at the store and didn't hesitate to tell her to go ahead. People were always coming out to see my animals. I thought it was safe with the protective outer fence around the animals.

The next thing I knew—it was about one o'clock in the afternoon—I received a phone call from my neighbor, Mrs. Troglin. I can still hear her words, clear as a bell: "Jack, you've got to come home right now—a little boy has lost his arm to your lion."

"What?!" I thought I was hearing things.

"Daisy's taken a little boy's arm off," she said. "The police are on their way to pick you up."

The police came by, not to arrest me, but because the arm was inside the enclosure, and they could not get in there to get it out and take it to the hospital with the boy, where it might be reattached. The police cruiser arrived, I jumped in, and we screeched off down the road. We pulled up in the driveway about the same time as the ambulance.

The scene was unreal. The mother was in a complete state of shock, but I'll never forget the little boy as long as I live. He was standing there, not crying or anything, with a sheet wrapped around him. You could see the blood coming through, and there was no arm. I just couldn't put this all together, the flashing lights, the sirens—it was like a horrible nightmare. My grief and devastation was beyond belief.

Daisy was on the other side of the pen, looking no different than she ever did. I went into the pen, picked up the little arm, and brought it out, handing it to the medics. They rushed it to Children's Hospital. The boy had already gone ahead in another ambulance. Standing there, I felt totally lost

21

for the first time in my life. Kathaleen was the same age at the time, and I couldn't begin to imagine how I would feel if that had happened to her. What had I done to this three-year-old child?

The police took me to the hospital, and I waited and waited for news. It seemed like forever. Finally, around five o'clock, they came to tell me that they could not reattach the arm, that it wouldn't work because the little boy could wind up getting gangrene, along with other complications. Dr. Bill Patterson, head of the Knoxville Zoo board, and Guy Smith, the Knoxville Zoo director, were both there. In a time of tragedy, there is no greater gift than friends. Guy was a great animal lover and also had raised a lion cub. The two of them helped me through this extremely emotional time. They reassured me, telling me it wasn't my fault. There was also Dr. Albert Chesney, a longtime family friend, who had experienced a similar tragedy, involving a child's death in an auto accident. He'd gone through hell, and his words helped greatly. At the time, nothing meant much to me, but looking back, their support got me through.

My family was also very supportive, even though they were devastated. "What should we do with the lion?" my dad wanted to know. That night I went into the enclosure with my beautiful Daisy and cried. I told her she was going to the zoo. I'd had Dasy since she was six weeks old, but now she was two years old and over three hundred pounds, and a little boy had lost his arm. The next day the zoo truck came to take her away.

I visited the little boy a couple of times in the hospital, but it didn't work out. His family understandably didn't want me around, and the doctor and my attorney both thought it was best for me to stay away. Years later, in the early part of 1988, I was surprised by a wonderful letter from the mom. She had just seen an article about me in *People* magazine, and she wanted to let me know that her son was a freshman at the University of Tennessee, that he loved swimming and girls, and that he was a typical teenager. That's the best letter I ever received.

But at the time, naturally, there were lawsuits, and they were long and messy. I had three different insurance policies, but none wanted to pay.

Eventually, my attorney sued the insurance companies in order to settle for the boy's family. Of course, no amount is worth the price of an arm and the suffering endured by all.

The exact details of what actually happened never came out, and I didn't care much at the time. But when I replayed the episode, as I have so often over the years, I realized what probably happened. There were no bite wounds, only teeth indentations on the arm. Crossing a wooden fence, the young boy had somehow gotten himself up against the chain-link fence and stuck his arm through it, maybe to pet Daisy. She probably just grabbed the arm, and with her power, jerked it right off.

With the story all over the local papers, life was very difficult for my entire family. Not long after the accident, Suzi and I were in a grocery line when we overheard some people talking, something to the tune of: "There's that Jack Hanna. He ought to go to prison for taking that boy's arm off."

Well, I looked at Suzi right then and there and said, "We're leaving." We had to leave Knoxville because we would never be forgotten there, and it wasn't fair to my parents. We just had to start over. The question was, where?

CHAPTER 3

Starting Over

Staying with the animal business was a tough choice. Besides the lion accident in Knoxville, I'd gotten hepatitis that same year from infected chimpanzees and lost twenty-five pounds in three weeks while staying in the hospital; I'd also ruptured two discs moving animal crates at the pet shop, which also contributed to my first back surgery. So it was easy for me to feel that maybe I'd taken a wrong turn career-wise.

But when Stan Brock told me about a job opening down south, working for Jim Fowler, one of the cohosts of TV's *Wild Kingdom*, I just couldn't resist. Fowler was in the process of assembling animals for Mattel's Circus World, a complex that was being built next to Disney World in Orlando. The animals were temporarily being held at the Fowler family's thousand-acre ranch in Albany, Georgia, and they needed somebody to help manage the place.

Before moving, I sadly donated the large part of my animal collection to the Knoxville Zoo. My remaining lions—Matthew, Mark, Luke, and Sarah—I gave to a top-notch trainer from Europe, Wolfgang Holzmair, who was with the Ringling Brothers and Barnum & Bailey Circus. I had gone to see Holzmair's act and came away so impressed, I knew my cats would have a good home. Günter Gable Williams, also of Ringling Brothers, had the most beautiful cats in the world. You couldn't find any healthier tigers—or animals of any kind, for that matter—than Günter's. People have a general misconception about circus animals being mistreated and underfed. This may have been true in the past and may still be so in some smaller troupes, but by and large circus animals are as well cared for as champion show dogs.

Of course, all of our "household" pets, which were like immediate family, would move to Georgia with us. We packed up a pickup truck with two chimps, four macaw parrots, Jocamo the spider monkey, Willy the cat, Joe the mynah bird, our sheepdog, and I forget who or what else. Suzi drove the station wagon with the two girls—one was sick; the other was still breastfeeding. My mother was crying as we loaded up the truck, and I think, at this point, my dad was quite concerned about the direction my life was taking.

Without looking back, we headed out of Knoxville and down to Georgia. I'd already arranged to have a mobile home ready for us, but when we got there after a tiresome trip, there was nothing on the site but a spigot in the ground. Fortunately, somebody put all of us up for the night, and the next day everything was miraculously taken care of by our only neighbors, Linda and Lew Thompson. A sewer was dug, the water put in, the mobile home delivered and hooked up—everything. It had seemed like such a long time since something had actually worked out right.

We lived in that home the whole time we were there, with a bedroom about the size of a desk for the two girls and the animals bouncing around all over the place. It was like a dream—a good one. Outside, we were surrounded by this serene thousand-acre ranch. Hyenas, giraffes, zebras, and baby elephants roamed around freely, and more animals started arriving. Suzi took care of the kids, all my animals, and picked pecans, while I worked from daylight till dark with animals. When walking around the property, we always had to watch for rattlesnakes. Linda Thompson told me that one day as her children were playing outside, she heard a rattlesnake tapping at the window. The place was loaded with them. I loved it anyway.

One of my first assignments when I got to the ranch was to go pick up three baby elephants at Kennedy International Airport. I was twenty-four years old, and had been to New York once before with Suzi for a day, which was a disaster because the car I borrowed from my mother-in-law stopped running in the Lincoln Tunnel. I was like a fish out of water. Trying to navigate the Big Apple was a true challenge for a boy who had rarely ventured beyond the state of Tennessee. My job was to fly up there, rent a truck, load up the elephants, and transport them to Silver Springs, Florida.

With fourteen elephants in it, that jet was something else. They don't do this anymore—bring big jumbo jets from Africa with animals—but that day there were rhinos, zebras, elephants, and lions all getting off this plane at four o'clock in the morning. It was like an ark of the airways.

After the elephants cleared customs, we loaded them up and headed in the direction of New York City in order to go south. Not paying attention, I made a wrong turn and went somewhere where it said, "No Trucks Allowed." I was functioning on little sleep, and I didn't see the sign. All I wanted to do was point this big truck in a southern direction, but obviously I screwed up.

Next thing I knew, the top of the truck was stuck under an overpass. I really did a number on jamming it in there. Fortunately there was stop-and-go traffic, so it just slowly wedged in. If I had been going fast, I would have torn the top right off. Remembering an old trick, I was getting ready to let some air out of the tires. By this time, traffic was backed up a mile, and here came the police with sirens blaring.

The cop was one of those no-nonsense guys. He jerked me out of the cab and told me to get in the back of the cruiser.

"You're goin' to jail," he barked at me. "Do you know that this costs the taxpayers a lot of money?" he screamed, pointing at the long line of honking cars. He kept yelling at me, telling me what an idiot I was. I couldn't even understand him; he was going a mile a minute.

"Can I tell you what's in the truck?" I asked him really fast.

"Shut up!"

"If we don't get the back end open, those elephants are going to die." I slipped that in there quickly.

"What's going to die?" He looked at me like *I* was going to die.

"The elephants."

"Listen up, buddy. You get smart with me, you're gonna pay for it."

"They're going to die!" I said real excitedly. "There are elephants in the back of that truck!"

"That truck's too small for elephants."

"Baby elephants," I said. "That's what I've been trying to tell you."

"Now, you listen to me, son," the cop said, poking his finger in my chest. "We're going to open the back of that truck, and if there're no elephants in there, you're in real deep. You understand?"

Well, now he'd scared me, and for a split second I thought, *What if they're not back there anymore?* So he pulled open the back door of the truck, and these three blessed little trunks came squirming out of the dark. The cop's eyes got as big as grapefruits, and he said, "I don't believe this. Those are the cutest things I ever saw."

His mind immediately switched off the noise of the traffic jam, the horns honking, the people yelling. All of a sudden, it was like I was talking to a different person. He asked me how old they were, what they ate.

"They're real babies," I said. Now, *I* was talking, and *he* was listening. "I have to feed them a rice mixture every two hours, and that's why I'm worried, sir. My truck's stuck, but I don't care about the ticket—I've got to take these elephants down to Florida and get them their special feed."

Really concerned, he listened, then said he thought he could help. He called for a special wrecker, and it came and lowered the tires and jerked the truck back out. The cop even had traffic stopped the other way so that I could maneuver the truck around. I thanked him, and he never gave me that ticket. Amazingly, he even apologized, a testimony to the appeal of animals solving a sticky situation. So, once again, I was on the road, leaving the Brooklyn accents for the land of southern drawls.

On the way home, I picked up Suzi in Georgia. I'll never forget the two of us eating Thanksgiving dinner on the hood of that truck. We had parked at some forsaken gas station in the middle of nowhere, and the only thing we could find to dine on was cottage cheese and bologna. Of course, we missed the girls, but it was good to know that they were enjoying a nice, traditional Thanksgiving dinner with my brother and sister-in-law. Since then, we've never taken our turkey for granted when we celebrate that holiday.

We spent six fantastic months surrounded by pecans, peanuts, Spanish moss, and wildlife on that ranch. I learned a great deal about animals—especially giraffes and elephants—from Jim Fowler and from having a substantial amount of one-on-one contact with the animals. Still, things didn't seem quite right. It was something to do with not having total control in making decisions about these animals, and a lot of other little things as well. I guess if I was going to be responsible, I wanted to run the show. I was not about to quit, but I knew my future wasn't there. When I was offered the directorship of a tiny zoo in central Florida, I had to go for it.

Stan Brock turned me on to the zoo job in Sanford, Florida. It was 1973, and he had his own animal park in nearby Clermont. Down there, Stan and I became not just close friends but I guess what you might call "animal associates," in a business sense.

Stan was a former cohost on Marlin Perkins's *Wild Kingdom* and knew more about wild animals than anyone I'd ever met. He was a rugged guy, having spent seventeen years on a wilderness ranch in South America. It was so entertaining to listen to his adventures in the Brazilian jungle. Always jogging in bare feet, he once accidentally stepped on the head of a rattlesnake! I called on Stan often for advice in those days, and he was always there to help. I'm very thankful for that—I don't think you can make it in the animal business without some knowledgeable help along the way.

Again, I packed up the family and the animals and U-Hauled us all down to Sanford. When we finally arrived, my excitement waned a little. Having only seen the place once, I had forgotten how small it was. Any zoo on an acre and a half is a crowded situation, but you tend to overlook that kind of thing when you want to direct your own zoo. The zoo's office was a cubbyhole on the sixth floor of a bank building two blocks away. But as Lou Holtz said, "Life is 10 percent what happens to you and 90 percent how you respond to it." I loved the fact that this place was so small, and I dreamed of this place becoming one of the neatest little zoos in America. I also started thinking about ways to expand.

The first thing I did was get the employees fired up—all four of them. I told them what a great place we had here and how we were going to expand and improve conditions. One of the first improvements included the ceiling in the concession stand; one of the falling pieces broke a girl's foot! We did have a fantastic animal selection, even if it was overcrowded. There were lions, tigers, jaguars, alligators, chimps, all kind of birds, and a little petting zoo.

Oh yes, and rats. We really had a lot of rats. They're naturally attracted to the feed and the concessions, and being on a river, as the zoo was, made it even more desirable for these little varmints. One night Suzi and I needed to check on an animal and went in the back gate. It was dark, almost impossible to see anything, and we heard this little scurrying sound. The next thing you know, these black creatures—rats!—were running over our feet. It was the first time Suzi had ever seen a rat, and she was petrified!

Everything we accomplished in Florida was the result of plain-old blind, youthful enthusiasm. One of the first things I did was go down the street to a man named John Sobik, who owned a string of successful sandwich shops, and ask him if he would donate five thousand dollars to buy an elephant. I told him we would name the elephant after him and tie him in to all kinds of promotions. Without hesitation, he wrote out the check. So I drove down to Bill Chase and bought one of those baby Indian bull elephants that I had always wanted. We brought Sobik back up in a pony trailer.

Stan Brock gave me a baby hippo, but I didn't know where to put it in the small zoo. So I took this nice little monkey island we had, moved the spider monkeys off, and put Sobik and the hippo, Geraldine, out in the moated area there. They got along tremendously and became the best of friends. I don't know if I'd ever do it that way again, but it worked like a miracle, and for the survival of the zoo, we were due one.

We had some funny incidents with that elephant. Of course, animal incidents—especially the ones where no one gets hurt—are always funnier in retrospect; at the time they just seemed like chaos.

The "Pachyderm Pro-Animal" was one of my early promotional brain-storms. The idea was to have a charity golf tournament, a fundraiser for the zoo. Instead of a "pro-am," this was a "pro-an." We had little elephant badges, elephants on the golf balls, etc. To kick it off, I was going to have the golfers greeted by the star pachyderm, Sobik, and other animals on the first tee.

Just before the event was scheduled to start, Suzi and I loaded Sobik into his horse trailer, and someone else hooked it up to our brand-new station wagon. This was a big mistake—always hook up your trailer yourself!

Following behind us was a guy named Herbie Sullivan, a herpetologist. Herbie was my friend and coworker and quite a character. He had long side-burns and horn-rimmed glasses and drove a 1968 baby blue T-bird convertible with light blue angel-hair interior and a license plate that read: SNAKE DR. Herbie did know his reptiles and always went out of his way to take care of them when they were sick. On this day, Herbie had a pet raccoon with him, along with a boa constrictor in a box next to him on the seat.

Herbie was behind us as we approached the golf course, which was about four miles from the zoo. Riding in the trailer with the elephant was Robbie Campbell, a zoo worker.

Suddenly, as we turned up onto the clubhouse road at about thirty miles per hour, the trailer snapped off, sideswiped the back of my brand-new car, and went flying across the golf course. The trailer—elephant and all—crossed a fairway and crashed into a large white oak tree, popping the elephant right out the back. He took off running across the golf course, and I thought, *Oh no, mass destruction on the links—headlines of scattered golfers and ruined greens.*

Robbie staggered out of the trailer and said he thought his ribs were broken. Herbie, cool as a cucumber, didn't budge from his car and asked me why I let the elephant trailer go out on the golf course. I was beyond upset.

"Do you think I arranged all this?" I yelled at Herbie. "We've got big prob-lems. There are a hundred golfers waiting to tee off, the elephant's loose on the course, and Robbie's got broken ribs. Do you think I did this on purpose?"

Herbie never got excited. He just sat there and said, "Yep, I guess I'll go

Herbie Sullivan and me with the snake that almost took my hand as a souvenir. (*People Weekly,* Bob Frey)

check Robbie out and then go up and see how those models are doing." (He'd set it up to have four local models tee the balls up on the first hole.)

"You're going to help me catch that elephant!" I told him. "You're not going to chat with your models or play with your snake or anything else. If that elephant destroys this course, the whole thing's going down the tubes."

After immediately calling an ambulance for Robbie, we chased that elephant all over the course. We finally caught up to him after he'd calmed down and was eating out of the rough near the sixth green. It was two hours before any golfers teed off, but I never saw any of it. I was too busy apologizing to the greens keeper. The elephant was unhurt, but we had some hoof prints to repair on one of the greens, which cost us a couple hundred bucks. Robbie's ribs were also broken, but he recovered quickly. Of course, it could have been much worse.

I would do almost anything to raise money and awareness for the zoo. It was largely because of this, along with the support of the local press, that Sanford secured the new zoo site in 1975. Another one of the early fundraisers was a birthday party for Sobik that I threw at the old Orlando Sports Stadium. First, I arranged for a marching band. Then I got kids practicing gymnastics and called them a circus, which, of course, was a slight exaggeration. But they really were training at a circus school in Sarasota. This show was a real mix, from karate to attack-dog demonstrations, and, of course, I had a birthday cake, which must have weighed over two hundred pounds.

The day before the party, as my luck would have it, Sobik developed a terrible case of diarrhea. Crap was flying everywhere. Now, an elephant with diarrhea is a potentially life-threatening problem. Plus, I also had one of my biggest fundraisers scheduled for the next day, with a couple thousand tickets sold (the place held about sixteen thousand). I quickly called the vet over, and he examined the elephant. He told me that Sobik would be all right, but if I wanted to have our party, we would have to shove these pills down his mouth. That's when I learned how smart elephants are.

Sobik wouldn't swallow the medicine. We put it in an orange; he wouldn't eat the orange. So we laid out twelve oranges. I had placed the pills in one of them—I had them hidden so deeply that no human being could tell they were in there. That elephant ate every single orange but the one with the medicine—twice in a row. We finally got him to take his medicine by tricking him with some molasses on a big wooden spoon. By the time he realized the medicine was in there, the stuff was stuck to his tongue and had to go down.

Sobik's condition improved for his big day, but he still dumped on everything that moved. He even crapped on his own birthday cake. Obviously, this was one birthday cake that was never eaten. In spite of it all, though, the event turned out to be a huge success.

Because there was no local ASPCA (American Society for the Prevention of Cruelty to Animals) in Sanford, and because the Fish and Game Commission was so busy, people would phone me whenever there was any kind of animal emergency. A typical example was the call I received from the police early one morning about a bear loose in Winter Park, an exclusive community outside Orlando. I didn't really believe this story and told the caller it must be a mistake. That's when the chief got on the line and asked me if I would please come over and help them capture this bear.

As usual, I called good old reliable Stan Brock, who brought along a set of heavy ropes and a tranquilizer gun. The Winter Park cops sent us a motorcade, and within minutes we were speeding to an address fifteen miles away. When we arrived, there were already two fire trucks, a couple hundred spectators, Herbie, who was my assistant on everything (I had asked him to bring the zoo truck, but naturally he'd brought his T-Bird), and a television news crew. The star of the show, a three-hundred-pound bear, was halfway up a tall white oak tree. It was the biggest black bear I'd ever seen, right in the middle of this lady's manicured yard in this elegant neighborhood.

"I say, Jack, that's quite some bear," said Stan in his usual, calm fashion. "We'll take care of this—should be no problem." He was actually smiling.

My first thought was, if that bear comes out of that tree and heads for the crowd, he could do some major damage. The police had wanted to shoot the bear when they first got to the scene, but the neighbors had protested. That's when we were called in to help.

Stan fired his tranquilizer gun and hit the bear in the butt, but the dart had no effect. Even after the tranquilizer had plenty of time to be effective, the bear just sat there as if nothing had happened. After two more direct hits, the bear shot out of that tree, full speed, and, to our relief, ran away from the people. He ran around for a half hour before he slowed down from the sedative. (Grizzly bears, by the way, are as fast as their reputation—when panicked or angry, they can run a football field in six seconds. Black bears are somewhat slower.)

We were chasing him; the police cruisers were chasing him. I remember at one point feeling like Marlin Perkins on a *Wild Kingdom* episode running through these lush yards. I mean, here were the police letting us have the run of everything, telling everyone to stay away but us.

Stan was yelling stuff like, "Jack, you go that way. I'll go this way." Fine, sounded like a plan, but I thought, *What if I go that way and run into the bear? I don't have the tranquilizer gun—Stan does. All I have is a rope.*

When I thought I spotted the bear in another backyard, I yelled to Stan to stay nearby. Then, all of a sudden, in one big blur, I saw the bear burst into the open and go running right through the shallow end of this lady's pool. Just remembering the look on her face still cracks me up. She's sitting on her porch and sees a bear running across her yard, followed by me, with coke-bottle glasses and a rope, followed by Stan, with his gun.

So we chased the bear down to a nearby lake area where Stan gave him another blast from the tranquilizer gun. The frantic bear tried to swim away, but the fourth dart began to take effect. (We realized later that the other darts had not worked because they landed in the bear's fatty tissue.) We lassoed him from a motorboat, then dragged him up to land so he wouldn't drown.

By this time Herb was there with the zoo truck, and about four of us transferred the bear into one of these huge liquor storage cages I'd bought from the railroad. We took him to the zoo for temporary safekeeping. This whole adventure was big news the next day. Consequently, the day after that, we had a record-breaking Monday at the zoo.

The bear was thought to be the offspring of a rare Himalayan sun bear that had escaped from a circus several years back. More than likely, he came down from the Ocala National Forest forty or fifty miles to the north, probably just walking along the freeway. We released him back into the forest three weeks later. As it turned out, this incident generated tremendous publicity for the zoo. I guess everybody enjoys a good animal story, and if I hadn't realized it before, that idea certainly clicked in then.

In Florida we received a lot of problem calls about alligators. The expanding highway and building construction in the 1970s was often responsible for pushing alligators out of their natural habitats, sending them to all kinds of unlikely places—mostly swimming pools. They were often a nuisance and sometimes dangerous. But as a Floridian zoo director, I soon found that gator was as much a part of my daily vocabulary as cat or dog might be to a vet.

One night the phone rang about two in the morning. A twelve-foot-long alligator had its teeth stuck in the tire of a police cruiser in the Longwood Hotel parking lot. Apparently the cops had tried to corral this wayward creature by using their cruiser to back him into a corner against a building. The poor thing felt trapped and bit into the tire, and now its jaws were locked into the rubber. The police didn't know how to capture it. Since alligators were endangered at the time, they couldn't shoot it—not that they would have. Besides, that wouldn't pry the teeth loose.

It was like a scene right out of a police comedy. I had to laugh; I also had to call Herbie, since he was our herpetologist. Having had too much rum the night before, Herbie at first didn't want to get up. But once he caught the scent of adventure, he was ready to go. He showed up with some ropes and had thought out a plan to first lasso the gator, then pull him off the tire. But for some reason, I wasn't feeling much like a cowboy.

We roped the alligator's head and pulled him loose, but at the same time, he flipped backward, knocking us both to the ground. Herbie got all entangled in his own ropes, but with the help of the cops, we managed to get the ropes off Herbie and onto the alligator. Once he was tied tight, we got him into the back of my station wagon, which had just been repaired after the elephant fiasco. (Imagine, by the way, filling out claim forms and trying to convince an insurance adjuster that the damage was caused by an elephant escaping from a trailer on a golf course.)

The cops asked us where we were taking the alligator, and we told them the zoo, of course—which wasn't true. We were going to drop him off, as we always did, in nearby Lake Monroe. In my two years in Sanford, I must have sent more than a dozen rescued alligators back into that lake, since the zoo had no room for them. I liked to watch them waddle back into their watery home. "Bye, bye, boys. Have a fun time," I'd say as they swam away.

While in Sanford, I got well-acquainted with those police officers—and not necessarily by choice. In one incident, I had stopped after work, like I did every day, at this little convenience store on the way home to buy my daughters candy. But on this particular day, Suzi had called me earlier with Kathaleen's dentist report: a cavity. "No more candy," Suzi had told me. And yet, there I was, still heading to the store for candy.

When I walked in, I noticed a man with rollers in his hair, wearing a winter jacket in the heat of summer—in Florida, mind you—leaving the store. I turned and saw my friend, the cashier, on the floor. She yelled, "That man just robbed me!"

Without thinking, I took off racing down the road after him. He was running ninety miles an hour with money flying everywhere. Looking and yelling for help on this busy road, I was quickly tiring, and I was ready to throw up. Finally, the guy ran on to the porch of a house and stopped.

The next thing I know, he is pointing a gun at me, yelling, "Hit the dirt or I'll blow your head off!" I heard a click and then sirens.

The police swept in and took the suspect into custody. Then later, after inspecting the gun, they told me that his gun had just misfired! Someone was certainly looking over me that day. And the next time Suzi asked me not to do something, I was a little more willing to listen.

Zoo workers are generally dedicated and careful people, but as we found in another incident, sometimes animal thefts will occur. At Sanford, someone was stealing exotic birds from the zoo. The three missing macaws were expensive, yet replaceable. But when they broke into my office and stole Joe, my prized mynah bird, I was really upset. These birds went for four to six hundred dollars at the time, but Joe was priceless. His routine ran from "What's the matter?" to "Hello" to "I wanna take the man's order" to "Aw, sh**!"

The police wanted to help me on this since Joe was such a kick and all the zoo visitors loved him. The local paper helped with the headline story: "Mynah Bird Stolen: He's Mine a Bird, Not Yours."

Two weeks after the theft, I received a call from Michigan; it was a guy claiming to know where my bird was. He said that his cousin knew the person who stole Joe and that the bird was at a house on Pine Avenue near downtown Orlando.

I called the police and told them the story. They staked out the house for a couple of days and got some results. Then they came to get me, stating that they could not get a warrant, but that we were going to go knock on the door and ask the people nicely if they had my bird.

The lady at the door was nice enough; she said yes, they had bought a bird several days ago. The police told her they thought it might be mine. "Well, how do you know that?" she asked us.

I said, "Ma'am, I'll tell you what I'll do. I don't even want to see the bird. You put the bird in this room right here, and I'll go in the other room, and I will talk to that bird. He's going to say 'Aw, sh**' and 'I wanna take the man's order.'"

So they put the bird on the other side of the door, and I said, "Hey, Joe, what's the matter?" He didn't hesitate. "Aw, sh**!" he said. When I asked him, "What's the matter?" again, he came back with, "I wanna take the man's order."

Right then the policeman said, "That's it. It's your bird."

The lady was nice about it, and I went home with Joe. She could have refused, which would have meant a court battle. But I bet we would have had a few laughs in the courtroom!

To top it all off, the prison was right across the street from the zoo. One day an inmate started a fire, and fourteen prisoners died. I saw one inmate walk out safely—the very one who had stolen Joe.

Joe was invaluable; he went everywhere with me, especially on my fundraising speeches. Once I was about to speak at a church in front of three hundred potential zoo donors. "Before we hear from Mr. Hanna," said the minister after introducing me, "please join me in a little prayer. Our Father—"

"Aw, sh**!" Joe screeched, as loud as ever. Obviously, I never brought Joe to a church again.

During my last few months in Florida, I got involved in a movie deal with Stan and a group of other people. The film was called *The Forgotten Wilderness*, and I guess you could say it was like the title, pretty much forgotten. Eventually I would lose all the money I had invested in it, my whole life's savings. The good news was that I didn't lose my finger to the big snake that was one of the stars of the movie. It was a very close call.

The snake, a 14-foot, 120-pound anaconda, was used in an animal-capture scene that was being shot in a local pond. Most of the filming was done in South America, but some of the close-ups of the animal scenes were shot in Florida. I was helping out on location, and I noticed that the snake had a loose piece of skin dangling from his nose. I went to remove it, maybe a little too casually, and the snake just snatched up my finger, clamping right down on it.

"Don't move your finger, or you'll lose it," said Stan. I couldn't really move it anyway—it was like having it stuck in a vise with sharp teeth, about 220 of them. While I screamed in pain, Stan and Herbie, who we had called for snake advice, tried to pry my finger loose.

Meanwhile a guy from the local newspaper was going nuts taking pictures, instead of helping me out. Stan convinced him to put down his camera and go get something to jam in the snake's mouth so I could get the finger out. He found an old shoe to use, and I was able to pull my finger back while Stan and Herbie held the snake's jaws open wide.

Miraculously, the finger was all there. I mean, it was shredded like it had been in a meat grinder and had about two dozen punctures—some all the way through—but it was still attached. They took me to the hospital and insisted on giving me shots against infection, even though the snake wasn't venomous. The shots in my butt wound up hurting worse than my finger did. My good friend, Dr. Gary Dotson, was always trying to keep me patched up!

After two years at Sanford, we were able to turn the place around, creating a little haven for animals. In fact, things went so well that, with the help of the media, we wound up with a new zoo: the 104-acre Central Florida Zoological Park on the shores of Lake Monroe. Overcoming the challenge of limited space helped to instill a sense of satisfaction and pride among the employees. They were much more content as animal keepers knowing that their animals would live in larger and more natural habitats. Upon the completion of this project, I decided to move on to new adventures.

In 1975, I left central Florida without a lot of fanfare but with a very positive feeling. The new zoo had just opened, thanks to the efforts of many people, on the Fourth of July, and I had a large emotional investment in that. But my next project was calling: I was leaving to go into the animal-film business, a venture that I thought was going to set me off on a lucrative new career. I couldn't have been more wrong, but that's all right. Indirectly, it got me one step closer to Columbus.

CHAPTER 4

Back to the Wild

They say you can't go home again, which is something I found out on my second move back to Knoxville. While Suzi and our three daughters—Julie was the latest arrival, if you're keeping score—waited back in Florida, I also found out I wasn't going to be the next Walt Disney. Six months of going out on the road promoting *The Forgotten Wilderness* turned out to be an effort best forgotten. With the movie business behind me, I returned home to Knoxville, with the hopes of figuring out how to make ends meet.

My father suggested that I go into the real estate business, and with a family and no money, who was I to argue? My dad reasoned that since I was outgoing and a good salesman, I'd no doubt be a successful Realtor. The only problem was the difference between promoting something you love—in my case, anything to do with animals—versus something you're indifferent to.

I was very fortunate at the time to hook up with Harold "Bubba" Beal, a Knoxville Realtor who was interested in my dad's property, the beautiful farm where I grew up. For tax purposes, Dad wanted to sell, and as one-third owner, I entered into a limited partnership with Bubba. We decided to turn the old homestead into a restaurant (Hanna's), and we used the rest of the property to build seventeen homes. At first I was very excited and relieved, but it didn't take me long to lament the fact that I was totally removed from something I'd loved all my life: animals. Before long, I would remedy that situation.

Meanwhile, I purchased a modest brick house near my brother's farm and sent for Suzi and the kids. It was an unusual home built totally with bricks—not only on the outside, but on the inside too. Even the bathtub and shower were made out of bricks. And to add to the conversation piece, the bathroom ceiling had two old beer bottles bricked into it.

It was Friday, on Memorial Day weekend, when the moving van from Florida arrived at our new home. We had the movers put everything in the garage and decided to wait until the next day to bring it all in. But that Saturday would turn into a day I'll remember as long as I live.

Suzi and I got up early and began moving furniture and boxes around, making a fair amount of noise. After a while, we noticed that Julie, who had just turned two years old, was sleeping for an unusually long time on the couch. She would normally be up and playing by that time. Suzi felt her forehead, and it was practically on fire—she had a 105-degree temperature.

We rushed her to Children's Hospital in Knoxville, but our family doctor could not diagnose the problem at first and had trouble controlling the fever. On Sunday, her condition worsened, and the doctors decided to do a bone-marrow test. The results were devastating. They told us that little Julie had leukemia, a cancer of the blood. By this time, she had already developed pneumonia and a staph infection due to her lack of immunity.

Our doctor told us that since Julie was going downhill so fast, the best thing to do was send her to St. Jude's Hospital in Memphis, some 450 miles away, as fast as humanly possible. But that was so far and we had so little time. I called my friend Bubba, a pilot, and in a few hours he flew us in a twin-engine plane to Memphis. Time was so precious that if we had driven her, she might have died.

Upon Julie's arrival, we were told she might not survive because she had "zero resistance." She was placed in a sterile intensive-care unit, where she spent the next several weeks in isolation to protect her from infectious diseases.

In the meantime, we had two other little girls to take care of. And we were completely torn. The endless hours at the hospital left few moments for quality time with Kathaleen and Suzanne, but we couldn't leave our two-year-old baby without knowing if she would make it through to the next day. So we made the decision to send Kathaleen, the always independent and darling seven-year-old, to stay with Suzi's parents in New Jersey for the summer. They treasured the time with their beloved granddaughter and everyone fell in love with her southern accent. Sweet Suzanne, who was four, went to stay with the Ensleys, some close friends in Florida who completely adored her. Even though we knew they would receive more attention there than we would be able to give, Suzi and I struggled with the family being so far apart at such a difficult time. At one point, Little Suzanne said, "You don't care about me. Even if a Mack truck hit me, you wouldn't care." We were stunned and realized how truly tough it was on Suzanne and Kathaleen. (She must have heard about a Mack truck from her older cousin Ross.) Even though they were healthy, they weren't receiving our attention, and that wasn't fair.

It was a long, slow ordeal for everyone, but gradually the chemotherapy treatments, cranial radiation, bone-marrow treatments, and spinal taps were successful, and Julie beat the odds. Her leukemia has been in remission ever since, and for that, our entire family is very thankful. To this day, Julie and I both dedicate as much time as possible to supporting the fundraising efforts of the remarkable St. Jude Children's Research Hospital.

The Knoxville Zoo had always supported me, even at the time of the lion incident that caused me to leave town three years earlier. Now that I was back in town, they asked me to be on the board of trustees of the Appalachian Zoological Society, a support arm of the zoo. Of course I accepted, since this was just the boost I needed to get back into the animal world.

About that same time, Stan Brock called me with an idea that would also involve me in the kind of work I loved. His timing was perfect, and his idea was intriguing and exciting. Stan's plan was to take two adult jaguars from American zoos, where they were born, and transport them to the South

American jungle where their parents were born. There, after a period of acclimatization, they would be released into the wild.

Together, Stan and I founded the Freedom for Animals Fund, a nonprofit organization dedicated to the reestablishment of threatened and endangered species in their natural habitats in the wild. It's basically the opposite of what the old zoos did—instead of taking animals out of the wild, we were going to reintroduce zoo animals to their natural habitats.

This project would take over a year to realize, and before the final accomplishment, it would involved an entire community, two zoos, Alcoa, the U.S. Fish and Wildlife Service, the Venezuelan and Haitian governments, and most importantly, Bubba Beal, since he was the one who flew us down there in his own plane.

The longest wait was for the permits. During this time, I continued to work with Bubba, and like so many people who have been around me over the years, he was bitten by the animal bug. Even in his office, he had Boa Derek the boa constrictor, and Billy Bob the tarantula. One day, after he overheard me talking to Stan about the project, Bubba offered us the use of one of his planes, an old 1937 Grumman Goose amphibian. This was the perfect flying machine for our needs—now all we had to do was find gas money.

On the other end, Stan had made arrangements with Dr. Pedro Trebbau, a Venezuelan wildlife authority. Dr. Trebbau knew a conservationist rancher in the remote Apure Llanos region who would build a ten-thousand-dollar chain-link fence around a four-acre compound for the cats, where they'd be held temporarily before being released into a 190,000-acre animal sanctuary.

Guy Smith, the director of the Knoxville Zoo, offered Esther, a female jaguar, and we obtained the other one, Mato Grasso, a male, from the Central Florida Zoo. Both zoos were solidly behind our plan—and not every zoo would so easily give up a jaguar, which is an endangered species. Alcoa, located just outside Knoxville, gave us two beautiful aluminum crates that they had custom-built for transporting the animals. As for the gas money, that came from the Appalachian Zoological Society.

On November 14, 1977, Bubba, Stan Brock, Bubba's partner Ken Elrod, a newspaper reporter, and I finally took off from Knoxville's Downtown Island Airport in Bubba's Grumman Goose seaplane with one jaguar in tow and another to pick up. We ran into some minor engine trouble on the first leg of our trip to Florida, and when we finally left the States with our second jaguar, we were over a day late, creating a serious problem for our clearance papers to refuel in Haiti. That, and the fact that our cargo alarmed the Haitian authorities, created more delays.

If that weren't enough, while we were in Haiti, Ken Elrod informed us of a little trouble. "Um, Bubba, I've got to tell you something."

"What is it, Ken?" Bubba asked, cool as always.

"I didn't want to tell you this before, but I had a pack of Dramamine in my shirt pocket, and it fell into the fuel tank while I was filling it up."

"Hmm" was Bubba's only reply.

"Is that serious, Bubba?" Ken was a nervous wreck.

"Yeah, it could be serious, Ken. Let me think for just a minute."

Bubba came up with a little experiment. After filling a jar with fuel, he had Ken drop in another pack of Dramamine to see if it would float. If it floated, no problem. The airplane would have to run out of fuel before the Dramamine could clog the line. Everyone watched as Ken dropped the pack of Dramamine into the jar of fuel. And we all watched it sink straight to the bottom.

At this point, I was getting nervous. Here we were about to fly over the ocean with an endangered species on board, after two years of planning and the media following the whole effort, and there's a pack of Dramamine stuck in the bottom of our fuel tank.

"We'll be back in a minute," Bubba said, and he and Stan headed to the hangar.

After about an hour, Stan and Bubba came back with a plan. "According to our calculations," Bubba began, "we should be able to make it with this one wing full."

It sounded good to me; I was ready to get these jaguars home. A few hours later, we were flying along—I had almost forgotten about the whole incident—when the cockpit control panel lit up like a Christmas tree.

"Please put on your seat belt," Bubba announced calmly. "Apparently the left-hand tank is jammed."

Meanwhile, the plane was sputtering, alarms were going off, Bubba was calling in to the tower, and I was hanging on for dear life. But Bubba, tried and true, calmly landed us safely on an alternate airport on the coast.

We were more than two days late when we thankfully arrived in Caracas, Venezuela. Dr. Trebbau met us there in his own plane, and our next step was to "just follow him" for a two-and-a-half-hour flight over jungle interior. It was thick and mountainous, seemingly never-ending, until we suddenly came to a small clearing in the jungle, a little muddy grass strip with natives running all around.

Landing the two planes, we took the jaguars by tractor and trailer to their new enclosure a few miles away. I was very relieved that the animals were still in perfect shape after the journey, not a scratch or skin burn anywhere. We went to check out the pen, and it was ideal—situated around a swamp on some high ground.

At first, we couldn't get one of the cats to come out of its crate and into the compound. No one seemed alarmed, but I was concerned about getting out of there before nightfall. I was wearing L. L. Bean pants, and like Stan, I had on a safari shirt. I was trying to be Mr. Cool, but I was sweating like a monkey, and the insects were chewing me up. I couldn't have lived one day out there. I thought he was crazy, but Stan somehow reached into the crate and brought that full-grown jaguar out. I couldn't believe it—with one arm, he actually grabbed its tail and gently pulled it out.

The reintroduction, to be supervised by Dr. Trebbau, provided for the animals to be fed in the enclosure every night, just like in captivity. After a month, they'd still get their meals, but the gate would be left open. The idea was for them to stray a little farther each day, then come back at night. The next month they'd be fed only every other day, then after that, twice a week. One day they wouldn't come back.

Eventually, the cats would begin by eating some easy prey, like armadillos and turtles, then move on to the bigger stuff, like deer and tapirs. The jaguars were strong and adaptable and should make it. We hoped that ultimately they would propagate.

Feeling a great sense of accomplishment, we headed back to our plane to set out for home. Bubba had some hairy moments on his plane after he agreed to carry a half-dozen sick natives on the flight back to Caracas. The plane was overloaded and struggled to get off the ground. As it gained altitude, it mowed the top of the tree line. When Bubba brought the landing gear down in Caracas, bushes and branches came pouring out onto the runway. Drugs were just getting big there at the time, and the Goose was immediately surrounded by police, who were hardly impressed with any story about returning jaguars to the wild. After a couple of hours of fast talking—and checking up by authorities—they finally cleared everybody. I suppose their suspicions weren't all wrong, but the only drug we had on board was the Dramamine still stuck in the gas tank.

The return back to the United States was relatively uneventful. On an unannounced side trip to practice water landings, Bubba did have me white-knuckling the armrests. Otherwise, we were able to rest easy, which left me time to wonder if what we had done would have a successful ending. Unfortunately for these jaguars, it did not. One animal was found a year later, killed and skinned by poachers, and the other one disappeared, even though it was equipped with a radio collar. The wild just wasn't as welcoming to its old friends as we had hoped.

But in another sense the project was very successful. The concept was really nothing new and the work required by the project was formidable; obviously, we can't go releasing all sorts of zoo animals back into their natural habitats—there are too many physical and financial limitations. But with every effort zoos make to represent the wild world of animals, the better people can appreciate wildlife and do their best to conserve it.

Planning and carrying out the trip to South America was a big break for me. I had missed the excitement, the interaction, and the outreach opportunities that animals had always afforded me. But on my return, I went right back into the real estate thing and it just was not working. Suffice it to say that I was no Donald Trump.

Bubba was very supportive all the way. During that time, he even involved me in putting together a petting zoo on three acres behind a shopping center he had invested in near Gatlinburg, Tennessee. It was a beautiful little area built around a mountain stream, where people could enjoy watching a magnificent black bear relaxing in the grass habitat, beavers swimming in the water, mountain goats jumping on rocks, rabbits hopping about and wiggling their noses, and many exotic birds singing in the background. Bubba gave me the opportunity to sell real estate while still reading my animal books during working hours. He knew that my passion was animals and that I was in a very difficult period in my life, with no income and no zoo. And even though Julie was in remission, there was still the haunting knowledge that there was no such thing as a cure for leukemia. Things were very frustrating at the time, but Bubba understood.

One day I was sitting in my office reading *International Wildlife* when Bubba walked in and said, "Jack, you're not happy doing this. You wouldn't be happy doing this even if you were making a million dollars." I tried to hide the magazine.

"You love your animals," he said. "You can stay here as long as you want, but why don't you try and find something that deals with wildlife?"

The very next day, Stan Smulewitz, an old friend, called me from New Jersey. Stan and I had once made fish tanks together by gluing the seams of glass tanks. (The fish tanks eventually started blowing apart and I got sued, but that's another story.) Stan called to tell me that his sister, who lived in Columbus, Ohio, had seen an ad in the paper there for a zoo director and thought I might be interested. Was I interested? Does a monkey eat peanuts? Does a hippo like water? Does a bear sleep in the woods?

CHAPTER 5

Hello, Columbus!

Well, after that fateful first trip to Columbus—when I discovered this wasn't a prank and that there actually *was* a zoo in Columbus—I had to convince the board that I, a barely thirty-something, hardly experienced zoo director, was the man for the job.

"We wanted to know what his wife was like, so we invited him back with Suzi. And Suzi made a hit like nobody's business."

—BLAINE SICKLES, FORMER PRESIDENT OF THE ZOO BOARD
AND MEMBER OF ZOO DIRECTOR SEARCH COMMITTEE

When the zoo board invited me back for a second trip, I knew I might actually have a chance at this thing. And I was starting to feel really good about it when Blaine Sickles, the president of the zoo board and member of the search committee, asked me to wait outside the boardroom to be introduced to the entire zoo board. The board didn't know I was on the other side of the door—that was going to be Blaine's little surprise—and I didn't know that inside the boardroom, the board members started getting cold feet, asking iffy questions like, "Isn't he awful young?" and "Can't we go awhile longer without a new director?" That's when Blaine—who typically is a teddy bear of a guy—let them have it. He told them the search committee had met all the criteria and had worked very hard on finding a new director. And, he added, anyone who voted against me would be serving on the new search committee.

"He had these big, thick glasses; they're now on display at the optometry school at Ohio State."

—DON WINSTEL, ASSISTANT DIRECTOR, COLUMBUS ZOO

Fortunately, Blaine's argument eliminated their hesitations; I can't imagine what I would have done otherwise. They voted me in as the new director for fifteen thousand dollars a year, with the fringe benefit of an old, white city-owned station wagon with a beat up back door that eventually flew off. After packing, Suzi and I loaded up our three daughters, and like the Beverly Hillbillies, headed to Ohio. A new chapter of my life was about to begin.

The jump to being director of the Columbus Zoo was the biggest thing that had ever happened to me—like going from dogcatcher to mayor without even running for office. I had never been in charge of more than a dozen employees; now I was overseeing forty. When I got to Columbus, the annual budget was around $2 million compared to the $250,000 budget I had to work with back in Florida. I was really diving into this thing, and I remember thinking at the time, *Either I'll make it go, or I'll sink it like a rock.* I had nothing to lose, and I never was one for just treading water.

My first impression of the Columbus Zoo was a place in turmoil with numerous problems or, really, challenges that presented themselves. Sitting behind my desk in the back of an old bird house on that very first day, I thought, *Let's map this out. What's the perception here? How is this zoo perceived by the community, by the trustees, by the employees, by the zoo world? And how can I improve that?*

"The zoo was a mess when Jack took over. There were weeds everywhere, litter. He'd always pick up trash. And on weekends, the whole family would pick up trash. Employees started seeing that, and they started doing it. Suddenly a transition began, and employees started taking pride."

—BLAINE SICKLES, FORMER PRESIDENT OF THE ZOO BOARD
AND MEMBER OF ZOO DIRECTOR SEARCH COMMITTEE

I applied some common sense and a few simple business techniques—forget zoological techniques for now; somebody had already tried that, and it didn't work. My strategy was to just get back to fundamentals and try to get this zoo up and going.

First off, I wanted to get it painted and fixed up and get the employees in nice uniforms, encourage them to go out there and say, "Hi, how ya doin'? Can I tell you about the elephants . . . the giraffes?" Instill a sense of pride!

"Jack's got charisma. It just oozes out of him."

—GERALD BORIN, EXECUTIVE DIRECTOR 1992–2008, COLUMBUS ZOO

Whether it's the public or your staff, people will always be skeptical at first, but you have to fight against the skepticism; you have to build some enthusiasm by generating energy—and I've got plenty of that! (Everyone tells me that if I had been born today, I would have been the poster child for Ritalin.) You need to get people to believe. And they will. Enthusiasm is infectious.

Mel Dodge and Joe Cross, two men who greatly influenced the early development of the zoo, as well as the development of my career. (Michael W. Pogany/Columbus Zoo)

At the same time, another important change was taking place. Mel Dodge, then head of Parks and Recreation, had initiated the transfer of the Columbus Zoo from the Sewers and Drains Department to the Parks and Recreation Department. Why the Sewers and Drains department was ever in charge of the Columbus Zoo was puzzling in the first place. Sewers and Drains had just made sure the animals weren't starving and that the ASPCA wasn't going to close the place down—that was the extent of their concerns. As the new director, that transfer was instrumental in getting the zoo off to a positive start.

Mel Dodge was also one of the people responsible for hiring me and was like a godfather to me throughout my years in Columbus. We connected immediately because of the common bond we shared in our passion for lions. At that time, he and his wife, Norma, were raising a lion cub for the zoo. One of the most difficult losses in my life was when Mel died from cancer. As a special gift, I brought his lion to the burial.

Back in my first year, I went to Mel for advice on just about everything.

Mel Dodge and I going over the ten-year master plan for the new Columbus Zoo in 1979. (*Columbus Dispatch Photo*)

And if I didn't go to him, it was because I already knew he would approve. Of course, I've made some mistakes along the way, but Mel always supported me. As far as people and animals were concerned, we usually saw eye to eye.

Mel loved animals and loved people who love animals. He'd had a number of his own lions over the years, and unofficially, he'd been known to take an animal home overnight from the zoo now and then. But most importantly, Mel knew everything that went on at the zoo; he knew all the keepers by name, what their jobs were, what all their special projects were. He would stop to chat with them about the animals—about care, feeding, and breeding. There were major problems with morale at the zoo, and Mel knew it. But he gave me the confidence to go about things my own way, which is probably the same way he would have operated the zoo, if he'd been director.

The easiest way to run any organization is to shut the door and do it all by yourself. You can leave all the problems outside and let them boil up to the point where the whole thing explodes. With this philosophy, either you or your organization will end up in flames. And if you're lucky, you'll go first. I honestly don't know how they'd kept the lid on the Columbus Zoo. A zoo with disgruntled employees taking care of wild animals is a powder keg.

The important thing to do immediately was to win the respect of the employees. This was going to be a difficult task that would not happen overnight. Three-quarters of the employees were older than I was and had been there many years. And here I was, a nobody kid coming from a small zoo in Florida. Their main problem, as I conjectured, was one of self-esteem. They thought no one cared about them or their animals. They felt the public and some trustees considered them "sh** shovelers," which wasn't true.

> *"Jack started saying we were good before we were good.*
> *And I think it helped make us good."*
>
> —Don Winstel, Assistant Director, Columbus Zoo

The closed-door policy that existed had to go. In my first meeting with the zoo staff, I gave them a pep talk about how great this place could become—something none of them believed. Their eyes were like lasers boring through me. I realized why the trustees hadn't bothered to introduce many of the staff to me before I was hired.

I told them that I wanted them all—regardless of their function, be it keeper or garbage collector—to give me a list of their problems, to tell me how they felt the zoo could be improved. Only about twenty or so lists came back, but I went to work on each one right away. I didn't want anyone to think his or her problem wasn't worthy of attention.

Money was always needed for this and that—money we didn't have. I tried to get people to donate paint, materials, anything. I was giving fits to our treasurer, Ken Cooke. He was a zoo trustee and, like all trustees, a volunteer—only he had to work harder than most just trying to keep tabs on me. He would try to raise the budget, assisting in every way, but I was consistently creating a problem for him. He was always saying, "Jack, you can't do this—the zoo hasn't got the money."

> *"Jack has a real reverence for the animals and the people who take care of them.*
> *Because of his support and commitment to his staff, he made it possible to make many*
> *groundbreaking advances in the care of captive animals."*
>
> —Charlene Jendry, Founding Member, Partners In Conservation (PIC)

John McConnell not only offered financial contributions to the zoo, but also tremendous business advice to me as the director. (Michael W. Pogany/Columbus Zoo)

Now, I was well aware of the zoo's financial constraints. I had examples every day to remind me of them. One day I was sitting in my not-so-plush office, a room in the bird exhibit building beside the animal hospital. I must have been deep in thought, concentrating on solving the challenge of the day, because I didn't hear a thing. Then all of a sudden, this chimp drops down through the ceiling tile and lands smack in the middle of my desk. He had escaped from the hospital and was coming by to check out the new director, I guess.

One thing in my favor was that the zoo staff all cared very much about their animals. They would not be in this business otherwise, because the pay was low. I figured if I could produce something big and exciting for the animals, the staff would pick up on it, the public would benefit, and it would have a positive snowballing effect for everyone. The question was, what kind of splash could I make with little or no money?

If I didn't know then that anything is possible, I would soon find it out with a visionary plan that to this day makes me as proud as anything I've ever done. Yet it was only possible because of the willingness of one generous man: John H. McConnell.

The gorillas had always been the star attraction at the Columbus Zoo. Even with a run-down operation, our collection of great apes generally was held in high esteem throughout the zoo world. It seemed a shame to me that they were largely ignored by the community—like having Pavarotti sing to an empty house. It was zoologically important, but few people cared that Colo, the zoo's oldest female, who was then twenty-one, was the first gorilla born in captivity. She was even featured on the cover of *National Geographic* when she was born in 1956.

John McConnell gives the first major donation to Bongo to build a new gorilla exhibit, which helped turn the zoo around. (*Columbus Dispatch Photo*)

When I got to Columbus, neither Colo nor any of the other apes had ever been outdoors on grass or felt the sunlight in a natural habitat. This was not anything unusual in zoos at the time, but it was disturbing to me, and I wanted to do something about it. These magnificent animals certainly deserved better; any animal does. As an added bonus, I also knew that attendance usually jumped radically when you put animals in natural habitats.

When I came across an item in the paper about a man named John McConnell, the self-made multimillionaire founder of Worthington Industries, I thought, *Why not?* He seemed like a community-type guy. Maybe this man would donate the money for us to build a new gorilla enclosure.

Well, it looks like I wasn't the only one with that idea. Mr. McConnell had people from all sides asking for one thing or another, which made getting in touch with him nearly impossible. Fortunately, I was able to get to Joe Stegmayer, Mr. McConnell's vice president and right-hand man. After several of my phone calls, he finally made an appointment to meet me.

Joe was a man for detail, and I think my vagueness may have put him off at first. "Joe, I've got this idea," I told him right off the bat. "Our gorillas have never known anything but a concrete cage and bars; they don't know what grass is. I want to put the gorillas outside. It's going to be spring soon, and I've got to do something quickly." I realized later I was talking to a man who had never even been to the zoo. Later, he was to become chairman of our zoo board.

As I gave him more details, we struck up a dialogue. I told him about an old, out-of-use elephant yard, now housing kangaroos, that could be turned into a gorilla environment. I mentioned that I had devised a plan where we were going to raise the wall four feet on the outside, knock down the inside walls, and install glass for viewing inside, for a cost of forty or fifty thousand dollars

"What makes you think these gorillas aren't going to jump out?" he asked me.

"I just don't think they will," I said.

"You want us to give money in our name to put these gorillas outside. You realize if something happens, if they get out—it's our money that did it."

"No, Joe, they won't," I told him, but he didn't seem very encouraged or enthusiastic. He said he would call me.

Over the next three weeks, I called Joe numerous times. My excitement and enthusiasm finally got to him. Joe called and asked me to come in and meet Mr. McConnell.

John McConnell had a friendly look about him, not at all what I would have imagined. He had a warm, round face, like Santa Claus without a beard. When I walked into his office, he was smoking a pipe. He just sat there and looked at me for about ten seconds without saying anything. Nervously, I was praying for a miracle.

"I've been hearing some stuff about the zoo," he said at last. "Joe tells me you're trying to do some good things over there." He put me on the positive side right away.

I jumped in, "Yes, sir," and reiterated my grandiose plan about building an outside yard for the gorillas. At the same time, I went into my usual speech about how the zoo is there for the use of everybody in the community: children, senior citizens, and the disabled.

He listened, then told me he liked my plan, but he, too, was concerned about the gorillas escaping. "What makes you think they won't get out?" he asked. "I want somebody to check it out." Mr. McConnell had no idea that I had made this plan up on the spot!

"I'm going to check it out, sir," I told him. "I've got a heck of an idea. Chimpanzees are the most ingenious and agile of all the zoo animals. I'm going to turn a chimp loose in there, and if he can't get out, I know a gorilla won't. It's got to work."

What I didn't tell Mr. McConnell later was the chimp actually did get out. He ruined our test by going up and over the side of a portable wall. By that time, I had already announced the opening day of the new exhibit, so I didn't want to blow everything. We just put some hot wire over that corner, and everything was all right.

Building the gorilla yard took 120 days, and I think during that time I began to win the respect of my employees, or most of them at least. We were indebted to Mr. McConnell, of course, but the entire exhibit was staff-designed and staff-built. That's what made everyone so proud—we did it ourselves.

To the newspapers and television, I built up a steady stream of PR for our project. May 19, 1979, was our big day, and as people heard about it, they became involved. We were all pushing together to get this thing ready in time. During this period, we were becoming a team, working night and day and, in the process, getting to know each other.

Gorilla keepers, who never seemed to care too much about what went on in the rest of the zoo, now worked with maintenance people; aquarium people came in—nobody had ever known they existed. I was in there painting, shoveling sand, doing whatever I could. They all found out that everybody's success depends on everybody else's hard work at the zoo.

We finished just in time on May 18, and the next day was one of the biggest days of my life. At first, the gorillas were afraid and didn't want to venture out of their indoor enclosure. They would peek out, then maybe take their hand or foot and touch the grass, pick up little pieces and put it in their mouths. It was sad to see them afraid of a natural environment. The first day only two gorillas came out into the new yard. Airplanes above frightened them because they had never seen anything fly. When a bird flew close by for the first time, they ducked. But slowly they adapted to their new habitat. It was especially rewarding when I saw Oscar, my favorite gorilla, basking in the sun, kicking his feet in the stream.

The whole project was a tremendous beginning for me—from the day John McConnell gave us his commitment to the day the first gorilla saw sunshine. It was also a significant start for the community to become involved with the Columbus Zoo. Granted, I was pretty anxious those first days. I couldn't sleep at night thinking a gorilla might jump over that wall.

We've spent millions of dollars in construction since then, but I will never forget about all of our staff working together to build the gorilla exhibit for fifty thousand dollars. As for the donation from Mr. McConnell, it had set a huge precedent, paving the way for zoo charities and donations to come.

And if you're wondering, the gorillas never did get out—well, not from the outdoor enclosure anyway. But the indoor enclosure, now that's another story.

CHAPTER 6

Monkeys on the Interstate

While community enthusiasm continued to grow, I knew I had to keep coming up with new ideas and different ways to renovate the zoo. Just after the gorilla exhibit opened to such success, I thought, *Why not do the same thing with the snow monkeys?* But this is one scheme that really backfired!

Our ten snow monkeys, or Japanese macaques, were one of our finest attractions, but they were confined to indoor living. I thought, *Why not put the snow monkeys—who are very active and put on quite a show—out on this moated area called Monkey Island?* At the time, this exhibit, which was the oldest at the zoo, was being used for small primates and goats.

Before moving the monkeys, I had the moat filled with water and the outer wall raised. I knew these snow monkeys could swim, but the level of their abilities truly amazed me.

Japanese snow monkeys swim on top of the water and underwater; they could even swim in ice water! They love to swim. They can also—we realized a little too late—climb hoses that are left out to fill the moat. During a seven-month odyssey across central Ohio, they became the most notorious escapees the zoo has ever had.

I first heard about the "breakout" over my trusty little walkie-talkie that we all carry around the zoo. Animals seldom escaped, but if they did, chances were they would stick around near where they got out, since the zoo's their home. Our two monkeys (actually three escaped but one came back) were first spotted just off the zoo grounds on the edge of the river, high up in some big old willow trees, virtually unreachable.

Since we had no veterinarian on the grounds at the time, no tranquilizer guns that worked well, and no Tarzan on hand, I thought, *Let's get a chain saw, cut these trees down, and see if we can quickly capture the escapees.* Bad idea.

The tree could fall either way, so I had one guy next to it with a net, while a zookeeper and I were out on the river in a rickety old rowboat with another net. The tree fell into the water with a huge splash, just missing the boat. So eager to capture the monkeys, my keeper jumped into the water to grab them, forgetting he couldn't swim!

When I jumped into the river to try and save him, an underwater tree branch caught me in the groin area. Now I was moaning in pain, my keeper was gasping for air, and the monkeys were casually swimming upstream. By the time we got ourselves back together, they were long gone.

Over the next few weeks, the monkeys were spotted on farms a few miles from the zoo in an area near Seldom Seen Road, so I named them Seldom Seen Junior and Senior. They were foraging in people's gardens and having the time of their lives. By now, a lot of jokes were being made, the newspapers were covering it every day, and of course, local television newscasters were having a ball with it too. I wasn't laughing, and I wasn't sleeping much either.

Some calls I received were from irate people, some even threatening to shoot the monkeys if they didn't stay out of their gardens. I begged them not to, to please have patience; I promised that we would capture the monkeys.

Most of the calls I received were from people enjoying this "great escape." A woman told us she had been watching one monkey sit in her crab apple tree eating fruit; another said he was swimming in her pond. One man told us one of the animals had been sleeping in his tool shed at night. With every sighting, we would drive to the location and come back empty-handed; some of them may have been false alarms.

For about a month, we lost track of the monkeys. The story sort of died down, but I knew those monkeys were quite hardy, and I knew they could survive in the "wild" of Ohio in the summer. A big concern was that they were possibly developing muscles they'd never used before and could be quite dangerous, especially if cornered by people who were untrained in handling animals.

Then, one night, some five weeks after they first became fugitives, Senior somehow worked his way back to the zoo, to the original bunch of trees next to his enclosure. We called Dr. Gardner, our veterinarian, to the scene with tranquilizer guns. He managed to hit him twice, with no effect. With the help of twenty-two people and five floodlights, we cut down two more trees in an attempt to nab him before we wound up watching him swim to the other shore and head north.

Cutting down all these trees just added to my embarrassment. It wasn't long before I received a call from Mel Dodge: "What's going on up there? Now you're decimating our local woods again? I mean, what is this, the Keystone Kops? Can't anybody catch those monkeys?"

From time to time, truck drivers would help us keep track of Seldom Seen Senior and Junior. We put pins on a map in my office every day, as if we were charting enemy troop movements during a war. Gradually it became apparent that Senior and Junior were separately moving north along I-71, each on a different side of the interstate, about twenty miles apart.

One day a trucker called to tell us he had tried to get Senior inside the cab of his truck by offering him a sandwich. Senior ate the sandwich, then bolted to a nearby golf course. I sent some keepers to the course with a new plan. The keepers dressed up like golfers and put tranquilizer guns in their golf bags, along with golf clubs of course. I even told them to be sure they were playing golf, since Senior was so smart. It was evident that I was getting desperate.

When the keepers spotted him in a tree, they stayed calm, finished their golf shots, then went to their bags for the guns. The moment Senior saw them with the guns, he was off like a bullet.

Eventually, by late fall, the monkeys had traveled over a hundred miles from the zoo. With winter around the corner and vegetable gardens bare, it was apparent they were ready to return to civilization, on their own terms anyway. The sightings were becoming more frequent and always around people.

In the second week of November, almost six months after they had escaped, we received a tip from a county game warden. Junior was hanging out in a barn near Upper Sandusky. With a number of zoo staff, we surrounded the barn and took him in relatively easy fashion. With one monkey recovered, everyone felt relieved, but Senior was still at large. I remember telling the press, however, that it was just a matter of time until we'd get him. The question was, how long?

By this time, I was getting a little edgy with my staff. I was tired of people coming back empty-handed, of overtime pay, of nighttime hours, of the Columbus Zoo—and its new director—being the laughingstock of the entire community.

I'll never forget the night of the call from Elyria, a Cleveland suburb. The sheriff's department had called to tell us that Senior was trapped in a garage and that they would wait for us to come to get him. I really wanted to go, but I couldn't leave the zoo because of an important giraffe birth. Tommy Steele, one of our keepers at the time, was one of the "bounty hunters" I'd sent out occasionally. Tommy lived just across the river, was in his early twenties, and had worked around the zoo since he was a little boy.

Tommy said, "I'll get him. I promise." By his look of determination, you knew he meant business. He had a net, a crate, everything. I told him to call me when he got up there.

When Tommy arrived at the house (owned by an Elyria patrolman), there were about seventy-five people, three television crews, and a dozen reporters and photographers surrounding the garage. Some people were waving bananas. Tommy called and explained the situation, and I told him he had to keep that garage door shut and not let anybody in until the monkey was captured and secured.

Tommy told everyone to stand back and stay out, and he proceeded to have a slam-bam-and-drag-out chase with that monkey. In the process, Old Seldom Seen just about wrecked the entire garage. When Tommy came out with the monkey after almost an hour and a half, he looked like he'd wrestled a grizzly.

Later, Tommy told me that the man had just rearranged his garage—nails and screws in little jars and all that. The monkey overturned every single item in the entire place, making it look like a hurricane had been through there when they were finished.

After pictures were flashed and interviews were finished, Tommy and the staff were proudly on their way back to the zoo with Senior.

Needless to say, no more hoses were ever left hanging over the wall around the moat. Considering that each male monkey had about eight wives, life was pretty good. Makes you wonder why they ever wanted to escape in the first place.

One of the things I found exasperating in my first year at Columbus was that zoos rarely worked together. Zoos were remodeling natural habitats, raising funds, and doing all kinds of new things, but giving or getting advice or sharing information did not happen that often among zoo directors. The sad part was that the animals were the ones hurt by the lack of cooperation.

As I mentioned earlier, the Columbus Zoo was behind in the zoo field in the late 1970s. Knowing everyone has his own place to operate, I'm not saying the entire zoo community should have bent over backward to help little old Jack Hanna, but all zoos could have benefited more in the past by working together. I'm talking about calling somebody up and saying, "Joe, we're putting in a pond for our snow monkeys . . . any ideas?"

Edward Maruska, director of the Cincinnati Zoo at the time, ran one of this country's greatest zoos. I'm very thankful to be able to say that our relationship survived a strange incident back in 1980. Few people would have been as understanding as he was.

One hot August morning, "Unit One," my call number, blared in my ear. I heard a panicky call over my walkie-talkie—which I left on all the time. People found it humorous the way I left that walkie-talkie on twenty-four hours a day. Listening in kept me informed of everything going on at the zoo, from a dysfunctional boiler to a late-night visit from our head veterinarian,

A cereopsis goose, like the one that paid a high price for biting a zoo employee. (Earl W. Smith III)

Dr. Gardner, and I think the employees, in reality, valued that.

Anyway, on this particular morning, there was an emergency involving the cheetahs. I rushed over and got there just in time to learn that one of our employees had five minutes earlier fed an endangered cereopsis goose to the cheetahs. I was dumbfounded. How? Why?

It was tough to get the details, but the undeniable bottom line was that a zoo employee in maintenance had purposely fed a rare goose to the cheetahs. To make things worse, this goose was on a breeding loan from the Cincinnati Zoo.

As I found out later, the woman, I'll call her Jane, was deathly afraid of birds. This, together with the goose's nasty disposition—he liked to bite people—created a bad match. One of Jane's duties was to clean the bathrooms. In order to do this, she needed to walk through the holding pen for birds, and on this day someone had temporarily left the goose in the pen. The birdhouse people knew that the goose wasn't supposed to be in that area because it assaulted people.

Predictably, the goose bit Jane while she was cleaning, leaving a welt on her leg. Crying and upset, she ran over to her husband's office—he was head of maintenance—to tell him what happened. In his account, he told me later that he was busy with some other people and underestimated how upset she was. "Go feed it to the cheetahs," were his exact words, never looking up from his desk and never thinking his wife would take him literally.

Jane huffed out madder than ever. She went back over to the bird house, and with the help of a seasonal employee, managed to corral the goose and stuff it into a big garbage container. Now, this other worker was either intimidated, or didn't realize at first what she was up to, or couldn't stop her by himself, whatever. At some point, he ran back to maintenance to tell her husband what was happening, and that's when I heard the call over the walkie-talkie.

Our security chief, Dave Bricker, zipped over to the cheetah pen with his sirens going full blast. He arrived too late, just as Jane was lifting the garbage container up over the fence, sending the goose to its certain death. The goose never knew what hit him, which was a cheetah going about fifty miles an hour. The cat hit that goose like a bombshell and broke its neck instantly. The cheetah had no interest in eating it, and the dead goose was just lying on the ground when I got there.

After talking with everybody involved, I went back to my office and sat there, baffled. I was convinced the goose was on the endangered species list and thought maybe the woman could go to jail for what she'd done. It was that serious.

Then there was Edward Maruska and the Cincinnati Zoo. Here I was, new kid on the block in the zoo world, trying to win the respect of people like him. The man was noted for being tough. Now I had to call him and explain what happened. Didn't I have control of my employees? Didn't they value wildlife? I went home, jogged a couple of miles, and thought about it all night.

A curator came into my office first thing in the morning to tell me that this species of goose had been taken off the endangered list two weeks earlier, which was some relief for me and Jane. Now it was time to call Edward Maruska.

"Mr. Maruska? This is Jack Hanna."

"How are you doing?" he asked. "How's the zoo going?"

"Fine," I said, and not much more. "Mr. Maruska, I've got to tell you something. I don't really know how to tell you—this story's incredible. Your cereopsis goose is dead."

"How did it die?" was his first response.

At first, I blurted, "One of my maintenance people fed it to the cheetahs." Then I rambled, "It's a long story . . . she's deathly afraid of birds . . . her husband was busy . . . the goose bit her . . ."

"What?" He cut me short. "Slow down, please."

I went on, bumbling out the story, making very little sense, before he cut me off again.

"Listen, just put this in writing, okay? Just write in a letter what happened. Do that. Thank you."

"I'm sorry," I said to him. "I'm really sorry—I'll make it up to you. I'll get another one. I'll . . ."

At this point I didn't know what to say. Fortunately, Maruska knew that incidents like this, if prolonged, hurt everyone, and he considered the case closed once he received the written report. Of course, we also paid for the bird, or I should say, the zoo workers involved paid for the bird.

Looking back, I'm very happy that I did make the decision not to fire anybody. It's too easy to fire people. Jane was suspended for two weeks without pay, and she and her husband wrote letters of apology. They continued working for the zoo without incident for several more years.

Then the paper broke a front-page story, with the headline "Columbus Cheetahed Cincinnati on Goose." I hadn't even told the trustees yet. The Cincinnati Zoo had been very forgiving, and this negative publicity was terrible. Being rattled, I called Mel Dodge, who surprised me with his reaction.

"Jack, that's the funniest thing I've ever read. I'm still laughing." He could barely contain himself.

"Mel, I'm glad you see the humor in it, but it's not funny." I was dead serious. "It's a troubling situation and certainly doesn't help the zoo or me in acquiring any kind of respect in the zoological world, of which we're both lacking."

"Hey, mistakes happen," he told me. "You can't control what other people do."

As usual, I felt better after talking to Mel. He helped me get a grip on things, and though I still didn't see the humor, I got over my self-doubts.

One interesting result of this whole affair was that we had a huge crowd that weekend to see the cheetah that killed the goose. Of course, we didn't promote it that way, but that's the power of the media.

CHAPTER 7

To the Rescue

Things don't happen totally by accident; I'm convinced of that. If the trend of my getting calls for animal rescues followed me from Florida to Ohio, well, I guess I may have promoted that somewhat. Like most people, I like to help animals, and if this generates publicity that helps the Columbus Zoo or increases the appreciation and better care of wildlife or house pets, so much the better.

The first of my many animal rescues in Columbus happened in the fall of 1979, my second year at the zoo. As so often happens with these things, I was dog-tired and ready for bed when the doorbell rang. At the door stood a very panicked lady. She introduced herself as Charlotte Stukey from Citizens for Humane Action.

"Mr. Hanna, you've got to come help me," she said. "Someone has thrown a kitten over the O'Shaughnessy Dam."

"I'm sorry, ma'am, but there is no way that cat could be alive," I remember telling her right away. "You've looked down at that dam, right?"

The O'Shaughnessy Dam wasn't exactly Hoover Dam or Niagara Falls, but it's more than a hundred feet down, and it's safe to say that a human being wouldn't survive such a fall.

"No, it's not dead," she insisted. "This cat is stuck on a concrete ledge, ninety feet down from the bridge, right above the turmoil. Please, get in your car and just come look. No one will believe me."

"Why did you come to me?" I asked her.

"The Humane Society is closed, and the police and fire departments are too busy. No one will help me. Please come." She told me later that she and her family had spotted the cat while sightseeing at the dam.

Driving with her to the middle of the dam, I stopped the car and got out with my high-beam flashlight. It was pitch black outside, and I just knew this woman was out of her mind.

She pointed. "It's down there."

"Down where?" All I could see was rushing water.

After poking around with the flashlight for a while, I came across this little black form, way down at the bottom, dangerously perched on the ledge of a concrete slab that was maybe two feet wide.

How it wound up there is beyond comprehension. Talk about nine lives. It was so disturbing to think that somebody had probably just driven by and flung it out the window. Somehow the kitten must have slid down the concrete piling and managed to catch on to the ledge. I could not believe it.

What was even more amazing was that someone had to be walking across the dam and looking down from the perfect spot just to see the poor little thing. That cat could have stayed there for weeks without anybody spotting it—for all I knew, it had been there two, three days.

Not knowing exactly how to tackle this problem, I said I'd get a boat and we'd get him tomorrow when it was light. I knew that cat wasn't going anywhere.

First thing the next morning, I called Mike July, our animal curator. The two of us borrowed a boat and net from Art Hegedus, the aquarium curator, and went out in the boat under the dam at the same time many people were driving over on their way to work. We didn't call the media, but before we knew it, a crowd had gathered on the bridge above to watch our attempted cat rescue. And boy, did we give them a show.

From the boat, our net would not quite reach the ledge, which was about twelve feet over our heads. After flailing around for a while, I realized we were stuck in turbulent water and could not maneuver the boat. Now I was thinking we might be stranded in this precarious spot forever. This whirlpool had a death grip on us, keeping the boat in the same spot. The water was swirling, and it scared the fire out of me.

John Becker, our zoo operations manager, was on the bridge over the dam, and he came up with an idea to dangle some rope down to scare the cat into our net. That scheme did not work—it was difficult getting a rope that long anywhere near the cat. So we started throwing little rocks at it, trying to get it off the ledge. We proved to be bad marksmen, and we worried that a poorly thrown rock might scare the cat off the wrong way. If the cat went into the roaring water, it was all over.

After many failed attempts, the kitten is miraculously knocked into the net. (*Delaware Gazette*)

Then Becker came up with another idea: throw water balloons at the cat. He bought some balloons from a market near the dam and threw a half dozen of those water balloons. It was now two outs, bottom of the ninth, and a three-and-two count on the cat. Most of the balloons hit us, not the cat. I was trying to hold the boat in position, Mike had the net, and we were both getting splattered. And just as I was thinking this was hopeless, a water balloon hit the cat perfectly and knocked it into the center of our net. The crowd up on the bridge went nuts. They were still clapping and cheering when another boat came to pull us out of there.

The cat wound up in the home of a secretary who worked for WBNS-TV in downtown Columbus. I was honored that she named the cat Hanna, but I wasn't surprised when she told me it was the feistiest cat she'd ever seen.

Rescuing one little kitty from drowning didn't seem like a huge deal at the time, but it set the Columbus Zoo in a completely different light in the eyes of the community. The whole incident garnered heavy coverage in the newspapers, and the staff of the zoo became known as "people who cared." At the same time, it established Jack Hanna not just as a zoo director but as a caring person whom people could call on twenty-four hours a day—and that's just what they started doing.

One of my great misadventures, actually a *non*rescue, occurred on a cool, late-fall Sunday night when my brother had come to visit from Knoxville. My brother, Bush, had gotten sick of following me around all weekend. (Weekends can be my busiest time at the zoo.) He came up to see my family and me, and I really hadn't been able to give him too much of my time. By the time Sunday evening rolled around, Bush was just looking forward to a nice dinner at home with Suzi and the kids and a quick trip back home. We just had a drink, and I was putting the steaks on the grill when the phone rang.

"Mr. Hanna?"

"Yes?"

"This is the Columbus police dispatcher. We've received a report that a hippo is loose in the river in downtown Columbus and . . ."

"Yeah, right, and I've got the tooth fairy up on my roof talking to Santa Claus right now. See you later," I said, and hung up. Usually I'm not so rude, but I was trying to unwind and wasn't in the mood for any jokes.

Less than a minute later the phone rang again, and this time it was the sheriff's department.

"Mr. Hanna, there's a hippo loose in downtown Columbus, and we wondered if you knew anything."

"Wait a minute," I said. "This is for real?"

They assured me it was and wanted to know if I knew anything about it. I didn't, and whoever I was talking to didn't know much either. I went out and told Bush, and he looked at me like I was either nuts or drunk.

I immediately called Dave Bricker, my security chief, to see what the heck was going on.

"I just talked to the chief on duty," he explained. "Jack, they've got four squad cars up there. They've got a SWAT team helicopter up there. They've got *everybody* up there chasing this hippo."

"Did you check our hippos?" I asked him. "See how many we've got there."

"I just did that. They're all there. I counted three: Pete, Mama, and the baby."

"Well, where do you think this hippo came from?"

"Jack, I don't know. I'm not *supposed* to know where the hippo came from." Boy oh boy, I sure wasn't getting a lot of information around here. I told Bricker to pick me up, and we'd go downtown and check this out.

I went back out to the porch, told Bush the story and, trying to involve him a little bit, asked him where he thought the hippo came from.

"Jack, I don't really care," he said with his blasé attitude. He acted like this was somebody's idea of a bad joke—which, for all I knew, it was.

I asked him if he'd take a ride with us to see what was happening.

"I'm staying right here to eat a good steak," he told me. "And another thing—I'm never coming to visit you again while you're working."

"Fine," I said. "You don't have to go. But you know I can't shoot very well, and I can't lasso at all." Bricker was bringing along a tranquilizer gun and two sets of ropes. At the mention of shooting and lassoing, being the cow farmer he was, Bush decided to come along.

On our way downtown in Bricker's car, we monitored the situation over the police radio, and it was apparent that they were very serious about the whole thing. About two minutes before we got there, a voice addressed us: "Please have Mr. Hanna ready. We've got the helicopter and chair ready to bring him out over the river with his ropes."

My throat went dry. No way was I going out over that river dangling from a helicopter seat. "Bush, you've got to do this for me. You live on a farm; you know how to lasso," I said, trying to convince my brother.

"Okay," he said. "I'll lasso it—I'll shoot it too." He didn't care. He thought we were all crazy, and he wasn't far from wrong.

When we got there, it looked like the president had just arrived. There were squad cars, fire trucks, helicopters, spotlights, TV crews, fog lights. I wasn't three steps out of the car when a guy I knew, the head man on the SWAT team, took me aside and said, "Jack, I've got a big problem."

"What's wrong?" I asked him.

"You're not going to believe this," he said, "but we've just found out that it's only a river otter. I don't know who made the mistake."

"What? A hippopotamus weighs at least three thousand pounds; a river otter will go twenty or thirty pounds at the most—how could you guys get the two confused?" He couldn't answer me.

After hearing that, my brother and I thought about the steaks we had left behind for this mishap. On top of it all, they were asking *me* to make an announcement to the media.

Dana Tyler, who's the anchorperson for Channel 10 News in Columbus, was right there, asking, "Jack, what is it? What's going on now?"

"Dana," I said, taking a deep breath—somehow I knew ol' Jack was going to take the rap on this fiasco. "There's obviously been a mistake here. You're not going to believe this, but from what I'm told, it looks like it's a large river otter."

"A what?"

"An otter, a large river otter."

"How much can it weigh?" she asked me.

"Well, in prehistoric times," I said, and here I started making things up, "it could have weighed up to two hundred pounds." Of course, who cares about prehistoric times? This is today. "But today," I said, "a big one might weigh up to twenty pounds." I was doing the best I could to not make the whole rescue team look any more ridiculous.

"But, Dana," I added, digging a deeper hole, "have you ever seen a person swimming—you know how they come up with their back and make the water roll and everything? That otter was swimming, making the water roll in these big waves, and it looked like a hippo."

I was trying to explain all this on TV, and she just shook her head and said,

"Jack, what are you doing? I don't believe this. What do you think happened?"

"Don't ask me," I said. "I was called from home; you people were here forty-five minutes before I even knew about it." That's what I should have said in the first place. Next thing I knew, she was interviewing Bush, a man of few words, who of course had no idea what was going on. Nobody had any clear-cut answers on this thing.

The next day's newspaper ran a story headlined "River Monster Turns Out to Be Otter," and the television coverage of the incident led off the "year in review" news show on New Year's Eve—some kind of funny "Who can forget . . ." sort of thing. One thing's for sure, my brother Bush never forgot it.

Another crazy rescue call came on one of my busiest Saturdays ever at the zoo—this was a time when I had a lot of speeches and zoo tours to prepare—I got a call from some guy who was frantic.

"Mr. Hanna," he said, "I've got a big problem, and I don't know who to call. My German shepherd had puppies two days ago and one of them fell down the heating and air-conditioning vent in my house." If he really didn't know who to call, how come my phone ends up ringing?

"Can't you reach down in there and get it?" I asked.

"I can't," he said. "I've tried everything. He's way down in there, and I can't get him out."

I wrote down the man's phone number and told him I would see what I could do. After I hung up, I crumpled the note and threw it in the wastebasket. I had speeches and zoo tours scheduled for that day, and I wanted that note to just go away. But it wouldn't. I kept hearing the guy's voice.

Finally, I dug the number out of the garbage, called the guy, and told him I'd be out there. He lived about twenty miles away—a real pain in the butt.

So I went out there with Bricker and Glenn Baker, another character who had been with the zoo forever and worked in air-conditioning on the side. We pulled up to the house and there was already a group of people gathered—"Hey, Jack Hanna's here," and all that. A kid even came up and asked for my autograph.

The house was about twenty-five or thirty years old—nothing fancy by any means, just a nice little white house. The man showed me the vent, and I knelt down next to it and listened closely. I could hear little puppy sounds.

"Well, let's get a saw," I said, "and we'll cut a hole in the floor."

"It's concrete," the guy said.

I couldn't believe it; I didn't think they made houses like that. We pulled a little of the carpet back, and sure enough, the metal vent was centered into poured concrete, a foot thick. The vents went through that concrete to the heating and air-conditioning system about thirty feet away.

Glenn Baker knew air-conditioning, so I figured he could take care of this. He stuck his arm in there but couldn't reach the dog. We tried a sewer snake, monkeying it this way and that, but the puppy wasn't moving—had to be fifteen feet down. This was Glenn's first rescue call, by the way, and he was having a ball. He wasn't just going to rescue the dog; he was going to rescue the world.

"Tell you what," Baker told the dog owner. "We're gonna pull up some more of that carpet and we're gonna take us a hammer and chisel and take up some of that concrete down where we think that dog is."

The guy didn't mind; he just wanted his puppy back. So we pulled up about ten feet of glued rug, pretty well ruining it, and we hammered and dug a hole down through the concrete into the vent. Now we could really hear the dog yipping, but we still could not reach him—he had moved farther back.

"Aw, geez," I said. "Just cancel my whole day." It was now two hours since I'd gotten that call and we weren't any closer to the dog than when we arrived.

"I got an idea," said Baker. "Bricker, why don't you go out to your police cruiser and call the Sewers and Drains Department, have them bring one of their jackhammers over."

Baker's idea seemed all right, like one I would think of myself. Whoever showed up, I'd take care of them with a load of free zoo passes. A half hour later, the Sewers Department truck pulled up with a guy and his jackhammer.

He said it was a slow day and didn't mind coming over—he was probably getting double-overtime. So we went into the house, got that jackhammer going, and it was something else with that ear-piercing noise and cement particles flying. Everybody had to go outside. Within thirty seconds there was so much dust, you couldn't see a foot in front of your face.

"Whoa!" I yelled at the top of my lungs. "Stop! Stop! This is terrible! We're destroying your house," I told the guy. Not to mention that his puppy might be vibrating to death.

"This isn't my house," said the guy, dropping the bombshell. "I'm renting it."

"You're what?! You're kidding me, right?" Baker started laughing. "You're kidding this man, aren't you?" he said.

"No, I don't own it. I rent it," the guy repeated.

"I don't believe this is happening," said Bricker. Up till now, he'd just been standing by. Again, Bricker, my security chief, worked for me and the zoo, but he was officially on the police force, and this was hardly official conduct.

"Didn't you call the landlord and tell him what we're doing?" I asked the guy.

"No, I didn't call him. I don't ever talk to the guy," he said.

"You told me I could tear up your carpet and jackhammer your floor. There's got to be over two thousand dollars' worth of damage here," I said in a panic. Baker was still laughing, and Bricker looked sick—and I could wind up paying for this upheaval!

"Now listen," I told the guy, "we're going to get your puppy, but I want you to sign a piece of paper saying we're not responsible for this mess. Somebody's going to sign something, because I'm not paying for your house."

Well, we blasted that floor another three minutes or so, and the jackhammer noise made the puppy back all the way into the air-conditioning unit. Hearing him in there, Baker pulled him out, and suddenly he was a big hero.

We left the place in shambles, carpet and concrete lying all over the place. Baker didn't even put the guy's air conditioner back together. Since I had to get back to the zoo, he just left it on the floor. That landlord still probably doesn't know what happened to his house, but no one ever called me.

Another time I received a call, but it involved an animal that was a far cry from a cute little pup. When I get phone calls from various city departments, I try to give them as much attention as possible. As I've said over and over, the Columbus Zoo owes a debt to the entire community, and it's important that we all work together. Some departments I've never heard from and never will, and some come at me out of the blue—like the Water Department.

On one of those rare mild early spring days, I got a call from an official

at the Water Department. He told me that one of his meter readers had reported an encounter with a large alligator at a residence near the fairgrounds. The department head asked me to check it out. As it stood, his worker was frightened and refused to return to the neighborhood. It was a busy Friday, and it was difficult for me to get away. Not really believing the story, I didn't want to go, but I finally gave in because the man was politely begging me to go down there.

Dancing with Allie, the pet alligator. (Michael W. Pogany/ Columbus Zoo)

That area of town was tough, so I called Bricker to tag along. It's not the kind of place where you can walk up, knock on a door by yourself, and say, "Excuse me, but I want to see your twelve-foot alligator." I would have called these people first, but they didn't have a phone.

Bricker did not want to get a search warrant, and I agreed with him. A lot of times, people who have exotic animals don't know what the law is and could get in a lot of trouble. If I can talk to them and possibly get the animal to a zoo or a proper home without going through all of the legal stuff, I would rather do that.

So Bricker and I drove down to this address, a little house near the Ohio State Fairgrounds. An older man came to the door and asked what we wanted.

"Jack Hanna, from the zoo," I said, putting out my hand. The guy ignored it and just looked at us. "We had a report about an alligator being here."

Bricker was wearing his police uniform, and I know this helped. If it had just been me, the guy probably would have just lied. But he called back in the house and said, "Son, they're here to see your alligator." Just like that.

A man appeared, about thirty years old, and was very nervous. "Nothing's wrong with my alligator," he said.

"Look," I explained, "we're not going to hurt your alligator—all we want to do is see him. We received a report the water meter man stepped on a twelve-foot alligator."

"Okay—if you won't take him away from me."

"I won't take him away from you." I thought the guy was going to break down.

"All right, then," he said. "We'll go see Allie." He took us around the side of the house to a basement door and called down, "Here, Allie. Here, Allie."

It was the most incredible thing. We're expecting some two- or three-foot gator, and up the stairs came this eight- to ten-foot, four- to five-hundred-pound alligator!

Bricker and I both jumped back.

"He ain't gonna hurt you," the guy said. Then he patted the alligator on the head and said, "Come on, Allie. Let's go outside."

The alligator walked up those basement steps—so help me—went out in the backyard, and lay down in the sun.

"This is where it happened," said the son. "I had Allie out—I was sunning him—and I went inside the house for a minute. The man must have come across the fence and stepped on him. But Allie wouldn't hurt him."

"Maybe not," I said, "but that thing could eat a hundred-pound boy. How long have you had him?"

"Fourteen years."

Fourteen years. This guy had an alligator near downtown Columbus ever since he was a kid. He bought it when it was a foot long and had kept it ever since. What amazed me was the care he provided it. Most of those "pet" alligators—that you used to be able to buy in places like Florida—died from people not knowing how to care for them.

"What do you feed Allie?" I asked him.

"Rabbits," he said. He took us to the back of the yard and showed us these cages with about thirty rabbits in them. He said the neighbors thought he raised rabbits, and as far as he knew, they didn't know he had an alligator.

Then the guy showed us pictures of him and Allie taking showers and baths together. He was actually lying down in the water with this alligator.

"Allie just loves it when I take a bath with him," he said. Bricker sat there with his mouth open, shaking his head.

This created a dichotomy for me. I was impressed with this guy's care for his alligator. I was probably wrong, and it goes against my general beliefs about people owning exotic animals, but I wanted the guy to keep his alligator. Bricker and I went outside to talk it over.

"What are we going to do?" I asked Bricker. "I don't want to take that alligator."

"Yeah, but he might be breaking the law," he said.

"I know, but let's wait until somebody officially calls us to go pick up the alligator. I really don't need any more gators at the zoo anyway."

"Okay," said Bricker.

"What about the water man? What do we tell him?" I asked.

"Tell him whatever you want," he said.

So we left father, son, and Allie back there. When I got back to the office, I called the water man and told him to just be careful the next time he reads that meter!

Of course, I kept really quiet on this one. But the funny thing is, a few years later, the *National Enquirer* featured the story of a man and his alligator in an urban setting. I recognized him immediately. A lot of people probably thought it was bunk since it was in the *National Enquirer*, but I knew better.

Looking back, I probably should have compassionately explained why he couldn't keep the alligator. I empathized with this guy and his love of a unique pet, but I also knew what could happen when a wild animal—no matter how loved—threatened a stranger. To this day, though, I haven't heard any reports of an alligator attack in the area, so I guess it all turned out for the best.

CHAPTER 8

Sssnakes

Of all the animal world, snakes are probably the most hated, ill-regarded, misunderstood creatures there are. I've found that people are generally deathly afraid of any kind of snake. Forget the fact that most snakes are hardly more harmful to humans than a housefly—let's face it, they're victims of a reputation that goes all the way back to Adam and Eve.

Knowing how David Letterman dislikes snakes, I don't try to get him to hold them, like I do with other animals on the show. Recently I appeared on the *Late Show* with the largest python I've ever seen in captivity—it weighed about 310 pounds, was twenty-six feet long, and took seven of us to hold it up. This enormous python, Fluffy, is now on exhibit at the Columbus Zoo. She sure is something! Dave stood all the way across the set and turned nearly bleach white before we got that thing off.

I personally like snakes, but more importantly I respect them too. A spitting cobra can blind you in a split second; a bite from a coral snake can be deadly. I've learned a lot about snakes from Dr. Joe Cross, a reptile expert who was also my personal doctor and has treated me for all of the bites, scrapes, scratches, and claws I've gotten in this crazy business.

I also don't mind if responsible people own snakes, even venomous ones, provided they care for them properly and are cautious toward the general public. Unfortunately, this isn't always the case, and that's when somebody can get hurt—be it the owner, an innocent bystander, or an innocent snake. And that's when the zoo gets a lot of phone calls.

On a late autumn afternoon in 1984, I was just getting ready to leave the zoo when I received a phone call from the Columbus chief of police.

"Jack," he said, "we've got a little problem with some snakes in an apartment down on the Ohio State campus. Can you come down and help us out?"

"Yeah, I know—this kind of call comes in all the time," I told him, trying to cut him off, "but I'm real busy, and I can't get down there right now." I was meeting a good friend Don Malenick, the president of Worthington Industries, for dinner. It was his company that had given us money to remodel the gorilla exhibit, my first large donation, and they had remained one of our steadiest contributors.

"Well, all right," he said, "but if you could get down there later—these are venomous snakes, mostly cobras and . . ."

"Cobras?" That got my attention.

The chief went on to tell me that a neighbor had noticed a terrible odor coming through the vents for over two weeks and had called the landlord. The landlord had gone into the apartment, seen the snakes, and called the cops. I was concerned because cobras can be deadly, and that smell probably meant mistreated animals.

The chief told me he could send a cruiser right away to pick me up, so I called Don and asked if he would mind coming along to look at some snakes before we had dinner. He was tickled when we pulled up to his house with the police car. Don was a rugged individual and runs a large company, but this was a change from his daily coat-and-tie world. Me, I just wanted to get away from the animal world and go eat dinner. Don was ready for whatever arose.

We were taken down to this typical university apartment complex—a group of buildings with duplexes. There were already four squad cars on hand in one of the parking areas, one with its lights flashing. The captain walked over and introduced himself.

"Jack, I appreciate your coming down. We've got a real problem here," he said. "There are over fifty snakes in this house."

"Did you go in and count fifty snakes?" I asked him. I didn't mean to be a wise guy, but people always seem to exaggerate and get alarmed when it comes to snakes.

"No," he said, "but I walked in the front room there, and this guy's got spiders on his mantel, and it's dark in there, and it's plenty weird. We have him under arrest now."

So now we're into spiders. I couldn't help thinking that this whole thing was a joke, except for the poor guy under arrest.

"What have you got here, a cult or something?" I asked the captain.

"None of my men want to go upstairs into the guy's bedroom. One of them got halfway up, saw this cobra on the bed, and came back down."

I realized then that it was stupid not to have my reptile people along. They handle snakes all day long. I hadn't considered it that big a deal, maybe one or two snakes. But what if I was wrong? I know a little bit about snakes, but I wasn't really ready to handle a venomous one.

So we went into the apartment, which was in semi-darkness. The lights didn't work—the electricity had probably been turned off. There was still some daylight left, but curtains or sheets had been nailed to the walls over the windows. The stench was overpowering, beyond anything I'd ever experienced, and I've been around a lot of animal dung in my life.

Sitting on a couch, just as we entered, was the snake owner and a policeman. Roy Dulin was the snake owner's name, and he was something else. In the dim light, I could just make out the long, dark wig he was wearing, pulled back from his shoulders in a ponytail. He was in his early thirties, wore metal-rimmed glasses, and had a faraway look in his eyes.

On the mantel were live tarantulas in little boxes. Don and I looked at each other and didn't say anything.

"Upstairs, that's where the snakes are," said the policeman.

"Well, why don't you have him go up there?" I said, pointing to Roy. "They're his snakes."

"Nooo, nooo," said Roy, shaking his head. He wasn't about to help—he was in a trance.

The policeman handed me his flashlight, motioning me to go first.

"Don, you want to go with me?" My buddy Don—I don't know why I asked him. Maybe I was getting the willies myself.

"Sure," said Don, "but I'm not going to touch any snakes!"

So we proceeded up the stairs, and I nudged open the bedroom door. On the bed was an aquarium tank with just a piece of cloth over it, and in it was a six-foot-long cobra—that's the first thing I saw. As my eyes got accustomed to the dark, I realized that there were actually three Egyptian cobras hooding in that fish tank with just a flimsy sheet as a cover.

"I don't believe this." That's all I said.

Behind me, the cop looked back and said, "Jack doesn't believe this." Then there was another cop behind Don who said, "Jack doesn't believe this." It was like the Three Stooges—the word went on down the stairs and out the door to the rest of the police.

"I can't believe they don't get out," I said.

"They're not going to get out," said Roy—he had heard me from downstairs—"because they're my friends."

As I looked around the room, I realized Roy had a lot of "friends." In another container on the floor were two rattlers, both overfed. One was easily six feet long and had to weigh ten pounds. There was a garbage can in the corner with a nine-foot python in it that weighed over sixty pounds. In a chest, in the drawers where most people keep shirts, he had three copperheads. In another aquarium he had a boomslang, a dangerous African tree snake.

It was mind-boggling. Here were about twenty snakes in this little bedroom, all venomous, except for the python, which probably could swallow a medium-sized dog. The guy couldn't possibly sleep in here. It was like the pit in *Raiders of the Lost Ark*, or worse.

Surprisingly, the snakes were in good condition, though some were overweight. For feeding his collection, Roy had live rats and mice all over the place, which added to the smell. He worked at an animal research lab, which is probably where he got his snake feed, although he claimed he bought them. There was also a thirty-gallon container half filled with chirping crickets, for feeding his spiders.

It took Don and me a few minutes to settle down and regain our senses, but after that, I literally got the chills—I didn't want to be there. It was pretty creepy, but we couldn't just leave. The police wanted the snakes out.

"Roy," I yelled down. "Come up here."

"They won't hurt you," he said.

"Get him up here," I told the officers. "We're not touching these snakes."

Roy came up, and I was relieved to see that he had a snake hook. I had the cops get me some silver duct tape, and Don and I started taping down whatever covers were on the containers, while Roy moved the snakes as we told him to. Some of those aquariums had cracked glass or holes in them, and we had to tape those too. The other snakes were transferred to garbage cans that Don and I had borrowed from the apartment complex.

I'll say this about Roy: he knew and loved his snakes. He would just reach in and pluck a cobra up by hand. He knew how to do this just like the professionals who worked with snakes all day long. We packed the snakes up to the best of our ability, and once I felt they were secure, we moved them down to the parking lot next to the apartments.

Apparently I had neglected to put the lid down tightly on the container holding the big python. The lid fell off, and the snake started slithering out. The cops were screaming all over the place. But he was nonvenomous and well fed. We just shoved him back in and waited for the paddy wagon.

When the paddy wagon showed up, the policewoman behind the wheel refused to take this cargo. "I'll drive drunks, rapists, and murderers," she told the captain, "but I won't drive these snakes."

So they had to find a substitute driver. Meanwhile, I had called the home of Dan Badgley, our head reptile keeper, and told him to meet me at the zoo. It was almost ten o'clock at night.

"What are you doin', Jack?" Dan asked me.

Julie and a chimp named Emily monkeying around. The animals offered Julie a joyful escape from the reality of ongoing leukemia treatments. (Greg Miller)

Our family gathered in front of the Scioto River on my first day of work at the Columbus Zoo in 1978. (Columbus Zoo)

My four beautiful granddaughters: Brittany is holding Gabriella, Caroline is on the left, and Alison is on the right. (Jack Hanna)

My two handsome grandsons, Blake and little Jack. (Jack Hanna)

The Four Musketeers were reunited at a Kiski twenty-year reunion. From left to right, Lee Cohn, Ken Hinkle, Joe Handrahan, and me. (Jack Hanna)

In my eyes, Larry King is the king of the news world—very fair and unbiased, and for me, always interested in learning something new about animals. (CNN's *Larry King Live*)

The whole family gathered to take a Christmas card photo, with Taj, the white tiger cub we raised. (Rick A. Prebeg)

Kathaleen and her husband, Julian, gathering firewood for the home in Montana. (Jack Hanna)

The girls and I hanging out with an African elephant, Belle, at the Columbus Zoo. (Rick A. Prebeg)

I met up with a couple of mountain goats while hiking through Glacier National Park in Montana. (Suzi Hanna)

While at Jack's Camp in Botswana, Julie and I were able to help care for this orphaned zebra that had been taken in by the camp staff. (Rick A. Prebeg)

Kathaleen and I, filming on safari, with these white rhinos in South Africa. (Rick A. Prebeg)

I couldn't resist saying hello to this rare spectacled bear cub at Jambeli Animal Orphanage in Ecuador.
(Rick A. Prebeg)

Suzi bottle-feeding little Taj. (Rick A. Prebeg/Columbus Zoo)

And me with my hands *full* of white tigers! (Marine World Africa USA)

From Antarctica to Africa, Suzi and I have shared unbelievable adventures together. (Rick A. Prebeg)

In 1993, I had my first experience of giving a daughter away in marriage.
(Jan Brown)

In return, Billy and Suzanne have given me four precious grandchildren, who now adventure with us while
filming. (Rick A. Prebeg)

We met these two baby orphaned elephants in Kenya at the Sheldrick Animal Orphanage. (Rick A. Prebeg)

Amazingly, this family makes their home in the barren Namibian Desert. (Rick A. Prebeg)

The Maasai people taught me one of their interesting customs, the jumping dance, or "adumu." (Rick A. Prebeg)

Our family in 1978, mesmerized by the roar of one of my favorite animals. (Susan Scherer/Columbus Zoo)

Testing for myself the skin-care benefits of the Dead Sea in Israel. (Rick A. Prebeg)

I met President Clinton in the Oval Office to discuss conservation issues. (White House Photography)

To Jack and Suzi Hanna
with best wishes

Suzi and I met President Bush Sr. at a fundraiser in Columbus, Ohio. (White House Photography)

Behind Suzi and me is one of the most amazing sights on the planet: the critically endangered mountain gorillas of Rwanda. (Rick A. Prebeg)

"I'm bringing a bunch of snakes up there."

"We don't need any more snakes."

"Look," I said, "we get our money from the city, and the police asked me to take the snakes. Who else is going to take them?"

Dan saw my point and agreed to meet me at the zoo. In the meantime, Don and I went with them in the back of the paddy wagon; Roy was in a police car. We hadn't gone a hundred yards when Don looked up in that cool, calm way of his and said, "Whoa, Jack, those copperheads are getting out."

I jumped up and looked back at the box, and those copperheads had pushed the top off! Copperheads are very aggressive snakes, and I didn't want to be bitten.

Don was laughing.

"Don, this is no joke," I said. "Get the driver to stop!"

Don banged on the glass and yelled, "A snake's out!" The driver slammed on the brakes and that knocked about six more snakes out of their boxes and onto the floor of the wagon. I tried to get out from the back door of the paddy wagon, but it locked from the outside so that prisoners couldn't get out. When the driver came to unlock it, I was pushing on the door so hard she couldn't get it open.

"Quit pushing," Don told me.

I eased up, the door opened, and I went flying out. I was getting a little panicky—this whole scene was getting ridiculous.

"Everybody calm down," Roy was now telling us in this really weird voice. "Everybody calm down. I'll catch the snakes."

He reached inside the wagon and casually picked up a copperhead by the tail and held it upside down. "See?" he said. "It's not going to hurt anybody."

I ran back to the apartment for the snake hook and had Roy round up the ones that were flipping around on the floor of the wagon. We repacked and resealed the crates and containers, and this time Roy rode alone in the paddy wagon with his snakes, while Don and I rode in the police car. We finally got to the zoo around eleven o'clock that night.

Before going home, Don and I decided to have that one drink. I got home around midnight and took off all my dirty, smelly clothes at the front door. Stark naked, I walked into the kitchen. There stood my wife, Suzi.

"Have you been drinking?" she asked me.

"Suzi," I said, "you are not going to believe this. I've only had one drink. I captured twenty-two snakes. You'll read about it in the paper tomorrow."

"You did what?"

"Smell my clothes if you don't believe me. I'll tell you about it tomorrow; I'm going to bed."

She knows me well enough to expect anything by now. I went to bed and fought off dreams about snakes.

Owners of exotic pets have to understand that someone—a repairman, anybody—can come on their property and be in serious danger, or that the animals themselves can get loose. What if Roy's cobras had slithered off into the building's air-conditioning vents? I've seen it happen. That apartment building would have been a time bomb. Roy's bedroom was not the right place for those snakes, no matter how healthy they were or how much he loved them.

The year 1984 was a good one for exotic snakes in Columbus, Ohio, at least for our zoo. We kept getting them free, from the community, no less.

A few months before meeting the illustrious Roy, I got a call one late-spring night from a Franklin County sheriff's deputy. He told me that a man had seen a twelve-foot-long snake crawling around his back porch and that it had brushed up against his leg and scared the daylights out of him. He said the man had a two-year-old daughter and sounded really scared. Would I check it out?

The place wasn't close by, and Suzi and I were about to barbecue some chicken. It probably wasn't anywhere near a twelve-foot snake, but it was the sheriff calling, and he did mention a two-year-old girl, so I didn't hesitate.

I grabbed a couple of pillowcases and a rake—my snake-catching kit—and took off in my white Columbus Zoo station wagon. I drove about forty miles, following the directions the man had given me, and pulled up at this nice-looking farmhouse.

Right off, I noticed a lot of people outside holding beers; I think they were having a barbecue or picnic, but nobody looked too happy. Everybody was standing around a big metal hog feeder that had a big piece of plywood on top of it with a dozen cinder blocks holding it down. They were all staring at that big bucket looking anxious.

"Thank goodness you're here," said Phil Corbitt, the man who'd called the sheriff. "We just don't know what to do. Maybe there are more of these running around."

"More of what? Where?"

"That thing in there," he said, pointing at the feeder.

"You could keep a gorilla under all those cinder blocks," I told him, trying to lighten things up.

"No, there's a snake in there," he said, seriously.

"Well, let's take these blocks off and see the snake."

Nobody wanted to lift up that cover—I even heard a few people say, "No way." I told them that I couldn't very well transport the hog feeder, whatever was in it, and the cinder blocks back to town in the station wagon. Besides, I had my little pillowcases and my rake. Reluctantly, they agreed, after I assured them that we could catch the snake if it escaped again, which was very unlikely.

They lifted up that board, and I thought I was going to drop my teeth—I wanted to put those blocks back on. It was a much bigger snake than anything we had at the zoo. It was a python, about ten to twelve feet long, and had to weigh seventy to eighty pounds, a lot of weight for a snake. It was also in magnificent condition. I'm not sure how it had survived in the cool spring weather, but it didn't have a runny nose like some snakes have when they have respiratory problems.

How it had gotten there was a mystery to me since there were no houses within two or three miles. Later on we found out that one of the nearest neighbors who had recently moved away had indeed raised snakes, so that's obviously where it came from.

Anyway, we put the cover back on, and the folks helped me put the hog feeder into the back of the station wagon. I put four cinder blocks on top so I could rest easy and be assured that the snake would be secure for the trip back to the zoo.

About twenty miles up Interstate 270, listening to country music as I always do, I felt something up against my leg. That snake had somehow slithered out of that hog feeder, squeezed itself out, and come up to the front seat.

I shuddered, and my heart went down to my stomach, because I didn't know if the snake would bite me. He couldn't kill me—he wasn't venomous—but I knew that he had a couple hundred teeth shaped like fishhooks. If it bit me, there wasn't going to be much I could do about it.

I couldn't get out and handle a snake that big, and besides, I was on the interstate, so I just kept on driving, and I waited to see what the snake would do. For a while, he just lay there against my knee. But after a few minutes that seemed like hours, he started moving again. That thing crawled right across my lap—the entire snake—on up over my shoulder and into the back. He just laid down and curled up on top of his big bucket and didn't move the whole drive back.

Suzi and I had a big argument when I got home over this snake. I've brought my share of animals home over the years, but this snake was too much. She didn't want it staying around the house, not even locked up in the car.

"What if that thing gets loose and harms a child around here?" she said.

"Suzi, that thing isn't going anywhere; it's impossible."

"Well, then how come it got loose in your car when you were driving?" Suzi asked. I couldn't argue against that.

Unable to unload the snake at the zoo by myself, and because it was now too late to call people in from home to help me, the snake would just have to stay there. Of course I locked the car doors, but I must admit, I went out and checked on him a few times during the night, since I had left the windows cracked for ventilation. When I came out in the morning that snake hadn't moved an inch from the top of the hog feeder. It was amazing our neighbors never got upset with us, but of course they probably didn't know the half of it.

Back at the zoo, we put the snake in quarantine for a week and then put him on special display. You know who I'd like to see on display? The crazy guy who let that snake loose in the first place!

One summer evening I got a call from a lady who was frantic. She said that she lived out in the country with three other women and that there was a snake in her commode. None of them had dared use the toilet for the last eight hours and they didn't know what to do. Could I come help?

We turned this into a family affair, with Suzi and the girls all piling into the station wagon. Of course, I took my trusty old snake rake and pillowcase. Driving about six miles into the country, we approached a very meager little farmhouse that looked abandoned except for a beautiful, well-cared-for vegetable garden.

The rickety screen door was open, and as we walked in, I saw four nervous ladies all sitting on the couch. You'd have thought the Lone Ranger had arrived from the way they greeted me. They were glad to see Jack Hanna, the great snake handler. The funny thing is, I'm just as leery of snakes as the next person. They showed me to the bathroom, but none of them would go in; in fact, they stepped back a safe distance.

I went into the bathroom and saw that the lid to the commode was shut, with a ten-pound pot lying on top of it. I called Suzi so we could check this out together. I took the pot off, and Suzi, fearless as ever, lifted up the toilet lid. What we found was a big old corn snake, maybe four feet long. It looked quite comfortable, all coiled around in there like an Italian sausage.

I didn't realize it at the time, but that snake had probably come up through the rotted floorboards in the bathroom. A toilet bowl is a cool, enticing place for a snake on a hot summer day.

Suzi used the rake to get the snake out of the toilet and into the bathtub, then somehow steered it into the pillowcase I was holding. The girls were watching, giggling, and making fake screams the whole time. The snake was harmless, but I wouldn't like to find it in my toilet. In Africa, we are always checking the outhouse toilets for snakes—just part of the routine.

The ladies were ecstatic when we got the snake out of their house. One of them kept trying to give me fifty dollars, which I refused. It was a nice gesture because they were so poor. I immediately noticed that the others were all lined up waiting to use the bathroom.

They kept insisting they owed us, so I told them we'd take some vegetables out of the garden I'd noticed as we drove up. They said fine, and we drove home happy with a bag of potatoes and another snake for the zoo.

At the Columbus Zoo, we have one of the finest reptile facilities in the world. It's noted as much for its displays and layout as it is for a reptile breeding program that includes turtles and just about every kind of snake and lizard there. It's certainly a nice place to visit, but I wouldn't want to spend the night in there . . . especially not on my first date.

One Monday morning, the phone rang at six thirty. George Merritt, our nighttime security man, was calling, and naturally I knew something was wrong or he wouldn't be calling at that hour.

"What's up, Merritt?" I asked him.

"There's been a big mistake at the zoo—I don't know how to tell you."

"What mistake?"

"Security . . . uh . . . somebody locked a young couple—college kids— in the reptile house last night. A groundsman found them when he went over there to clean up this morning. They were pretty upset and are at my office now."

"What'd they say when you first saw them?"

"The guy said he wanted to call his boss, the girl asked to use the bathroom, then they asked to see you."

I rushed over to the zoo to meet the two kids, and they were very nice about the whole thing—more relieved than they were scared or angry. The boy was hoarse from yelling for help all night and anxious to get to his early-morning job. He had no way of knowing that we have a Honeywell system that controls lighting and temperature automatically. During the night, the lights will go on and off in different exhibits at random, and I imagine it can be quite scary. That, combined with the sounds of rattling rattlers and alligators splashing around, was no doubt nerve-wracking.

Apparently, at six o'clock the previous night, the couple had heard the keeper's call at closing time, but they just hadn't been able to get to the door in time. They saw the door closing and yelled, but nobody heard them.

From a security standpoint, it was embarrassing to me because that's the one animal area security doesn't enter at night. We only check the temperature controls on the outside of the building. The young man had plans for law school, and he told me that was why he didn't try to break out through the glass entrance. He didn't want a police report, which I was thankful for.

The story has a happy ending for the couple too: they got married a year later. Coincidentally, we saw them at the zoo ten years later, surrounded by four children, and they said, "Hey, Jack. Remember us? We're the couple who got locked in the reptile house!" Boy, will that be a first-date story to tell their grandkids!

CHAPTER 9

Handle with Care

Once I met a man at a luncheon who had just been appointed head of insurance regulation for the state of Ohio. "How do you know," he asked, "that one of your animals isn't going to get out on a busy weekend afternoon and hurt somebody?"

The man was kind of arrogant and ready for an argument, but he probably never expected an honest answer.

"I don't know that they won't," I told him.

"What? You know that your rates are based on that, don't you?"

"I know all about my rates, pal," I told him. "I just don't know what tomorrow will bring at the zoo any more than I know when a race car will crash or a football player will get a concussion, and neither do you."

I combat risk the best way I know how: prevention. Our first priority at the zoo, as well as on the road, is safety: the safety of the people and the safety of the animals. We take every possible precaution to ensure that the public will be safe, and, of course, we can never be too careful. But it's a balancing act trying to protect the animals and the people, while at the same time trying to allow the public a decent view, which in turn benefits the animals.

"Why risk it at all?" some have asked in criticism. "Why lock those poor little mistreated animals up in cages?" When I hear questions like that, I just wonder if those people are really paying any attention to the animal world at all.

It's completely acceptable to buy a Chihuahua and feed it beef tartar and carry it around in a handbag just to be trendy, but boy oh boy, does the criticism arise when we take an exotic animal, give it excellent care, a naturalistic habitat, and show it to the world for educational and conservation purposes. It just doesn't make sense to me.

First of all, animals have been held in captive environments ever since Noah had all those animals on his ark . . . and saved them *all* from drowning into extinction. It's one of our earliest examples of conservation that continues to this day. The very basis of my work at the zoo and in the animal world in general is that animals at the zoo are the ambassadors to their cousins in the wild. I fervently believe this, and you'll hear me say it time and again. In today's modern zoological parks much of the animal collection comes from other zoos, mainly through breeding loans.

If there were no animals in captivity, no Columbus Zoo, no animals romping on David Letterman's set, would the general public even know what a panda or a manatee or a snow leopard was? And if people didn't know what a panda or manatee or snow leopard was, how would they know and why would they care if these animals were endangered? And if people didn't know or care that these amazing animals were endangered, would they support any efforts to conserve them? Of course not. And with no efforts to conserve these animals, would they still be on this earth today? No, I really don't think so.

Second, these "poor little mistreated animals"—well, that's just another book within itself. But suffice it to say that if the animals were being mistreated, I wouldn't be in this business—nor would any of the people I work with. Both in the zoo and on the road, our animals receive the best care possible, and we're always working on ways to improve.

Despite our greatest efforts, however, accidents happen when you put humans and wild animals together. Just as a human might protect itself from a venomous spider or snake, a wild animal's instinct is to protect itself from threats in its environment. We just don't always know what an animal might consider a threat.

Most zoo animals have all of the defensive and aggressive instincts of their free-ranging cousins. It can often be misleading when the public sees keepers and handlers interacting with the animals—scratching a zebra's ears while the other hand rubs its back, mowing the cheetah yard as the cats roam freely, romping with the baby orangutans in the nursery, or handling young exotics and native wildlife on television.

What the public usually doesn't see (and what we try to teach) is that the keeper may have raised that animal from birth, may have years of relationship with the animal, and most certainly is trained in animal handling and behavior. Keepers know the behavior of the species and, in most cases, the behavior of the individual animal. Some animals seem to enjoy and solicit interaction. Others are never touched under any circumstances.

Even the most tractable, reliable animal may behave defensively or aggressively under out-of-the-ordinary conditions. The bull elephant in musth (a period of aggressive behavior) gives no second chances. The bull moose in rut (breeding season) is not the same creature that browses in his habitat at other times of the year. Mothers (and sometimes fathers) with young may be instinctively willing to protect their offspring to the death. And then there are the individual idiosyncrasies at Columbus: some of our primates engage in sexual discrimination, with the gibbons disliking men and the capuchin monkeys disliking women.

Fortunately, since I've been in Columbus, very few accidents have resulted in serious lawsuits against the zoo. In some ways, I guess this might be considered acceptable, since we live in an age where if a guy chokes on a Coke from your machine or spills hot coffee on himself, you'll wind up in court. But I've known all along that the zoo business comes with it's own set of risks. We do what we can to prevent accidents, but sometimes they still occur.

One of the first major incidents came in February 1984 while I was in Africa enjoying animals out in the middle of the Serengeti Plain. I received a message via shortwave radio garbled in Swahili. Translated, it simply said, "Call U.S.A.—there's been an accident at the zoo." That's all.

My heart sank to my stomach. I was thousands of miles from home, hundreds of miles from a phone. Over the radio, they didn't have any details about what had taken place. I called back over shortwave and asked them to please find out all they could for me and said that I would radio back in two hours. During that time, I walked around the camp thinking how ironic it was to feel safe surrounded by wild animals while back home something awful had happened with captive animals.

My worst fears were confirmed when I finally learned that a tiger had mauled a woman, that her condition was still undetermined. And that was all I would know for two days; it seemed like forever.

The woman was a zoo volunteer who had hardly been there four months when she was attacked by Dolly, a three-hundred-pound Bengal tiger. Volunteers provide an important contribution to many zoos, and in the past volunteers performed tasks that only zookeepers would perform today. On the day of the attack, this volunteer was helping clean the tiger exhibit. Of course, this was done while the animal is removed to a separate, caged enclosure.

"All clear" is what the zookeepers yell before releasing an animal back into its habitat. Just prior to the attack, keeper Ernie Tuller called "all clear" and checked the enclosure—just as he had done for twenty-five years—then came back in and raised the lever on the steel guillotine door that lets the tiger out. Moments later, Ernie heard the terrible screams coming from the yard. He yelled for help and was quickly joined by another keeper, Dan Hunt. They went running into the yard and found the tiger all over the volunteer.

Dan grabbed the only weapon he could find, a broomstick, and began beating the animal off her. The tiger was distracted for a few seconds, long enough to allow them to drag the woman to safety. She lay there bleeding as they hurried to call an ambulance.

She suffered multiple lacerations that required numerous stitches on her arms, legs, and head. To this day, we do not know exactly how it happened.

Ernie told me that he thought the volunteer was already safely back inside, since he didn't see or hear her in the enclosure. Logically, the only place she could have been without being seen was behind some rocks. And since we chose to settle out of court, we never heard all the details that we would have learned through a trial.

It was a devastating ordeal, and I felt horrible for the volunteer, even after she sued us. But after the lawsuit, we had to totally revamp our program for volunteers. Because of one accident and a major lawsuit, the entire program has suffered.

Some animals are a liability no matter how many precautions you take. Coco, an Asian bull elephant, is one of our most prized animals at the Columbus Zoo—he is also one of the most dangerous. At almost five tons, he would be fearsome with his weight alone, but in his younger days he was plenty ornery to boot.

Coco is skilled at throwing things with his trunk, and he used to hate moving objects. We found that out several years ago when he heaved some rocks and knocked out two windshields on our old tour train. He also smashed my truck windshield the same way when I was driving by his habitat.

An elephant's trunk has about thirty thousand muscles in it, and with it he can do anything from picking up a peanut to moving a thousand-pound log. The day before our Zoofari fundraiser, Coco lifted up a manhole cover and flipped it like a Frisbee through a five-thousand-dollar viewing window. If it had been one day later, it could have resulted in a major catastrophe. Since then, we have had those covers welded shut. But that is Coco.

The amazing thing was his accuracy. It was uncanny. Not only could he zing anything he could find, but his delivery was like Nolan Ryan's. He'd pick up a rock and hide it in his trunk, like a pitcher with a ball in his glove, before letting it fly. Naturally, we still try to keep his area as missile-free as possible.

One summer day, the front gates opened maybe a few minutes early, or maybe Coco was a little late going back in. At any rate, a man and his family managed to go over by the elephant yard when Coco was still out. While the man was walking around, Coco reached up his trunk and pulled a rock out of one of the decorative planter boxes that are about twelve feet over his head. That elephant fired one of his patented fastballs, and from about forty or fifty feet, he nailed this poor guy right smack in the middle of the forehead.

The victim, Glen Honaker, immediately went down. No one had any idea what happened. All that his wife and kids knew was that Dad was suddenly on the ground bleeding. I was on the scene almost right away, and just as soon as I saw that rock, I knew it was the work of Coco.

The Honakers were understanding, and fortunately they didn't sue. Maybe they saw some humor in the situation. For one thing, the guy will always have an unbelievable story to tell with the punch line, "I never knew what hit me. Who could imagine an elephant being the culprit?!" They seemed happy with the zoo passes and posters that I offered them. And of course we paid for Mr. Honaker's stitches. I hoped they would visit again; I didn't want their last experience at the Columbus Zoo to be getting whacked in the head by our star-pitching elephant.

Believe it or not, the same thing happened with Jack and Barbara Nicklaus's grandson, Stevie. During the week of the Memorial Golf Tournament, some members of the Nicklaus family were visiting the zoo on a private tour. Adam, the elephant keeper, said that Coco found a rock, and without warning hurled his weapon at Stevie. Thank goodness he was okay! The Nicklaus family is still very supportive of the zoo. In fact, Gary and Amy Nicklaus gave us our beloved yellow lab, Tasha.

We certainly didn't take the forgiveness of those families for granted— especially juxtaposed with other less-than-ethical characters who visited the zoo. The same day that Coco beaned a visitor—about a half hour afterward—I received another call concerning an accident with a visitor.

Apparently a man had broken his arm trying to steal a Coke from a machine up on the Nature Trail. He had his arm halfway up the machine, and the whole thing fell on top of him. Bricker called me on the radio from the accident scene to tell me the guy was going to sue, but I told him to throw the guy out. It wasn't my fault that slob was trying to steal a Coke.

That's the difference between people—on one side, you have an innocent gentleman pelted in the head by a rock-throwing elephant who gets up smiling; on the other, you have some jerk who wants to sue you after trying to steal from you.

Another frivolous threat of a lawsuit occurred just before I got to Columbus. Jim McGuire had been the zoo attorney for twenty years, and he told me he was glad this one didn't go to court.

A woman and her kids were walking through the children's zoo when her shoelace came untied. She bent down to tie it and was mounted and humped by a donkey. Her kids all started laughing like crazy, and though there was no physical harm she was both frightened and humiliated. When she got home, she was still so mad she called the zoo and said she wanted to sue. But when she realized the whole incident would have to be made even more public through the proceedings, she had to drop it—she couldn't take any further embarrassment. To say the least, it would've been an interesting trial.

When it comes to lawsuits, I'm forever thankful for the attitude of our employees. There are few animals here that don't involve some type of risk in just simple, everyday care. Even some of our cute little penguins love to bite. The staff accepts minor (and sometimes major) injuries as part of the job, not as an excuse to go running for a lawyer.

Now, I'm not saying that if an elephant like Coco were to kill a keeper, we wouldn't be sued. Don Winstel, who's now our assistant director, was thrown against a wall ten feet in the air during one of Coco's fits. During that same brouhaha, Brad Booth had his head gashed. Harry Peachey's had his arm crushed so badly that the bone was protruding through the skin. I've even been shoved in a corner by an elephant, and it's not fun. But what I like about these guys is that they don't complain about these things—they know the risks come with the job.

Once one of our red pandas got out during a snowstorm. These are small, cute animals, weighing at most maybe ten to twelve pounds. This one didn't go very far and crawled up into a snow bank. Ernie Tuller, a zookeeper, netted it, then tried to grab it with his free hand. With its razor-sharp teeth, that little thing about tore his thumb off, ripping up his whole hand.

Anything with teeth can bite. Anything with claws can scratch. Anything with horns can gore. Anything with talons can tear. And anything that is wild is wild. Our keepers and handlers never forget this, and we hope to instill this same caution in the public. A wild animal is like a loaded gun, capable of going off at any time with just the slightest pull of the trigger. Behind the scenes, each department has its own set of transfer, cleaning, feeding, and safety procedures that must be followed by everyone working there. One person's carelessness could cause a fellow employee and/or an animal to be injured. They must work as a team, looking out for one another to help insure the safety of all.

For zoo visitors, the fences, barriers, and warning signs are not there just so we can impose meaningless authority. The visitors who do not obey these restrictions, placed there for their own safety, may be injured or at the very least asked to leave the park if they do not heed the warnings. We want each visitor's stay to be safe and pleasant, and we must and do take precautions very seriously.

Recently, a tragic incident occurred partly because it is believed the visitors did not obey such restrictions. I'm sure you heard about the teenage boy killed—and his two friends mauled—by a Siberian tiger at the San Francisco Zoo. In my forty years in this business, as far as I know, this is the first time there's been a death of a zoo visitor due to an animal escape.

When the story first hit, the media painted a dramatic scene of this innocent teenage boy mauled to a grizzly death by this ferocious, blood-seeking tiger that escaped from a negligent, unsafe zoo. The networks started calling to get my take on the matter, and I started getting questions like, "Jack, do you think keeping caged wild animals is unsafe?" and "Should people think twice about visiting zoos?" What?

Don't get me wrong. I like the media in general. I have made a lot of dear friends on news networks, but sometimes it seems like the media stirs drama for drama's sake. And when I started getting those questions, I just had to be honest. First of all, the majority of animals aren't "caged." If you've been to a zoo in the last decade, you know that. They have amazing habitats created to make them feel at home, while still allowing them to be in a protective environment. In the case of the Siberian tiger, that protective environment was particularly important because they are on the endangered species list.

And are zoos safe? Well, I'm no statistician, but I do know about 150 million people visit zoos and aquariums each year, and this is the first time I've heard of a zoo visitor killed by an animal. So, let's multiply my forty years in the zoo business by a low estimate of 100 million visitors per year. That's a one in four billion risk of death! I'll take those odds over driving a car any day.

As the story of the attack unfolded, the most important fact remained—there was still a young man killed by a tiger—but a more accurate picture of the night's events came into focus. One of the three guys (two teenagers and one man in his twenties) reportedly later admitted they all smoked pot and took a few shots of vodka before heading out for—what else?—an enriching zoo experience. At the zoo, they were allegedly standing on the fence, waving and yelling at the tigers.

Now, when I see a fence, whether it's at a race track or a zoo, it says to me, "Stay back." I don't stand on the fence. I don't cross the fence. And if I do, I know it's at my own risk. And it's not just a precaution with race cars and animals. If someone's in my backyard, standing on my fence, yelling at me—a threat to me and my kids or grandkids—it's very simple what I'm going to do . . . run after them!

This tiger somehow cleared a twelve-and-a-half-foot wall to get to those guys. At first they thought someone had let the tiger out, but once those allegations were dismissed, it left many people scratching their heads. Think about the stories you've heard of humans lifting cars to save people and that sort of thing. When humans and animals are in threatening situations, adrenaline kicks in and gives them an almost supernatural boost. There's no doubt in my mind that tiger said, "There's something wrong here. I'm not taking this anymore." And that adrenaline took him over the wall. The San Francisco Zoo is now making plans to build a much taller, nineteen-foot wall.

I'd love to see legislation passed that makes taunting animals illegal. I believe, in this particular case, they're able to prosecute if they can prove that taunting did take place, since it's illegal to intentionally put an endangered animal at risk. I still believe a law should specifically address taunting and should apply to all animals. If a person is over the age of eighteen—plenty old enough to know better—there should be consequences for taunting an animal and engaging its defensive instincts. Had that law been in place and regularly enforced, there might be one more Siberian tiger and one more young man still enjoying life in California today.

So, was the wall too short? Yeah, it was too short. Can you blame the zoo? Sure, you can blame the zoo. But something out of the ordinary caused that tiger to attack. Wild animals, namely Siberian tigers, are powerful creatures, and you have got to show respect for them. Most people go to the zoo to observe the beauty and majesty of amazing creatures, and if you're not at the zoo for those reasons, well, you just don't need to be there. As the San Francisco Zoo case shows, if you're disrespectful to the animals at the zoo, you're risking your life, the animal's life, and the lives of other people there who truly value the animals.

Traveling with animals carries its own unique set of risks and responsibilities. In the beginning, I knew my job was to bring the public to the animals, but I never really planned to make a career out of bringing animals to the public. Yet, from early on, it's been a natural extension of my work at the zoo . . . even if it did get off to a really bad start.

During my first year in Columbus, I was involved in a freak accident at a church speech that I should have never agreed to. It was a case of my trying to do too much for too many people. And I was very lucky it did not cost me my job.

On short notice, I was called to speak at a community church and present animals before a group of preschool children. Dianna Frisch, who was in charge of apes, had worked with the chimpanzees, and we decided to take two of them along. They are, as everyone knows, very intelligent and entertaining animals and have the ability to instantly capture people's hearts. Most of the time, the chimps added a lot of value to our presentations, but this is one time when they did not.

We put the male, Cocoa, up on a jungle gym set outside the church to show the kids his climbing ability, with Dianna standing right there next to him. She was pointing out his features and characteristics, and he seemed to be all right, not tense or stressed in any way. We did this all the time. The kids were, as they always were, very excited, and I was keeping them back. I didn't see one little girl sneak around behind Cocoa.

Before anyone could react, Cocoa grabbed the girl's little finger, jerked it toward him, and bit the end off. It was terrifying and lightning fast. With quick thinking, Dianna rescued the fingertip from Cocoa's mouth, the young girl was rushed to Children's Hospital, and surgeons reattached the fingertip. We all hoped for the best, but eventually the doctors realized the finger was not healing properly and had to remove it altogether.

As expected, we were sued by the girl's family. After a year or so, they settled out of court, but the money was meaningless. How do you price a little girl's finger? I was sick for that innocent girl, and naturally a lot of people came down on me. But I cannot stand the Monday-morning quarterbacks. The same people who had begged me to come to their church were now attacking me. Why did I bring a wild animal? Why did I go to a church where small children were going to school?

I went before the zoo trustees and stressed that I still believed in taking animals out to the public. I said that you have to take systematic chances in life and still try to do what is safe for everybody. You don't stop driving because you hear someone was hurt in a car accident, but you certainly try to drive more safely. Thankfully, the trustees allowed us to continue with certain programs, with limitations of course. For one, I no longer take chimps to schools. Yet together we still believed that taking the zoo out to the people benefits everyone in the long run.

Since then, we have come a long way with our animal outreach programs. We now have a promotions department, and under the leadership of Suzi Rapp, that department has developed a science around the best way to raise and care for animals that travel exclusively for educational purposes. Other zoos often consult with us about our animal outreach programs, and we are happy to share the knowledge we've gained through experience.

The animals that travel with me are not just yanked out of their habitats at the zoo and put in a van. In most cases, these animals are raised from a young age by top-notch professionals in order to acclimate to them. They're so well-adjusted, in fact, that when many of them come of age, they go straight into a breeding program. That's a definite sign of their good health. On the road, they have a set feeding schedule of fresh meat or fruit or whatever dietary requirements are necessary, and they have time to exercise and roam (which can sometimes cause quite a stir for bystanders . . . but that's another chapter). The bottom line is that the animal's well-being comes first. If our trainers should have medical questions, we have veterinarians on call at the zoo, and if there is any doubt that the animal is perfectly healthy before we leave, it simply does not travel.

Still, it's so much more than just basic physical care of the animals on the road. These trainers get to know their animals; they talk to them; they know their moods. And the animals, in turn, learn to trust the keepers.

I'll be the first to admit, though, that things don't always go as perfectly as planned—like when you try to figure out how to get a flamingo through an airport turnstile. It was midnight when my daughter Julie, Suzi Rapp, and I finally arrived back at the Ohio State University Airport after a fundraiser at the Niabi Zoo, for my buddy Tom Stalf. None of us expected the airport to be closed, so none of us expected the only exit to be a turnstile. Animals of the human variety typically have no problems making it through the rotating contraption, but flamingos in large crates, on the other hand, tend to pose a problem—a fact I realized a little too late.

When we had eliminated all other means of exiting the airport, I told the others, "I'll just go in with him and push him through."

"Jack, that crate's not gonna fit," Suzi Rapp predicted.

But I assured her it would, and we started scooting the flamingo's crate into the narrow space, the metal bars closing in behind us. That's when I realized there was a little bit of geometry I hadn't figured into my calculation. Crates are square; turnstiles are round. As I pushed that square peg into the round hole, Marty the flamingo and I became wedged, in pretty close quarters. At that point we realized the turnstile didn't go backward. And now, it wasn't budging forward either, leaving Suzi and Julie trapped helplessly in the airport on the other side. I couldn't move, and the bars were pressed into my face. My only option was to wiggle up like a worm to the top of the turnstile and go for help.

When I got out, I drove to a nearby fire station. The door to the fire station was locked, so my next option was to call 911. "You've gotta help us. There's a flamingo stuck in the turnstile at the airport!" I exclaimed. The operator thought I was nuts. But when I finally thought to tell her my name, the whole thing made a little more sense, and she called the fire station.

When the firefighters arrived for what had already been dubbed "Operation Flamingo," they couldn't believe their eyes. (Embarrassingly enough, one remembered me from another animal incident several years prior when transporting a baby gorilla to Children's Hospital.) After overcoming the initial shock of seeing this big pink flamingo standing there in his crate in the airport turnstile, the three firefighters worked to get Marty's crate open and hoisted him over the top where we carried him safely to the zoo van. Marty waited patiently inside the van while we worked to remove his crate from the turnstile. In the midst of the confusion, Suzi Rapp said, "Guys, stop. You have to see this. Look over at the van."

And there was Marty, up in the driver's seat of the van with his face pressed up against the glass, watching us, obviously thinking, *Now this is what I call a zoo!* Of course, after all the chaos, the pilot found the access code, and the large gate magically opened.

Another thing you can never really predict is the poop. That's right, poop, feces, dung, whatever. When you're on the road with animals, well, poop happens. And if you're thinking we have a van full of animals walking around in their own mess, think again. On one trip, we were driving through downtown Detroit around five in the morning when a familiar aroma filled the van. No one really needed my pronouncement: "The cheetah crapped." Before I could even finish my sentence, the van was heading off the next exit in order for us to clean up the cheetah poop.

While we're on the subject, pee happens too. And cheetahs are pretty amazing in their peeing abilities. Did you know they can shoot a stream of urine up to about twelve feet? I guess I had that information filed somewhere in my brain, but I never considered it really useful knowledge until the day we forgot to put the sheet of Plexiglas behind my seat, in front of Kago the cheetah. We were driving along when I felt a light mist, followed by a musty smell. "Hey, guys, I think that cheetah just peed on me!"

"Nah, Jack," one of them answered, stifling laughter, "you're just imagining things."

About that time, the cheetah let loose with a spray that hit me in the back and shot all the way up to the windshield. The guys up front had already leaned out of the way and by this time were laughing hysterically. Man, I was whooping and hollering like nobody's business. I was soaked, head to toe, in cheetah pee. And do you think they pulled over right away for me to get cleaned up? Nooo, I had to wait until the next bathroom stop. Let me just set the record straight: the only animals that are mistreated when we travel are the humans. Now, why can't I find anyone to protest that?

CHAPTER 10

Gorillas in Our Midst

Many people, and some zoo directors, will argue that gorillas are the most fascinating and intriguing of all zoo animals. They've got a good argument, but I don't want to make that statement, because I have too much respect for all the animals. Hey, it may sound corny, but I love 'em all.

Still, there's no denying that the gorillas here in Columbus have always been a favorite for zoo visitors. It all dates back to Mac and Millie, two wild-caught gorillas that were brought to the Columbus Zoo in 1951. Mac and Millie hit it off, and the result was Colo, the first gorilla ever born at a zoological park. That day, December 22, 1956, made zoo history. With some outside help from breeding loans, Colo now has seventeen descendants—ranging from her own three children to her great-great-grandchildren!

Breeding animals in zoological parks is one of the main purposes of zoos today. This goes a long way toward the survival of many species. We don't want to put animals in a sterile environment and let people gawk at them—that was the old zoo. Today we go beyond their basic needs and ensure their comfort so that they can behave naturally within a family structure. We try to pair up animals in environments conducive to breeding. When the males are allowed to lead and protect females being submissive, breeding can occur.

Maybe it's something in the water here, but there have now been over thirty gorilla births in Columbus. That's a phenomenal number when you consider how difficult captive gorilla breeding is. With every new birth at the zoo, I feel like a proud father. And yes, I do pass out bananas.

Each gorilla birth is a major event. Our local (and sometimes national) media await the birth and treat it just like they would any celebrity's. Then after the birth, on a weekend, thousands of people visit the zoo to see the new gorilla mother with her baby. It's a zoo phenomenon, always fascinating to watch.

Many of our visitors are increasingly respectful and knowledgeable about our gorillas, recognizing them by sight, asking for them by name, and following their fortunes and misfortunes like they do soap operas. This appreciation and affection is very much due to the educational efforts of staff and volunteers and also the result of seeing babies being raised by their moms and dads.

Inevitably, you'll have visitors with the King Kong thing. They'll be crowding around the habitat, beating their chests and scratching their armpits, and saying stuff like, "That big guy can break that glass anytime he wants. I'll be the first one out of the building!" They probably really would like to see a real-life King Kong escape, at a safe distance, of course. There's no difference from wanting to see race cars crash. I raced cars for two years in the Fire Hawk Series and never had that crash, but I was charged by a silverback gorilla. And there's no doubt that gorillas are extremely powerful animals, and it is frightening when they do charge. However, contrary to the King Kong image, they really are considered gentle giants.

Once, during a gorilla's physical exam—they get yearly physicals, just like people—I had the keepers measure Bongo's waistline. Of course, this was done when he was anesthetized—a gorilla would no more let you put your hands around his waist than he would let you pick his nose! People were always impressed by the girth of the pants we had designed that technically would have fit Bongo. When speaking to school groups, it was always exciting to see the children's amazement when I would select three or four kids to come up to the stage and fit into Bongo's trousers. We did the same thing with shirts (size 22 necks). People would love to compare their hands to the molds we had made of the gorillas' hands. We find different ways to try to help people relate to the immense size of the gorilla and see what a magnificent animal he is.

The unique combination of gentleness and power is what makes gorilla watching so fascinating to me, whether it's in the wilds of Africa or at the Columbus Zoo. Having a four-hundred-pound lowland gorilla come up to within two feet of you and look directly into your eyes is mind-blowing. You're trying to figure out what he's thinking; at the same time, he's probably trying to do the same with you.

One of our gorillas took a master padlock—that I wouldn't be able to dent with pliers and a blowtorch—and squashed it like a marshmallow. I've seen a gorilla take a green-shelled coconut and pop it open like a peanut. At the same time, I've witnessed the wonder of Bongo, a 420-pound, thirty-two-year-old patriarch, raising Fossey, his son, after the mother, Bridgette, died when the baby was just a little over a year old. When Fossey was maybe fifteen pounds, Bongo played with him the same way a human being might handle delicate crystalware.

All zoo animals have controlled diets, and a good indicator of how healthy the animals are is how well they breed. Our gorillas eat a quality of produce that is probably equal to what you might find in New York City's finest restaurants, maybe better.

A typical day's feed would begin with a breakfast of grapefruit, apples, sometimes a boiled egg, lettuce or spinach, cooked sweet potatoes, bananas, carrots, and vitamins. For lunch, there would be a snack consisting of yogurt and a special protein drink developed by the staff. During the day, they are kept busy foraging for sunflower seeds, which they shell with their teeth, monkey biscuits, and willow branches. Sometimes they have a special treat of sugarcane, coconut, or watermelon. For dinner, they are served bok choy and endive, more sweet potatoes and carrots, onions, fruit, and a white potato. Pregnant females and sick gorillas also receive broiled liver, while those with colds get hot onion/garlic soup run through a blender and served in a glass.

Despite the four-star diet and all the care we can provide, there will always be problems. One of the most trying experiences in my zoo career was a year-long struggle to keep a baby gorilla named Roscoe alive.

Oscar, Roscoe's father, was so popular with the ladies that we had a hard time keeping tabs on his offspring. None of us were expecting it when Joansie, a nineteen-year-old gorilla on loan from the Buffalo Zoo, gave a surprise premature birth to a male in July 1980. Pregnancy was a possibility, but we also thought she might be overweight. Besides, Oscar seemed to ignore her.

A practice we often implement is not to name zoo babies until they make it to two or three months, because we would rather announce, "The gorilla baby died today," than use a name. Roscoe, Joansie's baby, lasted a year, so he was named for Ross Hall at Children's Hospital, where he spent most of his life.

Roscoe had to be "pulled" from his mother because of inadequate maternal care. Some people think we raise gorillas in the nursery so that the public can walk up to the window and go, "Oh, isn't he cute! Look at that little gorilla in his diaper getting a bottle." That's not it at all. We don't like to pull babies unnecessarily because natural motherhood and family bonding is best, and nursery care is also prohibitively expensive.

At first, we tried to keep him on formula, but his condition worsened and he did not gain weight. He seemed to be suffering from a bacterial infection, an illness we unfortunately knew little about at the time. One morning Roscoe seemed to be going down the tubes pretty fast, so we decided to rush him to the animal research wing at Children's Hospital.

It was confirmed that Roscoe was suffering from a bacterial infection in his stomach and intestines. Before he was five weeks old, he had to go on a life-support system. Over the first months of his short life, his condition improved enough a few times so that he could be brought back to his non-sterile environment at the zoo, but he would always deteriorate and have to return to the hospital.

Everyone involved—doctors, veterinarians, and zoo staff—soon realized that Roscoe could not live without life support. It was an expensive proposition to keep him alive, due to reach over two thousand dollars a month in medical costs alone—this was with all personnel donating their time. Our yearly medical budget at the zoo totaled only about eighteen thousand dollars at the time, so if we wanted to keep Roscoe around, we would have to find more money, which we did, mostly through fundraising and donations. It was a tough, controversial decision.

In my mind, there was never really any choice about what to do. Aside from the basic "keep living things alive at all cost" philosophy that I have, there were other factors: (1) gorillas are endangered, vanishing fast, and must be protected for future generations, (2) gorillas are economically quite valuable and were worth quite a bit of money at the time, and (3) primate research has been invaluable in saving human lives—here was our chance to repay the debt.

My youngest daughter, Julie, was fighting leukemia at the same time in the same hospital as Roscoe. Her disease was in remission, but she still had to undergo bone-marrow tests, spinal injections, and chemotherapy. Every night Julie would ask me, "How's the baby gorilla?"

Thanks to community support, we kept Roscoe going. Throughout all of his rallies and setbacks, the people of central Ohio were wonderful: the doctors—like Richard McLead, who was with him from day one—and nurses who donated their time, not just treating Roscoe but training zoo staff to aid in noncritical care; the zoo staff and docents, who spent long shifts and sleepless nights caring for the little guy; working people who donated money to defray costs; schoolchildren who helped with the fundraising—all these and many more not only kept Roscoe going but kept a positive spirit alive around the zoo.

After just two days short of one year of intravenous feedings and intermittent life support, Roscoe's life mercifully ended. He died of congestive heart failure in Chris Pendleton's arms. Chris, a zoo employee who had probably spent more time than anyone with him, told me often that Roscoe had such a personality, she'd always consider him her special friend. She wasn't alone. Dr. McLead was too upset to do the autopsy.

With his courageous struggle to stay alive, Roscoe touched many hearts, but his hospital stay was not in vain. We learned a great deal about gorilla infancy and dehydration that would go a long way toward saving similarly afflicted animals in the future. It had only been two years since we had given the gorillas their new habitat with grass, trees, and a pond, but I realized now, more than ever, how important these animals were to our zoo, our community, and the animal world.

And in the animal world, life goes on. Just two days after Roscoe died, on what would have been his first birthday, Joansie, his mother, gave birth to another male, also fathered by Oscar. This little tyke survived just fine, and we eventually sent him to the Buffalo Zoo to honor a prior breeding-loan agreement.

A hallmark year for the Columbus Zoo was 1983, when we witnessed the

Suzi and I with the rare twin gorillas, Mosuba and Macombo II. (Columbus Zoo)

exciting and unusual birth of twin sons to Bridgette and Oscar. These two bright-eyed, "smiling" little guys put the gorilla program on the map once again and ultimately brought about the beginnings of our relationship with *Good Morning America.*

But births mean more animals, which means more and better space. In 1984, we remodeled the interior of the old Ape House and built a new outdoor habitat complete with jungle canopy for our gorilla families. The enclosure opened in front of television cameras, a small crowd looking through the large viewing windows, and an anxious zoo staff.

In addition to the wire mesh we had installed for climbing, there were yards of ropes and swings. Before it was opened, my family and I crawled and swung around in there, trying to mimic what we thought the gorillas would do. But I was surprised to observe that for the gorillas, a rope didn't mean something to swing on; it didn't mean anything at all. They had never seen a jungle vine. Plus many of them, due to age and habit, didn't particularly feel like climbing. So when those gorillas entered their newly revealed habitat, it took several months for them to get used to these surroundings and do what they would naturally do in the wild. Juvenile gorillas learned to entertain themselves by climbing and gliding in the air on a rope. Females discovered that climbing the apparatus was a protective means of escaping an aggressive male gorilla.

Later that summer, we received a new male, nineteen-year-old Mumbah, on loan from Howletts Wild Animal Park in Canterbury, England. Mumbah was coming over to try to breed with Toni and start a new family, but the media made a big thing about how Mumbah would come over and "show our gorillas the ropes." I thought it was possible, since he'd had ropes for years. But Mumbah got in there and never swung on those ropes either, although he did use the swag ropes as a hammock for afternoon siestas.

It's a popular theory that gorillas learn by imitation, by copying, but it doesn't always work out that way. I guess we're probably influenced by the verb *ape*, meaning to imitate, to mimic. And Dian Fossey had proven with her studies in Africa that the gorilla is a very social animal and, like human beings, can learn by watching others. But one of my many brilliant ideas backfired.

I was getting very frustrated watching baby gorillas being pulled from their mothers who couldn't nurse. It was a catch-22 situation—we could not leave such valuable and endangered infant animals at risk, yet how was the mother gorilla ever supposed to learn?

So one day I looked into the possibility of having a woman nurse a baby—live, not on film—in front of the gorillas. Maybe then they would learn how to do it. I knew it sounded wacky, but I didn't think I would have any trouble getting volunteers. When Roscoe was sick, we received numerous calls from women asking if we needed their milk.

I called La Leche League, the breast-feeding organization, and they said they'd love to help out. I assured them there would be complete privacy, except for a few zoo staff members. They sent over a young mother who was very nice and, most importantly, enthusiastic. This wasn't an everyday thing—Mel Dodge had already told me I was nuts on this one.

Of course, we had a window separating the lady from the gorillas, and I told her she should get as close as possible. Well, as with Mumbah and the ropes, those females, Toni and Joansie, weren't interested. They looked up, the same as when visitors came in, but they didn't really pay attention.

Oscar, the magnificent silverback, was another story. He moved in for a ringside seat. He was definitely fascinated—had his nose flush against the glass. So the whole thing kind of fizzled out. Again, we got some national attention on this one, with the newspapers, Paul Harvey's radio show, and what not.

Oscar, without a doubt, was my favorite gorilla. He was definitely a character and reminded me of myself. I called him "Oscar Mayer Wiener." If I'd had a hard day, I might wait until the zoo was empty, take a walk, and go sit down in the bleachers opposite the gorillas. I'd call out, "Hey, Wiener, how ya doin'?" He'd look over at me, and if I had some grapes, he'd come over. I'd feed him the grapes and he'd grunt, which is a friendly vocalization.

Oscar and I had an understanding. Since I don't have a lot of time to spend with most of the animals at the zoo, they don't recognize me, and I don't expect them to. But Oscar is one who did, and I appreciated it. However, there was one day when he wasn't on my appreciation list.

We conduct an annual exercise to prepare for potential animal escapes. The zoo staff coordinates with local law enforcement in case anything ever happens. Only a few people know about it in advance, and, of course, the public gets upset since we have to evacuate sections of the zoo. But in the end, it's a necessary exercise that will help to protect the zoo visitors, staff, and animal collection.

One late August day in 1982, I was talking to someone about rhino insemination when the call came over the radio that a gorilla was loose. My first thought was, there's no practice today, and then it hit me that this was the real thing. I tried to find out more, but everybody was screaming all at once. I flew out of my office and went running across the zoo grounds to the Ape House. Once I got there, I saw security people already beginning evacuation.

Bricker was there, and he had his tranquilizer gun ready. In our business there's a rule that if a human being is in danger of being attacked, there's really no decision. With zoo rules, human life takes precedence—no matter what. If you can tranquilize the animals, that's fine, but a lot of times tranquilization takes quite awhile. The animal may not be trying to hurt anyone, but he's in an atmosphere he's not familiar with and he can be very dangerous.

So Bricker, the curators, and the keepers were all there within minutes, people were on their way out, and I remember thinking, *Thank goodness for our practice sessions.*

Meanwhile, Oscar was loose in the Ape House—not running around the grounds or anything, just loose in the keeper aisles outside his cage. A mistake had been made; a cage door had been left unlocked. It sounds crazy, I know, that a cage door gets left open, but with what I know about human error, I'm surprised it doesn't happen more often.

The keeper aisle is behind the enclosures; there are phones, sinks, hoses, all kinds of stuff back there. There's also one door separating that area from the outside world—one door with one little doorknob. All Oscar had to do was turn that doorknob.

Oscar was having a ball in there—we could hear that much. He was tearing spigots off sinks, pulling pipes off the wall, ripping up rubber hoses, preoccupied with everything. He'd been watching the keepers for years; this was his shot to do anything he wanted.

I wasn't sure what to do about the door—it was only a matter of minutes until he got bored with what he was doing, and I knew we couldn't hold that door. There was a worker nearby with a backhoe, and it occurred to me to commandeer that thing and push it up against the door. Ten, fifteen seconds after we blocked the door with the backhoe, we saw the doorknob start to turn, and then all of a sudden it disappeared—Oscar must have pulled it through the door. We all stared at it like it was something out of an Alfred Hitchcock movie. When Oscar realized something was jammed up against the door, he pounded and pushed, trying to get out. He couldn't, so he went back to making his mess in there.

By this time, Dr. Gardner, our veterinarian, had arrived with a blowgun and tranquilizers. We like to use a blowgun rather than a rifle because it's like a bee sting and there's no noise to scare the animal. Dr. Gardner went up into a loft area above Oscar, shot the dart into Oscar's shoulder, and watched him get sleepy. We moved in, put him back in his enclosure, and only then did I call the newspapers.

But I really don't think Oscar would have done anything to anybody. Just a few years ago, there was a report of a little boy who fell into a moat in a gorilla exhibit in England. A big male gorilla went over and touched the boy, who was unconscious, looked at him, and when the child roused and cried, he backed off. That's more the way Oscar is. I was more worried that he might somehow hurt himself on a utility wire or a hot wire in there. But Oscar blew his big chance at a breakout, and I'm glad.

Gorillas respond to body language. Sometimes I have to remind myself not to move too fast or talk too loudly, because that can irritate them, and they can't really deal with that. They're primates, a term that comes from the word *primary*, and they're very basic in everything they do.

Male humans are often threatening to gorillas, especially to male gorillas. They can feel threatened by beards, which fortunately I don't have, and they respond better to women. I would really have to watch myself when I went in the Primate House—I'd have to slow down, cool my heels, but sometimes I'd forget. Once, right after Christmas, I went in there wearing a brand-new suede coat that I had received as a present. I wasn't in there two minutes before Bongo had thrown crap all over it and ruined it. It's one of their favorite defenses. And at close range, they're very accurate—they can throw right between the bars. They'll pick out a person as their target and splatter him. One target was yet another member of the Nicklaus family—this time Jack got whacked! If only Bongo played golf!

The success of our great apes speaks for itself. Somebody has to be doing something right. I knew this as far back as 1983, when we had a visit from Dian Fossey, who was doing a worldwide book tour at the time. Although she did not approve of captive gorillas, and a zoo was probably the last place she wanted to visit, I took a chance and asked her if she would do a lecture for our gorilla staff. Surprisingly, she agreed. As we showed Dian our gorillas, she made vocalizations to the animals, and they answered her. The staff had been hearing the vocalizations all along, but did not know what they meant. After seeing the gorillas, she turned to me, not looking at the staff, and said, "I don't know what they're doing with these animals, but the gorillas are in great shape." After that first visit, she changed her travel arrangements to stay in Columbus four more days! She told us things about the gorillas that she hadn't even published. She explained how they built nests in the wild, so we immediately brought over hay. She told us about different types of vegetation that gorillas ate, and we started giving them lots of browse (freshly cut branches and plants) to supplement their diet. By accepting an invitation from an unlikely friend, Dian Fossey vastly improved the care of captive gorillas, in addition to her work with gorillas in the wild.

All captive gorillas worldwide are western lowland gorillas, rather than mountain gorillas, like those seen in *Gorillas in the Mist*, the film about the late Dian Fossey. There are few behavioral differences between the two subspecies; physically, the mountain gorillas are stockier-looking with more and longer hair.

Western lowland gorillas and mountain gorillas are both found in Central Africa. The critically endangered mountain gorillas are certainly the scarcer of the two, with an estimated population of around six hundred individuals. In 1981, the Rwandan population of mountain gorillas had dwindled down to about 250, and it seemed that this subspecies might not make it into the twenty-first century. Today, due largely to anti-poaching and habitat conservation efforts, their numbers have risen, but their future is still uncertain. Even with the vast differences in population, all gorillas are endangered animals.

Several organizations have been established on behalf of the mountain gorilla. The Columbus Zoo has long been associated with the Dian Fossey Gorilla Fund, an effort to continue the work begun by Fossey. The Mountain Gorilla Veterinary Project (MGVP) is another organization, where I'm honored to serve as a board member, that had its origins at the request of Dian Fossey. Beginning as a small veterinary clinic, it has now grown into a complete conservation initiative that, among other efforts, provides life-saving medical care to mountain gorillas. We do fundraising on its behalf and attempt to publicize its efforts whenever possible. Partners In Conservation (PIC) is organization that has been formed within the Columbus Zoo. Their incredible work supports both the people and gorilla conservation efforts in Rwanda.

I'm proud to say we continually strive to make advances for our primate friends both in the zoo and in the wild. In 2000, the Columbus Zoo expanded our gorilla exhibit again with the opening of the African Forest region. It includes big cats, an aviary, and other mammals indigenous to the African forest. But the highlight of the exhibit is, of course, the multiple generations of western lowland gorillas.

One member of the third generation of gorillas made his debut on January 2, 1987, my fortieth birthday. Turning forty is a real downer for some people, but I received one of the best presents ever. At about three thirty that afternoon, I got a call that Toni had just given birth to a male. A baby gorilla on my birthday!

The keepers decided that the Columbus Zoo wasn't ready for two Jungle Jacks, so they named the baby JJ, in my honor. His mother wasn't able to raise him, so he was reared for fourteen months in the nursery and then turned over to his grandmother, Colo, who took over as his surrogate mother. I don't know what was more satisfying—seeing Colo with baby JJ or seeing that nursery-raised baby acting "all gorilla" in a large family group. I do know that, wherever I go, it will always be satisfying to know that a little part of me will always be a part of that special family of apes.

CHAPTER 11

Monkey Business—Promoting the Zoo

When I was hired as director of the Columbus Zoo, I was charged with generating interest in the zoo among the people of central Ohio. They did not need a zoological expert, a PhD, or somebody who knew all the Latin names for animals—so I guess I fit the bill. I only know a few of those Latin names, but what I do know is how to promote a zoo.

Since I've been in Columbus, zoo attendance has grown from 350,000 to about 1.5 million visitors a year thanks to a lot of people's hard work. The annual budget shot from $1.7 million in 1978 to about $29 million today. In 1985, 70 percent of the citizens of this county voted in favor of a five-year $2.2 million county property tax levy. Ever since, that levy has continued to be passed every five years. The most recent levy—passed in 2004 with a two-thirds vote and 98 percent of the precincts having a majority—will provide $180 million over a ten-year period to support the zoo's growth and development. There's no way the Columbus Zoo would have been able to expand, improve, and support seventy conservation projects in thirty-four countries around the world without the gracious support of our taxpayers.

The people of the Columbus area truly love their zoo and see supporting it as an investment. And that investment has proven to pay off. I've heard estimates in the $30 million range when it comes to the amount of revenue the zoo has brought into the county from outside the Central Ohio area each year.

"One of the things we're really proud of is how the community supports the zoo, to the extent that they even vote to tax themselves to support it."

—GERALD BORIN, EXECUTIVE DIRECTOR 1992–2008, COLUMBUS ZOO

However, the bottom line remains that most zoos need visitors and donors to survive. Only a few zoos are self-sustaining. State, county, and city funds are a huge help, but you also need solid, consistent attendance and corporate donations to pull through. And the only way to get and keep money coming is to make people aware of the zoo, make them feel as though they're contributing to a necessary part of the community, a part of the community that's just as important as the symphony, the arts, libraries, or even the school system.

Like many zoos, the Columbus Zoo is operated by a zoological association. This is a nonprofit corporation composed of a varying number of trustees and an executive board that is appointed to manage the zoo. The property is owned by the city and county, but the zoo is basically association-run and free from politics; most important, it is nonprofit, which helps bring in corporate dollars—providing somebody finds the donors.

Today many zoos have adopted more of a "theme park" approach to compete with the current entertainment options. There's really no getting around that. Walt Disney set the standard, and that's what people have come to expect. By this, I don't just mean having Mickey Mouse and Donald Duck running around; I mean clean grounds, friendly and outstanding people who work for you, clean exhibits, good food, that sort of thing. All those qualities we didn't have when I was hired are all standards we now expect as routine, thanks to the hard work of many people. Some people even tell me the zoo doesn't smell anymore, but I wouldn't go quite that far.

Every year in the theme park business, you put in a new ride or attraction to get the visitors to come back. In the zoo business, we don't have the kind of money to build a new animal exhibit each year—you're talking millions of dollars. But every two or three years, you'd better have something new at your zoo. I can always count on each spring's new animal births to boost attendance, but any new animal (like the panda) or a spectacular new exhibit will all but guarantee you a successful season. In the meantime, you do little things that keep people coming to the zoo. High attendance at the zoo not only means increased revenue but also increased opportunities for educating the people of central Ohio about animals and, ultimately, generating interest in their conservation both at the zoo and in the wild.

Almost every weekend from April through September, there's some sort of promotion at the Columbus Zoo. It might be Go Wild! For Opera, Earth Day, Boo at the Zoo, Zoofari, or Family Nights. Even in the winter, we regularly offer half-priced admission to keep the momentum going when it's cold outside. And for the holidays, our Wildlights display has become a long-standing tradition for many Ohio families. The beat goes on and on—that's what zoo promotion is all about, keeping the momentum going. We can't sit still, and I've never been able to anyway.

I'm the first to admit that not *all* of my promotional ideas have been successful. For the sake of promotion, I've probably had more harebrained ideas than I care to admit. I just get carried away. Then by the time I realize a mistake has been made, it's too late—like in the case of the Great Zucchini.

The zoo's attendance for 1978 was a dismal 341,000—pitiful for a community of more than one million people. Since I had only been there a few months, I didn't feel personally responsible, but I wanted to start my first "zoo season," the spring and summer of 1979, off with a bang. The opening of the outdoor gorilla habitat was a step in the right direction, but now I wanted to add something commercial to attract the public.

One of my favorite acts at Ringling Brothers was the one where a guy gets shot out of a cannon into a net all the way across the arena. Reading about the act "The Great Zucchini" in a trade magazine, I thought this might be just the kind of "bang" I was looking for. So I called a carnival and asked how I could get in touch with the Great Zucchini. They gave me the name of his agent, and before I knew it, I had a date for a cannon shot in May.

The local media were alerted, and I told them all about how I was going to have the Great Zucchini shot from a cannon to open the season. (We're open 365 days a year, but it's always wise to have a special opener for the summer season.) The plan was to have this human cannonball go flying across the entrance lake and land in a big net in front of the zoo.

The day before the daredevil was supposed to arrive, my secretary came into my office to tell me that the Great Zucchini was here, that he had just pulled up in his truck. I was puzzled as to why he was here early, but I was anxious to meet him. The moment I saw him standing there in the parking lot, I knew something was a little off.

The truck was an old '52 pickup with a dirty metal cannon on top. The act I had seen in the circus used a huge truck, easily thirty feet longer, with a much bigger, gleaming cannon mounted on top. There was no assistant, no beautiful girl in tights, no agent, no entourage—just a guy in overalls, standing by his truck, smoking a cigarette outside my zoo.

"How are you?" he said in a thick accent. "I'm the Great Zucchini."

"I'm Jack Hanna, from the Columbus Zoo."

We talked a little, and I told him that if he didn't mind, we'd get the media up here and do a preliminary run. This was Friday, and I figured with a few calls to the TV stations I could get something on the evening news.

I always try to break an event—an animal birth, anything—on Thursday or Friday. Even if the animal is born on Sunday, I try to keep it a secret until Thursday or Friday so people will visit the zoo over the weekend. Of course, some jokers in the media are always saying, "Jack, we know it wasn't born on Thursday morning," but they'll usually go along.

On this particular Friday, the press and TV people showed up, along with a few trustees, and in the meantime, the human cannonball pulled me aside and let me know that he wasn't going to pull the trigger on the cannon now, because it would take all the suspense out of his act for the next day. He had a point, but I had all these people there who wanted to see the shot. I told the media he was going to practice—I just didn't say what.

Zucchini himself told the press that he was only going to lift the barrel and simulate what happens and that they could have pictures of him crawling out of the barrel or sitting up on the end of it. By this time, Zucchini had changed into his striped rocket suit, which was all full of holes, and he was wearing an old beat-up World War I leather aviator hat with weird goggles. By this time, I was trying to keep him *away* from the press.

Well, if I'd thought anything was awry before, I knew it for sure when Zucchini asked me—correction: told me—to be his assistant working the cannon. He took me underneath the truck and pointed to these big levers.

"Pull this one to make it go up, this one to make it go sideways, and this one to make it go down," he told me.

It was dark, filthy, and greasy down there, and I didn't know what I was doing. I also could not see what he was doing up above; I was supposed to just react to his commands.

"Okay," he yelled. I could barely hear him. Was he down in the barrel? I pulled on a lever and heard this whirring sound. Then I heard, "Stop!" So I stopped. "Get ready," he yelled. The next move was to pull another lever, just a little bit, to make it go sideways. I heard, "Okay," again. So I pulled. Then I heard this awful crash, followed by Dave Bricker's, "Oh no!"

"What's wrong? What happened?!" I called to Bricker from under all the machinery.

"Zucchini just fell off the cannon and went through the windshield of his truck!"

"Is he okay? What do I do with the cannon? Should I move any more levers?" I asked him.

"Just leave it all alone!"

As I emerged from under the truck, I saw broken glass all over the ground. The news cameras were rolling, catching the Great Zucchini in all his glory as he lay halfway through the broken windshield. Miraculously, he wasn't cut, but he was groaning. His aviator hat had blown off. Somehow he had slipped off the end of the barrel and fallen some fifteen feet down into the windshield below.

"I think I'm all right," he moaned.

I couldn't believe it. This guy's the daredevil, and he goes and falls off the cannon before it even shoots. I'd already given him a five-hundred-dollar deposit on two thousand dollars, and all I had gotten so far was a battered Zucchini. A song began circulating around the zoo, and the first line was: "The Great Zucchini lost his weenie one fine summer day!"

The press people wanted to know what was going on, so I told them Zucchini was all right. I really didn't know—he said he was, and I had to tell them something. "He'll be doing his stunt tomorrow," I told them. I didn't know that either.

I walked over to Mel Dodge, who was standing with the other trustees.

"He's not going off here," said Mel. "We'd have a lawsuit."

"Mel, we've got to do something." I had this thing all announced, all planned for opening day.

"Jack, he can't even get in his cannon," said Mel. "The guy will land across the lake and kill somebody."

I had an idea. After checking with Mel, I went over to the amusement park next to the zoo and asked the owner if he'd like to have the Great Zucchini, free of charge. It wasn't on the zoo property, but it was right next to it. I knew attendance was terrible over there, and I devised some story about how we couldn't do it at the zoo because of the trees and everything.

"I need to get the Great Zucchini over to your place to have him shot out of the cannon," I told the owner. "We'll pay for everything, no problem."

"You got it, Jack," the guy said. He obviously hadn't seen the news that night.

About 2,500 people showed up over there the next day—by no means a great turnout, but at least we had something. I had to practically beg Zucchini to go on—I think he was a little rattled and embarrassed about his practice fall. But I must say, he pulled himself together pretty well. To add ambience, he had some little speakers with music, but he still did not have an assistant. He set the net up in a spot that seemed to be miles away, and I started to really worry about how this would turn out.

"Five, four, three, two, one . . . ," Zucchini shouted from inside the cannon.

My heart stopped. Zucchini pulled his trigger somewhere down in there, that ol' cannon rattled, and with a huge BA-BOOM, and in a cloud of smoke, the human cannonball went flying through the air about fifty yards and plunked down in the middle of the net. Bull's-eye. Talk about relief.

Afterward, when I went to shake his hand, I had to ask him something.

"By the way," I said, "when I saw you at Ringling Brothers, that truck was a lot longer and the cannon was all chrome and polished. Did you have to sell it or something?"

"No," he said, looking kind of sheepish. "I might as well tell you. I'm not the Great Zucchini—I'm his cousin."

Probably the greatest fundraiser my first year at the zoo was Emily the chimp. Mel Dodge purchased Emily from the Cleveland Zoo for something like $2,500; in two years, she helped us raise nearly $200,000.

Emily was trained by Skip Butts, a young keeper who was, at that time, working with sea lions. Before the Cleveland Zoo, Emily had lived with a family, but they had to give her up because she was too destructive. Skip did a good job, but it took him about three months just to calm her down enough to be able to take her out in public. But once she caught on, she was a real ham.

Skip taught Emily to roller-skate, to ride a bike, to eat with silverware, to wear clothes—in short, all the things you would never do today. Today, we would never train a chimp in such a fashion. In fact, California is trying to pass legislation preventing the use of chimps and other great apes in projects such as movies and commercials which I now agree is the correct move to make. But at the time, it was Emily's entertaining, "humanized" personality that enabled us to raise money for the zoo and her cousins in the wild.

If Mel and I could not manage to get an appointment with the CEO of a bank or corporation, we would take Emily over to that man's office with a note in her hands. The note would say something like, "Would you please help the Columbus Zoo?" It never failed; Emily would walk away with ten, fifteen thousand bucks a pop. But like most chimps, she became ornery as she grew older, and her days as a cute little animal gradually ended. It's a hormonal change chimpanzees go through, and it can make them very aggressive. So Emily went back to her zoo habitat and eventually to a breeding program at another zoo.

Every Christmas Mel and I would take an animal around to the offices of the various people who'd made donations during the year. We would thank them for their help and support and have pictures taken of them with a baby lion, a baby elephant, whatever. We weren't there to ask for money; we were there to thank them.

One year Mel and I were going around with a full-grown camel. In the middle of our appointed rounds, we happened to be driving by the capitol. Mel turned to me—we were in a zoo truck—and said, "Let's stop in and see the governor."

"Mel, we don't have an appointment," I said, as if we could bring a camel up to see Governor Rhodes *with* an appointment.

"Don't worry about it," he said. "Let's go see him."

We got out of the truck, and Mel pulled the camel out of the back. We started up the steps to the capitol. He was leading; I was trailing, cleaning up the mess. The state troopers stopped us at the entrance, but the governor's secretary called down and said it was all right. I figured Mel knew the governor, but I didn't know how well or how much the governor wanted to have a visit from a camel.

When we got up there, the secretary said, "Mr. Dodge, the governor is in his final cabinet meeting right now. If you'd like to wait . . ."

"That's no problem," Mel said, pushing the door open before the secretary could stop him.

We got in there, and Governor Rhodes looked up without smiling, like this kind of thing went on every day. His cabinet members were in hysterics, but I was fearful for my job. Mel was about to retire; I was just getting started.

"Governor," said Mel, bringing the camel up behind him, "we've just come by to pay our respects and thank you on behalf of the Columbus Zoo."

"Why, thank you, Mel," said the governor, "but I believe you're on the wrong end of the camel!"

In the early spring of 1980, I had another promotional idea to get the kids back out to the zoo around Easter. An Easter egg hunt is nothing new as far as promotion goes, but I thought it would be a natural, nice thing to usher in the spring season. Simple, right?

Mel advised against it. "It takes a lot of organization, a lot of planning, Jack," he said. "Lots of things can go wrong. I wouldn't do it."

I told him that we needed to get more people in the springtime, and even if the weather wasn't great, an Easter egg hunt would bring the people out. Mel would not deny that, but he still said he wouldn't do it. I should have listened.

We ordered about fifteen hundred marshmallow-filled chocolate eggs, and I announced the event in the papers and on the radio. I said I was going to give big prizes to the one who could find the first twelve eggs. That was my first major screw-up: not giving every kid a prize. The next was not dividing the kids into age groups. And the third, of many, was not expecting a very large crowd because of the forecast for a rainy, cold day.

On the day of the hunt, a *beautiful, sunny* pre-Easter Saturday, kids and their parents started coming to the zoo earlier than ever before. Dave Bricker radioed about nine o'clock to tell me there were three to four hundred people outside the gates. The zoo didn't open until ten; the hunt was scheduled for eleven. I said that was great, tremendous. I remember being really excited, pumped up by the gorgeous weather. And of course all these kids are jumping up and down and screaming—they were excited just to be out.

A half hour later, Bricker called to tell me there were now about a thousand people gathered at the gate; he said we'd better open early. Little did I know that there were still floods of egg-seeking children to come, and I had completely forgotten that our eggs only numbered fifteen hundred. I was just reveling in the big turnout.

So we let everybody in, and we took them all down along the river to this acre-and-a-half area where we had the eggs hidden. There were about a dozen volunteer docents helping and just a single rope around the area. We had Gabe Ritter, a nice man (and a sucker like me) who likes to play the Easter Bunny, lead all the kids in a bunny hop. Around the zoo, I saw all the kids hopping to the music, and I just grinned proudly.

By ten thirty there were almost three thousand people there, and we could barely hold them back from the ropes. At that point, the danger began to set in. The kids were going nuts, dying to get at those chocolate eggs, and the parents were doing little to control them. We knew we had to start this thing soon.

I picked up my bullhorn to start the countdown, but before I could even count to one, a couple of parents and their kids came through the ropes. That started a mass stampede, and within thirty seconds there wasn't one egg left. In fact, there wasn't anything left. They'd sucked up the earth!

It was a terrible scene. Kids everywhere were wailing because they hadn't gotten even one egg. One kid's ear was cut—he had blood all over his face; another had a black eye. Even the Easter Bunny was injured—he was covered in mud, and someone had pulled his ears off! And a local ABC news crew was getting it all on film.

All of a sudden people came toward me. Who was responsible for this? Who can we blame for this mess? They didn't have to look far. One mother grabbed me by the shirt and ripped the epaulets off my safari shirt. "I can't believe you're this dumb, that you'd have an Easter egg hunt for all these kids without enough eggs!" she yelled at me. I couldn't believe it either.

Bricker escorted me back to my office, and I asked him to announce over the bullhorn that we'd give every kid who didn't get an egg or a prize a free pass to the zoo. We were there for hours handing out free passes.

That night Mel called me at home.

"What'd I tell you?" he asked, but that was all he said. Mel was right 99 percent of the time. He laughed about it a little, which was good, because I felt terrible.

I was almost asleep when the phone rang again. It was a guy from the Associated Press wanting to know what happened. Besides being half-asleep,

I didn't mind, and I knew I couldn't run away from the incident. But I should not have spoken my mind quite so bluntly.

"You wouldn't think that the adults would go out and hunt eggs," I told him. "Off the record, it was like placing cheese under a bowl, and suddenly lifting the bowl and watching three thousand rats that haven't eaten in weeks."

Well, that did it. The next day—Easter Sunday, mind you—everybody was in an uproar reading about how the Columbus Zoo director called the people of Columbus rats! My mom, in Florida, even read about it and was mortified. Then Paul Harvey announced it on his radio show and went through the whole story again. I didn't think I'd ever live it down.

The next year we had another Easter egg hunt, and I was determined to do it right. We got five thousand eggs—and it rained. I had to eat or give away forty-five hundred eggs. The following year I got another five thousand eggs—it was 85 degrees, and they all melted. The ants got those.

Today, I am proud to report, we have the Easter egg scene very well organized. We call it Eggs, Paws, and Claws, and the kids go to stations throughout the zoo where they can pick up candy at the animal exhibits. They even get to see some animals have their own real (hard-boiled) egg hunt. Everybody gets something. As always, I learned the hard way, and to this day, I am not a fan of Easter eggs!

As for bonehead plays, no chapter would be complete without the infamous Great Wallenda episode. This was actually a very successful promotion—it brought fifteen thousand people out to the zoo—but it failed for me personally, by bringing practically the entire zoo community down on my head. Yes, I was in the wrong, though I did not realize it at the time.

The Great Wallendas were considered the greatest aerial act in the world. In 1980, the grandfather, Carl Wallenda, tragically fell to his death in a high-wire accident in Puerto Rico. Since then, people were leery of booking them. But in the spring of 1982, I read an article that Enrico, the grandson, was trying to make a comeback. I found out he would be touring in the area, so I thought, *Hey, why not have him perform his act over some wild animals at the zoo?*

I wrote to Enrico Wallenda with my proposal, and he responded right away, saying he thought the idea was ingenious and that he loved zoos and animals.

"The Wallendas like to do dramatic things," he told me when we first met here in Ohio. "We have walked across canyons, gorges, waterfalls, tall buildings." Now he said he wanted to walk above the lions, tigers, and gorillas.

We settled on a price and a date, and once again I announced my plan to the papers. With cutbacks in federal funding, I emphasized to the media, we needed more promotions to generate revenue. The zoo desperately needed more money.

Wallenda also talked to the media. He told one newspaper that he was going to toss a banana to Bongo the gorilla to get his attention. Of course, Bongo, who had never seen people in the air before, would not need much to get his attention. The same article mentioned that police teams and an ambulance would be there—a just-in-case kind of thing. It already sounded risky, and I knew this wasn't the way we wanted to go—not with the gorillas.

The next day my primate keepers came to me with grave concerns. Fearing for the safety of the animals, they told me they were worried about how the stunt might trivialize the gorilla collection at the zoo, as well as those of other zoos. I agreed with them; I'm not all promotion oriented. But I still wanted Wallenda, so we agreed to do it over the tigers. My mistake, or one of them, was not respecting the tigers in the same way.

Wallenda put on a great show for the huge crowd that came to the zoo; he's not just an aerialist, he's a performer. When faking his fall over the tiger pit, I just about had a heart attack. Afterward, he gave Suzi and me lessons on a wire two feet off the ground, and I could not go three feet without falling off.

Even though I had police standing by, I really felt quite confident about Enrico or I would not have done the show. Only growling occasionally as they typically do, the tigers didn't seem to be bothered. A reporter asked me what I would have done had Wallenda fallen into the pit. I could not really answer that, since Enrico had emphatically stated that he did not want the animals harmed under any circumstances.

Several days later I heard it big-time from Robert Wagner, the executive director of the American Association of Zoological Parks and Aquariums (now the AZA, Association of Zoos and Aquariums). Wagner is a good man, a serious man, and he explained to me what I had done was wrong according to AAZPA ethics.

With the act, I had exploited the Bengal tigers through showmanship, not zookeeping, and it could have resulted in the uncalled-for injury or death to either performer or animal. Feeling badly about the whole situation, I sincerely apologized for going outside the standards of zookeeping. But deep down inside, I was still thrilled about all those people we drew. Looking back today, however, I would rather have no visitors than initiate a performance like that again.

In the zoo world, it would be easy to argue that the piéce de résistance is the giant panda, or the Ailuropoda melanoleuca. It's like the Mona Lisa of the zoo world. Now I'm not one who typically goes around spouting Latin (or French, for that matter), but in this case, I learned a Latin name that I would not soon forget.

With fewer than one thousand surviving in the wild, the giant panda has become a symbol for all endangered species; the struggle to save the giant panda has become a challenge to save all wildlife. The panda's primary threats are poachers and loss of habitat. A panda consumes up to forty pounds of bamboo, its primary food source, daily, and the animal's sole natural habitat is a rapidly diminishing region of bamboo forest in central China. To complicate matters, bamboo goes through a periodic die-out, causing food shortages and starvation for some pandas. Pandas are also carnivores, but are generally too slow to catch prey. They are fragile animals in a fragile environment and face almost certain extinction if our commitment to their survival is halted in any way.

In 1986, we took a twelve-person Columbus delegation to visit China. Earlier our mayor, Dana Rinehart, had approached a Chinese minister with the hope of exchanging "breeding technology," which was a polite way of opening negotiations for a panda loan. It was a nice idea, but the Chinese are not about to exchange a pair of pandas for anything short of the state of Texas.

At one point in the trip, we were all sitting around a big table, and this one guy kept looking at my arm. When I finally realized what he kept eyeing—a watch engraved with a tiger—I told him, "If we can have the pandas, I'll give you my watch!" Well, I'm not sure if the watch really had any bearing on the deal, but we came home with a promise of a panda loan in 1992 (when the city would be commemorating the five hundredth anniversary of Christopher Columbus's arrival in the New World), along with an agreement for golden monkeys in 1988.

At the time, the scramble by zoos nationwide to borrow giant pandas from China had created considerable controversy. There were two issues raised: (1) Was the shuffling of the animals from zoo to zoo (and continent to continent) in any way endangering the survival of the species? (2) Were the funds generated by these "rentals" being properly applied toward conservation efforts by the Chinese?

Despite the jury being out on these issues, I received approval from the AZA in 1988 for the short-term loan of the pandas. We immediately began to prepare for our giant, furry visitors. Central Ohio pulled together to raise and spend millions of dollars to build a habitat in which the pandas could feel right at home. Even President George Bush Sr. wrote to congratulate the mayor of Columbus on the achievement.

In 1992, weeks before the pandas were to arrive—they had already begun transport—we were in a federal court in Columbus with the World Wildlife Fund (WWF). The case was heard by an older man, U.S. District Judge Joseph Kinneary, maybe in his eighties at that time. At the beginning, Judge Kinneary asked the WWF attorney to state his case, and the guy said something like, "We're here on behalf of the Ailuropoda melanoleuca."

The judge pounded his mallet. "Excuse me a minute. Can we use the word panda bear?"

"Well, it's actually not a bear," the attorney enlightened him. "It's a giant panda."

Judge Kinneary was not fazed. "Okay, from now on, please refer to it as a giant panda."

As the attorney made his case, he continued to use the Latin name. The judge said, "I thought we talked about this. I want the words giant panda used, not the Latin name."

"Okay, I'm sorry your honor," he conceded and began to build his case about why the Columbus Zoo shouldn't have them—how it would affect breeding and how we were just using the animals to make money.

After a while, Judge Kinneary interrupted again. "Excuse me. You're telling me it's going to affect breeding. I don't quite understand this," he mused. "Columbus is getting two pandas that are both males and both under the age of three. Now, I'm not a zoologist. I'm not a person really in this field, but I don't think two males can breed."

All of a sudden you could feel a shift in the packed courtroom. I heard one of their attorneys say something like, "Let's pack our bags." They knew it was time to get out of that courtroom. And sure enough, they only lasted another ten or fifteen minutes.

When it was his turn, our attorney, John Kulewicz, got up and made our side of the argument. He told the judge how we had gone through the proper approval process and had received permission in 1988 from the AZA for the loan of the pandas. He also pointed out that ever since we had received permission, we had been making preparations for the giant panda. Why had the WWF waited until three weeks before the pandas arrived to suddenly try to prevent their journey to the Columbus Zoo? And what would we tell the citizens of Columbus who had rallied around us and helped to raise millions of dollars to build the habitat, who were expecting this rare treat on the five-hundred-year celebration of the country?

In the end, the judge ordered that the pandas could come, and naturally I was relieved that all of the work everyone had put in was not in vain. The citizens of Columbus—and really, the entire Midwest—would have the rare opportunity to see and appreciate the giant panda up close. It really was not about winning a lawsuit; it was winning what was right. I sometimes wonder about the judicial system in this country. But this was one case where: (1) there should not have even been a lawsuit filed, and (2) the people who were doing the right thing won. Period. End of story.

Except it wasn't really the end of the story. As a result of the judgment, in order to make a point to the zoo world—well, that's how I interpreted it—the AZA came down on me. A little while after the trial, I received a letter in the mail saying that I would personally lose my AZA membership—along with the Columbus Zoo—for six months to a year. That's like a lawyer or dentist losing his license for a year!

"There was a lively discussion. About half the board thought it was time to end the 'rent-a-panda' program, that it made zoos look too commercial and not conservation-oriented. The other half said, 'Jack's played by all the rules. He hasn't done anything different than any of the other zoos.' So he was sort of a victim of the times then."

—STEVE TAYLOR, FORMER PRESIDENT OF THE AZA

Personally, I was hurt by the action of the AZA. This time I had done my homework, and I had followed all the rules. With the backing and approval of the trustees of the zoo, I knew I was doing what was best for the conservation of pandas and for the zoo and the people of Columbus. During those days I was greatly encouraged by a quote from Ralph Waldo Emerson: "What lies behind us and what lies before us are tiny matters compared to what lies within us." Despite everything that had happened and would happen, I knew that my intentions were genuine and had to believe that everything would eventually work out for the benefit of all—especially the pandas.

In retrospect, I can now undeniably say I was doing what was best for the giant panda. Much of the money we paid in the agreement went directly to support their habitat development and conservation in China, and that's saying nothing of the awareness raised and support garnered from the 1.6

million visitors who came to visit the giant pandas at the Columbus Zoo.

Pandas make people become instantly aware of conservation. People are profoundly affected when they see firsthand this lovable creature that might become extinct. The effect comes from seeing it up close and live, not on a slide, the Internet, or in a book.

Regardless of the incident, I knew then and know now that the AZA is important to this business, and I've continued to support them to this day. Some people say, "How do you do that, Jack, when they kicked you out?" Well, I don't do it for redemption; I do it because I believe in what they do.

"It was a slap in the face to him initially, but he handled it like a gentleman. Later, when the AZA needed his help, he never even considered saying no."

—SALLY SOUTH, FORMER ADMINISTRATIVE ASSISTANT, COLUMBUS ZOO

Since that time, zoological and conservation leaders have come together and revised the loan program. It's now a longer, ten-year period and is seeing much success. There are four pairs of giant pandas on loan in the United States today, and three of those pairs are breeding.

Ironically enough, the whole panda fiasco was the start of one of the Columbus Zoo's largest conservation programs. And through that we have saved the lives of many, many animals, and many, many people with the conservation fund that all started with the pandas. And that, to me, is the bottom line. That's the end of the story.

Today I travel extensively for promotion—to promote both the Columbus Zoo and the animal world in general. I'll take animals from our promotions department at the Columbus Zoo, as well as invite area zoos to bring their own animals. And it's a personal policy of mine not to accept a speaking engagement unless I'm allowed to plug the Columbus Zoo and any other zoo involved in the presentation. After all, the animals are the stars of the shows, and there's really no point if they don't benefit in the long run.

Promotions can be serious or silly. What I do know is that they serve a number of purposes, including bringing more people through the gate, boosting support for endangered animals, and educating the public about the other inhabitants in the world around them.

CHAPTER 12

The Circle of Life

Spending my entire life in the animal world has given me a front-row seat to the amazing circle of life. And even after all the years of witnessing every stage of the cycle, again and again, I am still awed by the birth of a baby giraffe and overcome when I learn of the loss of the smallest creature.

The birth of any animal is probably the single most rewarding aspect of being a zoo director. And not a week goes by without a birth happening at the zoo. In a sense, it's like being a grandfather: most of the time, you can just sit back, appreciate, and enjoy.

Anyone who knows the zoo business also knows that newborns are great attractions. Naturally, high-profile animals like gorillas, lions, and elephants receive top billing from the press and the public, but around here we're tickled with each and every birth, from cougar to centipede, from hippo to hyena.

One reason our births captivate the public so much is the anthropomorphizing of animals. Whether the "purists" in the zoo field like it or not, zoo animals take on character in the public eye. After the average patron has visited the zoo two or three times in one summer, certain animals become favorites, become family. The zoo visitor feels like he knows the animal, and in his own way, he does. When the animal has a baby—and zoo patrons are kept informed by newsletters, television, newspapers, etc.—it becomes a big family event.

And getting down to basic sentimentality, baby animals are just plain cute; there's no denying it. They're especially appealing when they're small and playful, even if they're guaranteed to become ugly when they're older. A polar bear cub or a baby elephant will draw huge crowds. One of the most gratifying sounds to me is the "*Awww*" chorus around a newborn animal.

Most important of all, zoo births are a means toward continuing propagation and the preservation of many species. Breeding has become an all-important activity in zoos, if not the most important. It's what we're here for. We don't want to sit around and watch Clyde the endangered black rhino die in his habitat after forty years, then go out to the Serengeti Plain in Africa and net another rhino. Thank goodness those days are over. We're now here to help make a lot of little Clydes so that future generations can see and learn about these creatures.

Furthering a species like Clyde's does come with a price . . . and the need for a bit of discretion, as one incident years ago proved. Making my way through a pile of paperwork, I learned of the incident when I noticed an insurance form with a claim for a lost contact lens from our curator Don Winstel. The claim said that the lens had been knocked out of his eye while he was ejaculating a black rhinoceros to collect semen.

What?!

It was the first I'd heard about this, so I ran up to the pachyderm building to see what was going on. The guys nonchalantly told me they'd been collecting semen from Clyde, our black rhino, once a week for about three or four months. They would drive his semen down to the Cincinnati Zoo, where it could be frozen and preserved for artificial insemination.

Their method was archaic, but quite ingenious. At the front end, someone would feed Clyde monkey chow. (To my knowledge, Clyde was the only rhino in the world who would eat monkey chow—which is like a sweet biscuit—and at the same time stand still for this type of research.) At the other end, they had this contraption made from two two-by-fours that held a soft rubber femur cast. The rest of the process, I hope, is self-explanatory.

Apparently, at some point in the process, Don's contact lens was knocked out and unable to be recovered. Now, while I understand the importance of the artificial insemination process and Don's need for a new contact lens, there was no way I was going to ask the insurance company for sixty-five dollars for a lens that was lost while ejaculating a rhino! I just reimbursed Don for his contact lens out of petty cash and spared our insurance company the claim, along with this newfound knowledge of rhino propagation.

When it involves an endangered species like the black rhino, the birth of an animal can have worldwide significance. There are fewer than three thousand black rhinos left in Africa, with the most endangered subspecies numbering under ten. Their ability to be propagated in zoos could determine the fate of their species.

With any captive birth of an endangered animal, the benefits of that newborn are two-fold: (1) the population of that endangered animal just grew by one, and (2) there is an adorable, big-eyed newborn that will now serve as the poster child for this endangered species, raising awareness (and funding) with every bat of its tiny eyelashes. The public, in turn, becomes better educated and more engaged in that species' struggle for survival. Look at the giant panda: everybody is aware of (and many are supporting) the conservation of that species, and there have been only a few born in zoos worldwide.

When a gorilla becomes pregnant here at the zoo, we go to great lengths to ensure the well-being of the animal and her future offspring. People used to think we were crazy anesthetizing the pregnant female, but it's the only way to examine her. The information we learn not only tells us whether she and the fetus are all right or not, but just as in humans, it helps pinpoint the birth date. Then we can start our gorilla watches accordingly, a few weeks ahead of the due date.

Back in the summer of 1983, we were doing a typical exam on Bridgette, the gorilla on breeding loan from the Henry Doorly Zoo in Omaha. The ape staff, our veterinarian Dr. Harrison Gardner, Dr. Nick Baird (my wife's gynecologist and our good friend), and, for the first time, Dr. Larry Stempel, who was administering the sonogram, were all present. After shaving Bridgette's belly, Dr. Stempel began scanning with his instrument, watching the monitor. He'd barely been at it a minute when he stopped suddenly.

"I can't believe this," he said. "Take a picture," he told his assistant. "Take another one . . . one more." He was very intent and seemed excited. None of us knew what was happening.

"Dr. Stempel, what's going on?" I asked. "Is the baby dead?"

"No," he said, and continued scanning. After a minute or so, he looked up. "I think there are twins in there!"

"Dr. Stempel," I said, "I don't know everything about gorillas, but I don't think twins have ever been born at a zoo." (I found out later they had—twice, in Germany and Spain.) "Are you sure about this?"

"Is this guy for real?" asked head keeper Dianna Frisch. All the keepers were shaking their heads in disbelief.

Nick Baird went over to have a look at the monitor. "Looks like two heads to me," he said. "Could you back up a little, Larry? . . . Yes . . . there are definitely two gorillas there."

"Now, Nick," I said, "I'm going to announce this, and I don't want to make a fool of myself, like we did with the elephant that was pregnant for twenty-four months and never had a baby!"

"No problem, Jack," Nick said. "You've got twin gorillas there."

"And they're in perfect shape," added Dr. Stempel, who was measuring their size, heart rate, everything. Now we were all ecstatic with the news.

That next October, on the twenty-sixth to be exact, someone phoned Suzi, my wife, to sub for them in volunteering on labor-watch duty. Little did she know this would be the big night. Suzi picked up on the most important thing: that Bridgette was going into labor. There were some tense moments because Suzi had trouble starting the video machine, and she couldn't seem to work the walkie-talkie to call for help. A security officer heard her screaming into the walkie-talkie and came right over to assist.

As always, all the vets, doctors, keepers, and I were immediately summoned. At a little after midnight, Bridgette moved to her nesting area, and with one long, hard push, the first baby was born.

The critical thing was how quickly the second baby would be born, since we had no research, no precedent. Bridgette immediately picked up the first infant (Baby A), and fifty seconds later the second baby (Baby B) was born. She leaned over to tend to this infant but became distracted by a cry from her firstborn. She then started consuming the placenta (a natural and important process), meanwhile forgetting Baby B, who was still enclosed in the amniotic sac.

The doctors said we could wait about three minutes, then somebody would have to go in and get that baby out of the sac. But you can't just walk in on a full-grown gorilla.

Dianna coaxed Bridgette, who was cradling Baby A, to a back enclosure while my good friend Dr. Nick Baird, the gorilla gynecologist, rushed in and tore open the sac. And there was Baby B, moving and breathing.

Nick Baird wrapped him in a blanket and headed out to the nursery, where incubators and staff were waiting. But Nick got lost in the zoo maintenance area and we had to go find him. What a scene it was, Nick lost in a dark maintenance room holding a rare twin newborn gorilla.

We had to pull Baby A as well, since that was the request of his owner, the Henry Doorly Zoo. With such a high-profile birth, no one wanted to take any chances, and it's possible that Bridgette could not have handled two babies anyway.

The twins were boys, in beautiful condition, weighing in at four pounds eight ounces each. They both had long eyelashes and little arms that were grabbing out at everything.

Because the twins were the result of a breeding loan, after the ultrasound it had been decided between Dr. Lee Simmons, the Henry Doorly Zoo director, and me that each zoo would own one twin, the firstborn going to Omaha and the second to Columbus. We eventually worked out an agreement whereby they traveled between Columbus and Omaha each year—about eight months in Columbus and four in Omaha—for the first four years.

It took months, but we finally got past "A" and "B" and named them Mosuba (for Molly, Sue, and Barb, the three Columbus volunteers who helped raised them in the nursery) and Macombo II (for Colo's father, Baron Macombo).

Every year for their first four birthdays, we had a party for the twins on *Good Morning America*. In fact, their birth brought about my first appearance on the show (more about that in the next chapter). For the first four years, the boys and I had cake together on the air, but by 1988, they were about a hundred pounds each and very powerful, quite capable of jerking me around if they chose. I

Mosuba and Macombo II stole everyone's hearts. (Doug Martin)

decided not to go in with them that year, but we wished them "happy birthday" on the air and did a program on the endangered gorillas.

It is quite possible that the twins would continue to get along throughout life, but even in the wild they might not choose to stay together. The Propagation Committee of the Species Survival Plan (SSP) of AAZPA recommended to both zoos that the twins be separated when they reach maturity and integrated into unrelated family groups for genetic reasons. In the captive gorilla world, the gene pool we have now is all we will ever have (because gorillas are no longer taken out of the wild), so genetic diversity is absolutely critical.

Some births are less glamorous than others, but as I said before, they're never any less important. You probably wouldn't think much about a couple of turtles being born, unless you realized how rare they are. But when two baby yellow-spotted sideneck turtles chewed their way through their eggshells on August 26, 1983, we again made zoo history.

These South American turtles were the first of their species ever hatched at a zoo (the eggs had been "dropped" two months earlier). They're endangered today because they have been overexported in the past, as well as overeaten by Amazon natives. We hope to see them make a comeback, and every little bit helps, right?

The people in the reptile department have done a fantastic job over the years. In a five-year span, Mike Goode and Dan Badgley managed to breed twenty-five different species of turtles—an unrivaled feat in the zoo world. And they never did it exactly by the book (whatever the book on reptile and amphibian breeding is). In the case of the turtles, they found that a diet of trout chow somehow increased fertility. The special care taken to create proper nesting areas plays a large part as well.

One of the most nerve-racking births we have at the zoo is a giraffe birth, but at the same time, it's one of the most rewarding. There are potential problems with giraffe births because the animal is so large and unwieldy and because the mother stands up while dropping her offspring four to six feet. That's right—the baby just drops from the mother, right to the ground. What a way to come into the world.

The baby giraffe is all neck and legs coming out. Eventually, like a newborn colt, it will push on those skinny legs and just wiggle itself up—a joy to behold. With its big brown eyes, the baby giraffe is just about unequaled in the cuteness department. After a couple of days, all cleaned off, it fluffs up and looks like a big stuffed toy. Gorgeous.

In the spring of 1985, we had a rare white tiger born to our two tigers, Duke and Dolly. Both parents carried the white and orange genes, so one out of four cubs had the chance of being white. This cub was one of a litter

The playful Taj, when we were still friends, before he lost Suzi's engagement ring. (Rick A. Prebeg)

of three and had black stripes like the others, but white fur and blue eyes.

Some white tigers have physical problems, and this one was no exception. She couldn't stand on her hind legs properly and risked becoming deformed if she stayed on the slick floor of the tiger den. She needed twenty-four-hour care in soft surroundings, but at the time, there was no room in the zoo nursery for her.

By this time, our kids were all at school during the day, and Suzi hadn't raised an animal since our Knoxville days. I knew she was capable, so I asked her if she wanted to raise the white tiger cub at home. She was elated, and for six months, that tiger got around-the-clock, tender-loving care.

Suzi disinfected the kitchen floor every day on her hands and knees until the cub had her shots. She held her and gave the cub her undivided attention, even bringing the cub to bed with her at night. I'm a light sleeper, so she slept with the cub in the guest room to accommodate the cub's frequent feedings without disturbing my sleep.

Wanting to give it the best name in the whole world, Suzi named the cub Taj after the Taj Majal; she thought that was the most amazing building with a name to match. Taj grew up to be a magnificent specimen, thanks to Suzi's attention. For a long period after the tiger had been returned to the zoo, Suzi would go in and feed and care for her every night. It turned into a very special relationship.

One early summer evening, Suzi was exercising Taj, who was now about a hundred pounds, in an outdoor yard at the zoo. Later, as it was getting dark, Suzi came home and sat down on the couch. When she felt her ring finger, she turned bleach white and screamed.

"What's wrong?" I asked her. Suzi is always calm; I had never seen her like this.

"The diamond's gone out of my engagement ring," she answered and started crying. Noticing a small scratch on her ring finger, she added, "I must have lost it playing with Taj."

"Don't worry about it," I told her. "We've got insurance. We'll get a diamond to put back in there." She'd had the ring for nineteen years, and I wasn't fazed by her losing that stone. But Suzi was inconsolable.

The next day she went back over to the zoo. On her hands and knees, she cut the grass by hand for hours, looking for the stone. Her hands were blistered when she came back, and there was still no diamond.

The same day I got my maintenance crew to mow, and we vacuumed up every blade of grass into some big green plastic bags that I was going to take home to search through. I left those bags outside the yard and went to my office for about an hour. In the meantime, the grounds crew came by, picked up the bags, and fed that grass to the elephants. I called Suzi to tell her—big mistake—and she fell apart all over again.

Suzi came back to the zoo, and together we went over to the pachyderm yard, where the elephants had already eaten about half the grass. At that point, my job description changed from looking through bags of grass to looking through piles of elephant poop. I'd already looked through Taj's dung, but elephant poop? Now that's a substantially different matter.

Even after all of that, we never found the diamond. Luckily for me, the insurance company did pay for a replacement diamond after a bit of a hassle. Still, for Suzi, no diamond could replace the original one I had given her back in college.

A very strange place to go diamond mining . . . (Columbus Zoo)

Somehow Paul Harvey got wind of this story and ended up using it on his newscast. Soon after, Mel Dodge ran into a substantial donor to the Columbus Zoo, and the guy said to Mel, "Hey, Mel, I'm not giving any more money to the zoo."

Mel was a little taken aback. "Why is that?"

The man answered with a grin, "Any zoo that can afford to feed diamonds to the elephants doesn't need any more money!"

While the birth of a white tiger was rare, eagle births are always critical, both in the wild and at the zoo. Each and every successful hatching helps offset their well-known status as an endangered species. They always hatch in a nest on high, usually after an incubation of thirty-six days or so. During incubation, the parents will share sitting on the egg. The weather plays a large part in whether the eaglet survives once it's hatched. High winds and harsh spring weather can be fatal; meddling by humans can spook the parents into harming the offspring.

George and Georgina, two Columbus Zoo bald eagles, were prolific parents. Georgina lived to be about twenty-five (she died in the summer of 1988) and hatched nine eaglets over a ten-year period. Of those, five survived, but one came through with flying colors. Freedom was born at the Columbus Zoo in 1982 and released in the Tennessee Valley before he could fly. Three years later he bred in the wild and hatched an eaglet. That was a big first.

At six weeks old, the bird was taken to a hacking tower high above the tree line surrounding Norris Lake. The hacking tower is a boxlike apparatus that allows the bird to be fed (by means of a pulley from another tower) for a few weeks until it can fish and hunt on its own. When the bird is old enough, it's released from the tower. This is a glorious moment. It'll take about a twenty-foot drop at first, then with a couple of wing flaps, it'll go soaring off against the sky. Just thinking about it gives me the goose bumps.

Freedom's release was part of a successful nationwide program (two years earlier, we had released an eaglet in upstate New York). We played our part by being one of a handful of zoos at the time to ever breed eagles in captivity. Tennessee ecologists did their part by diligently tracking the birds and their offspring. Freedom played his part first by surviving—he was tagged before being released—then by finding a mate and reproducing. Today he hunts and fishes over the Tennessee Valley in the grand fashion of our national bird.

Releasing such an endangered species into the wild is one of the greatest feelings to be experienced in all of the zoo business. It would be nice to say we're going to do the same thing with *all* the zoo animals, but you have to be realistic. Only a tiny percentage of animals born in the zoo will ever go back to the wild; most will live out their lives in the zoo. That's a fact of life, or death, if you will, and there's very little we can do about it.

We lose a certain number of animals every year, but some zoo animals have been around for such a long time that their deaths touch both the public and the keepers who've been with them all this time. Sometimes an animal loss is almost as difficult as that of a family member, but we deal with each one in the most sensitive and practical way possible.

Hippopotamuses are considered to be old at twenty-five years, but Pete, our oldest zoo resident at the time, somehow made it to forty-four. Pete came to us from Egypt in 1939; he died in March 1982. This old guy was one of my personal favorites. He loved having water squirted in his mouth with a hose, and I always highlighted every zoo tour with a visit to his habitat. Pete was an institution in himself.

Pete died on a Saturday night, and his death, in a sense, caught us by surprise. We knew he wasn't well, that his liver was in poor shape, but we hadn't planned on his leaving us so suddenly at such a time—by this, I mean four hours before the zoo opened for our busiest day. The public does not want to see a dead hippo, especially on a Sunday visit to the zoo.

When an animal of that size dies, people like to know what we do with the body. Well, we try to move it as quickly as possible. You can't take a two-ton hippo and bring him out the door as deadweight; you have to cut him up. I know it sounds gruesome, but how else are we going to do it?

In addition—and this is important—a necropsy (an autopsy of an animal) had to be performed, and we didn't want to hurry this unnecessarily. Some of the keepers had been with this animal twenty years. I told them they didn't have to assist with this if they didn't want to. They said no, the animal was dead, and they wanted to learn more about hippos. It's not every day of the week that a necropsy is done on a hippo, and this was an opportunity to learn more.

After an on-site necropsy, we found out that Pete died from a massively enlarged liver. That and other vital organs were given to the animal labs at The Ohio State University for further study, and the rest of Pete was cremated.

We weren't the only ones who missed Pete. Cleo, his longtime companion, knew something was wrong too. She was off her feed for months after his death.

But there's a nice postscript to Pete's death. Cleo was so sad we decided to get her another companion. We got Big Bake, a ten-month-old hippo from the Houston Zoo, about six months later. Big Bake was named after Glenn Baker, our maintenance foreman, who drove the 650-pound pachyderm straight through from Texas in a converted horse trailer.

The trip took twenty-eight hours and included ten stops at service stations along the way while Baker and his crew watered down the hippo to make sure his skin stayed moist. Gas station attendants, who got a big kick out of this, were very helpful, and Big Bake arrived in fine shape. When he finally arrived, he took a big, long drink of water and relaxed right into his new home next to Cleo. In fact, they produced a youngster much earlier than we expected.

Things can always suddenly go very wrong when you're breeding wild animals at a zoo. You just never know. You hope for the best, considering the risks but knowing that the rewards can be very great.

Rewati was a beautiful twelve-year-old female white tiger on loan to us from the National Zoo in Washington, D.C. Her mother had been a gift to the United States from the people of India, and Rewati was the first white tiger born in this country. Dr. Ted Reed, the former director at the National Zoo and one of the most renowned leaders in the zoo world, had raised Rewati in his home. It was through Dr. Reed's sister, who lived here in Columbus, that we were able to acquire Rewati for breeding.

Ika was a four-hundred-pound, three-legged former circus tiger that had lost his leg to an infection before coming to our zoo. Over a period of nine months, Ika began his courtship with Rewati in an adjacent pen. When the time was right, we introduced them, and for the first two weeks, it seemed like a marriage made in heaven.

One evening during their week together, I was playing tennis with Suzi when I saw head curator Mike July rushing toward me down the hill next to the courts.

From my earlier days with *Good Morning America*, Spencer Christian, Joan Lunden, and Charlie Gibson came to visit me at the Columbus Zoo. (*Good Morning America*/ABC)

Filming for *Animal Adventures* at the Columbus Zoo with one of our baby western lowland gorillas. (Rick A. Prebeg)

On our way to see the mountain gorillas in Rwanda, we discovered this giant earthworm in the jungle. At first, I thought it was a snake! (Rick A. Prebeg)

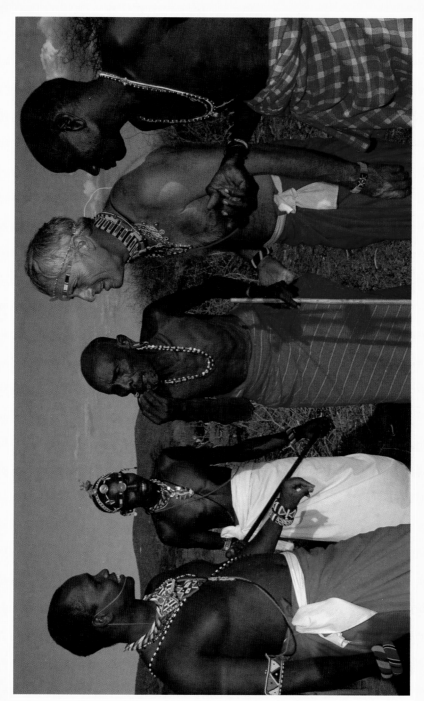

The Samburu people in Kenya were kind enough to let me try out their traditional dress. (Rick A. Prebeg)

My family and I were delighted to see little Bindi Irwin, flanked by her Crocmen, when we visited the Australia Zoo. (Rick A. Prebeg)

We also saw Bindi's mom, Terri, and little brother, Robert, who is cut right from his father's mold. Suzi is holding Bindi's python friend. (Rick A. Prebeg)

Swimming with the incredibly intelligent dolphins at Discovery Cove in Orlando is an experience like no other! (Busch Entertainment Corporation)

Natalie Portman and I while filming *Gorillas on the Brink* for the Animal Planet. Behind us, a mountain gorilla is about to sneak across the Virunga National Park border to grab a snack from the potato field. (Rick A. Prebeg/Animal Planet)

Each one of these people plays an important part in filming mountain gorillas in the wild. There are guides, park service trackers, and rangers, who ensure a successful trek for the film crew, my family, and me. (Rick A. Prebeg)

Just being one of the wombats at the Australia Zoo with the director, Wes Mannion, and the girls. (Jack Hanna)

While on safari, we met these children from a rural village in Rwanda. We took turns demonstrating how an elephant would drink water from the lake. (Rick A. Prebeg)

An early family photo, with a full-of-personality Suzanne. We didn't realize she had made that pose until we got the photos back! (Jack Hanna)

My dear friend, Betty White, with her Golden Retriever at her home in Los Angeles. (Jack Hanna)

Our family in 1974, including our Old English Sheepdog, Daisy, and our cat, Willy. (Jack Hanna)

Suzanne, Julie, Suzi, and I met these children at the base of the Virunga Mountains before our trek to view the mountain gorillas. (Rick A. Prebeg)

Rosamond Carr, founder of the Imbabazi Orphanage, upon hearing of a donation being made to the orphanage. (Rick A. Prebeg)

At Kathaleen's wedding in England—the first and last time you'll ever see me in a top hat. (Jack Hanna)

John McConnell's grandchildren, Porter, Jessica, and John, each played a special part in Kathaleen's wedding. (Jack Hanna)

Still on cloud nine after the Emmy Awards, where *Jack Hanna's Into the Wild* won for Outstanding Children's Series in its very first season! (Marc Bryan-Brown Photography)

The entire Hanna family! Second row: Julian, Kathaleen, Jack, Suzi, Julie, Billy, Suzanne; first row: Gabriella, Jack, Brittany, Blake, Caroline, Alison; in front: Brass and Tasha.

"Jack, Jack!" he yelled. "Come here, quick."

"What is it, Mike?" I yelled back at him. "What's wrong?"

"Ika just killed Rewati," he shouted, loud enough for players on courts next to us to hear. It was about seven o'clock, the sun going down—a beautiful, peaceful summer evening. Everybody stopped playing.

"What?" I walked over to the fence.

"Ika just killed Rewati—broke her neck."

"I don't believe it," I said. "They've been getting along fine."

"Well, apparently they were mating," explained Mike, "and he just snapped her neck. It's known to happen."

I dropped my racket and rushed over to the zoo. When I got there, they were just taking her body away. There were two small sets of puncture wounds on the skin, but her neck had been severely snapped. The strangest part of the scene was Ika, who just lay there in the corner purring, like nothing had ever happened. I felt terrible, and now I had to call Dr. Reed.

Fortunately, Dr. Reed understood the situation—in fact, much better than I did. I told him exactly what happened and apologized. He told me those things happen, not to worry about it, and to send him an autopsy report, which I did.

I still felt indirectly responsible, in that we put two animals together that would not necessarily have selected each other in the wild. Was there some way we could have known this might happen? And how could a three-legged tiger kill a four-legged tiger anyway? We try to be selective in our breeding process, but sometimes you just never know.

Like most of us, I have a difficult time at funerals; I hardly ever attend them. So I wasn't exactly thrilled when the gorilla keepers asked if they could pay their respects by having a small funeral for Mac the gorilla on the zoo grounds.

Mac (Macombo) was the clan patriarch when he died of a heart attack at age thirty-eight in June 1984. Dianna Frisch had called me to say that she'd found Mac dead when she came in that morning. She said it appeared that Mac had died quite suddenly, without suffering.

Mac represented both the old and new zoo; he had been wild-caught in Africa and brought to Columbus in 1951. Yet he was also an important granddaddy, having sired the first gorilla born in captivity. He was probably the most fondly regarded animal in the whole zoo.

It was after Mac's body had been transferred over to Ohio State for necropsy that the keepers asked me if we could bring him back for a zoo burial. I said I'd have to check with the trustees, and we would see. After thinking about it, I realized it would be nice to do something for all the people who wanted to remember Mac, but the last thing I wanted was for people to see this as a PR gimmick.

So we got the green light and went ahead with the memorial. At first, it was just going to be a quiet affair with keepers, and "members of the immediate family" type of thing, but then it began to grow. Docents, volunteers who had worked with Mac over the past twenty years, started calling and asking to come, the papers announced the "funeral," and some public showed up. I guess it was unavoidable.

On a beautiful weekday morning, about three hundred people were gathered outside the gates, waiting for the ceremony. The maintenance people had handcrafted a casket with "Mac" inscribed in rope on the top. They picked him up in a zoo truck, and it took eight sturdy pallbearers to lift it with him inside.

At the appointed time, I could hardly get near the gravesite, which we had decided would be next to the gorilla habitat. There were people crowded all around and piles and piles of flowers everywhere. I remember thinking this could be the funeral of a really important person.

Usually, I'm not at a loss for words, but here I was at a gorilla funeral, and I was stuck. Other people spoke first—it was informal and very touching, very respectful. Dianna Frisch said something about how Mac could be a colossal pain in the butt to all who knew him, and how you either loved him or you hated him, but you always respected him.

Finally I got up there and said, "We're all here today to pay respects to the first gorilla to breed successfully in captivity. Mac's contribution to the survival of the species will live on, long after we're all gone. Animals are usually not buried on zoo grounds, but we felt Mac and the community deserved it, because of what he had done not only for the zoo but for the gorilla species. We've learned a great deal from Mac, and that's why we're here, and that's why he'll be buried here where he spent nearly all his life."

The gorillas were outdoors, and Mac's two youngsters, Oscar and Toni, were looking on. It was really quiet. People later said that the apes knew what was going on. Maybe they did. And today, near their habitat is a plaque at the site to honor an animal that embodied both the past we were happy to leave behind and the future promise of the animal world. It's all in the circle of life.

CHAPTER 13

Lights, Camera, Animals!

All this television stuff started, unintentionally, after I got to Columbus. Seeing me in some colorful local news interviews, the producer of a cable talk show asked me if I'd host some animal episodes. As an opportunity to promote the zoo, I accepted.

My next stop on the local circuit was *Hanna's Ark*, a family-type show on WBNS (CBS) that featured my daughter Kathaleen and me as cohosts. With her trademark pigtails, she was only eleven but stole the show every time. She took the job very seriously, learning not only her lines but mine as well, to help me when I would forget. And she was completely fearless with the animals. She never flinched when a huge, black, hairy tarantula was placed on her arm, or when she was filming five feet from a spitting cobra. At Sea World one of the segments we filmed was the water skiing show. While one of the performers was skiing, he held Kathaleen, who then climbed on top of his shoulders. Suzi said the ballet and gymnastics lessons paid off—she even pointed her toes! Though she certainly had her share of scratches and bites, she never said a word about it.

We would open with an animal at the zoo, then go to footage of the same species in the wild, then come back and close from the zoo. I loved the concept, and it was fun while it lasted.

After two years and forty-eight episodes, *Hanna's Ark* was shelved. I was

Promotional materials for Hanna's Ark, featuring my fearless co-host, Kathaleen. (WBNS TV)

Kathaleen and I have an up-close encounter with a killer whale at SeaWorld while filming Hanna's Ark. (*SeaWorld*)

somewhat upset at the time, since the station announced that we didn't have enough animals to tie in to the wild because we were a small zoo.

But ending *Hanna's Ark* turned out to be a blessing. Shortly afterward, Channel 4, the local NBC affiliate, offered me a series of one-hour wildlife specials. These shows enabled me to learn (as I taught) about wild animals at the farthest reaches of the earth. We covered Egypt, East Africa, China, India, the Galápagos Islands, Alaska, Antarctica—you name it. And the result was an avalanche of invaluable publicity for the zoo.

A special bonus to our agreement was a small weekly bit every Friday

Patty Neger, producer for *Good Morning America,* launched my national television career in 1983. (Columbus Zoo)

called Zoo Day. I'd take an animal to the studio, or a crew came to us, and we just talked about what was going on at the zoo. It was a fantastic weekend reminder.

Angela Pace, the anchorperson for my first five years of Zoo Days, was, at the beginning, deadly opposed to the segment—she thought it had no place on a serious newscast. But we hit it off so well and had so many good times together that it did not take long for her to come around.

Soon to follow was my big start on national television. In 1983, Patty Neger, associate producer from ABC's *Good Morning America* called. She had seen on the AP wire service a story about twin gorillas being born here in Columbus. She asked if they could do a live remote with me from the zoo, and I said fine. It all went off very smoothly, but I have to say it's hard to miss with a couple of twin baby gorillas.

"I was the first person to put Jack on national television. . . .
You can blame it all on me."

—PATTY NEGER, COORDINATING PRODUCER, *Good Morning America*

A year later Patty checked in on us again with the idea of doing a birthday party for the twins. We had a birthday cake, the whole bit, and by this time the twins were total hams. They were all over me, pulling my earpiece out and chewing my safari shirt. The *GMA* people liked it, and Patty told me to call her if there were any more significant births happening at the zoo.

The following spring, while in New York on some other business, I told Patty about Taj, the white tiger cub born to yellow parents that Suzi was raising at home because of the cub's leg disability. Patty said they had a last-minute opening and asked if I could get Taj to New York immediately. Suzi wasn't home, but the *GMA* people somehow managed to track her down—before I did—on the golf course during Jack Nicklaus's Memorial Tournament. Hours later, Suzi and Taj were on their way to New York City.

Suzi carried Taj with her in a crate, and on the plane, Taj received star treatment. In an announcement, the pilot welcomed the "white tiger cub," aboard the plane, and the man sitting beside Suzi asked her for Taj's boarding pass. "My wife will never believe I sat next to a tiger cub on the plane," he told her. The next morning Taj joined me for my first Good Morning America studio appearance with Joan Lunden. And boy, did she "awww" them!

My next appearance was again in the studio, with two lion cubs and a sandhill crane. Kathleen Sullivan was the host and that crane was flapping its huge wings so much that Kathleen's hair was blowing like she was in a wind tunnel. The cubs were crawling all over my lap, and I just went on with the interview as though nothing was happening.

What I was going through was nothing compared to Debbie Casto's ordeal the night before. Debbie, our marketing director at the time, had just been kicked out of the Plaza Athénée Hotel. Around ten o'clock, she had taken one of the lion cubs for a walk on the marble floor of the hotel's foyer, and somebody got uptight. Debbie wound up sleeping in the manager's office on a cot with the two cubs.

Anyway, that particular show cemented *Good Morning America*'s relationship with the Columbus Zoo. Producer Sonya Selby-Wright suggested having me appear on a monthly basis, and at the same time *GMA* officially "adopted" the Columbus Zoo with the twins' second birthday party. An aardvark and a couple of baby wallabies were presented on the air to hosts David Hartman and Joan Lunden, with the understanding that *GMA* would adopt them, which includes the cost of feeding the animals for a year.

"Every single time Jack was going to be on, I'd come home and say to my kids, 'Guess who's going to be on next Thursday?' They would yell, 'Jack Hanna!' Jack was the guest, the star that they always wanted to see."

—Joan Lunden

For the first segment under the new arrangement, Joan Lunden traveled out to the zoo. We greeted her at the front gate with a welcoming committee that looked like a Noah's Ark with zookeepers. Joan loves animals, and aside from an embarrassing moment when Oscar the gorilla disrespectfully nailed her with his infamous crap toss, she had a great time touring the zoo.

It makes it much easier for everyone when a TV personality likes the animals that I bring on, especially on live television. There are no rehearsals, so it's hard to predict a tense situation, and, of course, it's a well-known fact that animals react differently to tension in human beings.

Charlie Gibson, who took over as cohost from David Hartman, had an uncomfortable moment once, just before we went on the air. It was Charlie's first week, it was a brand-new set, and it was my first appearance with him. There was a large group of television reporters on the set, and I'd brought along a cougar, a red-tailed hawk, and a fox for my talk about North American animals.

"People ask me, 'What's it like to be Jack's producer?' You can't produce Jack. You point him in the right direction, and you pray."

—Patty Neger, Coordinating Producer, *Good Morning America*

About thirty seconds before our cue to go on, I picked up the fox, and it tried to nip me a little, nothing too bad. I held it firmly in my lap, and as

Charlie sat down opposite me, he asked to hold the fox. I couldn't say no— actually, I *could* have and *should* have, but I didn't. I handed Charlie the fox, and it bit him hard on the index finger.

With only a few seconds until we were on, Charlie let the fox down without saying a word and reached into his pocket for a handkerchief to smother his bleeding finger. "Today, we have Jack Hanna with us from the Columbus Zoo," he said, cool and on cue, without any reference to the bite.

Meanwhile, I was holding a cougar, and the fox was running all over the set. Charlie asked me some questions very professionally, while I tried hard not to look at his finger, which was bleeding like a stuck pig.

"There weren't many things Charlie and I fought over; we didn't usually try to one-up the other. But every now and then we would fight over who got to do the Jack Hannah spot."

—JOAN LUNDEN

The minute the show was over, Charlie just asked me what kind of shots he needed before rushing out the door to a doctor. I told him tetanus shots, but I did not mention that foxes can carry rabies. A photographer from the *New York Post* was there, and Charlie got a lot of mileage from the bite in the next day's paper. I was on *Late Night* the following week, and, predictably, Letterman had a few laughs at Charlie's and my expense.

Since that first appearance in 1983, I've continued to appear regularly on *Good Morning America,* now about once each month. The agreement that we have with *Good Morning America* is a prime example of how the public has changed in its perception of zoos. We're more concerned with preserving species than we are with showing off exotic animals. *GMA* wanted the viewer to learn something about animals (often about threatened or endangered species) and still enjoy the animal as well. (For Letterman, you can just turn that around.)

Many people think that I earn big bucks from all the television shows I do, including *Letterman* and *GMA*, but I am there to represent the Columbus Zoo and the animals, not to make a million. The expenses—which, with animal travel, can be considerable—are covered by the networks, not tax-payer dollars. But the amount of TV time that we accumulate in a year would come to millions of dollars if we had to buy it in advertising.

Now, what I do on the *David Letterman* show is different. My philosophy is similar to that of Walt Disney: "I would rather entertain and hope that people learned something than educate people and hope they were entertained." I'm a character on *David Letterman*, and I accept that role—it's not all that much different from me in real life anyway, especially when I'm away from the zoo. It's also very different from what I do for *Good Morning America*, and it reaches a different audience, possibly an audience not typically exposed to animal programming. But on *Letterman*, people are mostly on the show for laughs, which is something we've managed to do for years now without demeaning or hurting any of the animals.

"It was fun television, but we were all impacted by Jack's love of animals, his dedication to educating people about animals, and his passion for protecting animals in zoos and in the wild."

—JOAN LUNDEN

And along with the laughs, people do learn about animals on the *Letterman* shows too. I'd like to think that even David Letterman, between all the jokes and the put-downs, has managed to learn something about animals, not necessarily from me, but from the animals themselves. They're the real stars.

My relationship with the *Letterman* show began about a year after I started doing *Good Morning America*. I received a call from Laurie David (now Laurie Lennard, former wife of Larry David), the talent coordinator at that time for NBC's *Late Night with David Letterman*. They were looking for an animal person who could get along with Dave, and Patty Neger had referred me, saying she knew just the guy.

Well, I hated to admit it, but I had never watched the show, mainly because of my job hours. I'd heard of it, but had never seen it. When the show came on, I was in bed. All the same, I told her, "Sure, I'll go on. Just tell me when and where."

Meanwhile, the local media all came to me saying, "Don't go on that show, he'll tear you apart." I thought Letterman was just a show host like I'd seen on Carson, and I wondered what they were talking about. Tear me apart? Why would he tear me apart?

On Valentine's Day 1985, my first *Late Night* date, snow threatened to cancel the whole thing. We were going to take the animals east in a zoo van, but the roads were mostly closed, and travel was impossible, especially with exotic animals. I was desperate, but I knew we'd get there somehow. If I called the *Letterman* people and said I couldn't make it, what were my chances of ever being asked back?

A friend of mine, Dale Eisenman, said he'd fly all the animals, no problem. Most of the animals were small, but I hadn't told him about Spinner, the eighty-five-pound baby pygmy hippo. The animals would not fit in his plane, so he found another one and pulled the back seats out so that Spinner, two capuchin monkeys, a pelican, a crow, a European hedgehog, and a pig could all squeeze in.

The animals got to the NBC studios in Rockefeller Center just in time for the show, and I was totally pumped up, ready to show our zoo to the entire country. David and I met on the air, the way it is with most of his guests. I brought the capuchin monkeys out and got a big laugh when I told him they didn't like women. I caught some flak for this, but, hey, it was true—they *didn't* like women. The pelican wouldn't eat the fish, Henry the crow flew up into the audience and wouldn't come back, and the pig was running around all over the place. We—my staff and I—just kind of let things happen. David was very polite and courteous, and I knew he liked the pygmy hippo. But I do remember him looking at me like I might be a little crazy.

At the Columbus Zoo with two young African elephants, Belle and Belinda. (Columbus Zoo)

Although I didn't plan it or realize it then, the helter-skelter, animals-all-over-the-place idea set the trend for future appearances. I'd found my niche. People who know me know that I'm at my best when I'm doing fifty things at once.

The producers were pleased and even asked me not to plan any other late-night talk-show appearances. The host seemed to have a good time too, and I knew this was important in terms of being invited back. When they officially asked me, a month later, if I could appear during ratings week in May, I was elated.

For the next show, I brought two young elephants, Boomer and Belle, who weighed in at two thousand pounds each. They barely fit in the freight elevators in Rockefeller Center; another six months and I would have been out of luck.

The pachyderms were a big hit, and it was on this show that David started to kid me a bit. He asked me how the lesser anteater I'd brought on the show got his name, and I said, "Because they eat less than other anteaters." He made a face, like "Sure, Jack," and everybody laughed. I wasn't trying to be funny or to set myself up; I was just kind of preoccupied when he asked—some animal had disappeared under his desk. It wouldn't be long before he'd be telling me that I wasn't really a zoo director, that there really wasn't any zoo in Columbus.

Everything on the *Letterman* show happens spontaneously; there is no script. But we still have to have the animal situation under control—you can't just bring them out in any order. Once we had a cheetah on the show, with a variety of other animals, half of which might be the cheetah's prey in the wild. As I was going over the list, the producer asked me where the "wow" animal was. We were start-ing with the cheetah and ending

Although I've been appearing on Letterman for well over twenty years, I still get really pumped up before the show. (CBS LATE SHOW)

with a Chinese pheasant, and I think he would have liked it the other way around. "We can't bring the cheetah on with those other animals," I told him. "We'd have a scene right out of *National Geographic*. It wouldn't be pretty."

We bring animals on the basis of their availability, their health, their temperament—how they'll react to music, for example—and we also try to vary the selection from show to show. Ideally, I'd like to have as many "wow" animals as possible on there. They're all "wow" animals as far as I'm concerned, but I know that if I bring a snail and a housecat on the show, my future in promoting the animals and the zoo wouldn't be too bright.

In a sense, I'm between a rock and a hard place on this. The producers would like to have wild animals running all over the place—that's the big payoff. But just as a singer knows what songs he can sing and in what style, as a zoo director, I know what animals I can handle, where I can put them, how fast I can pick one up, and a host of other intangibles that crop up. Dave obviously has to get the laughs, that's what the show's for, but I'm also out there to make sure nobody gets hurt; him, me or the animals. And in the process, I hope to educate the viewing audience a little as well.

One of our nuttiest visits ever was when I brought up a couple of full-grown camels. I weighed and measured them, like I do with all the animals before we come on, but I forgot to measure their humps. They had plenty of room in the elevator, but the ceiling where they got off was too low. And I learned a new animal fact: once a camel's walking straight in a narrow hallway, you can hardly turn him around. We walked them down the hallway to the studio, and their humps took out just about every ceiling panel—ruined them, lights and all.

"Jack's an unusual mix of someone who has always made us feel that everything's going to be safe and at the same time created the illusion of spontaneity and mayhem."

—MATT ROBERTS, JACK'S LONGTIME PRODUCER ON THE *Late Show with David Letterman*

The building manager came up and really let me have it. I apologized and told him I'd pay for the damage. He told me this would cost more than five thousand dollars. By now, a crowd of NBC personnel had gathered around like it was a big party—we probably cleared every office on the entire floor. I'd been trying to concentrate on the show coming up, and now I was a wreck about the damage.

Barry Sands, who was *Late Night's* producer then, came out and told me not to worry about it, that the building people don't run the show. I told Barry I was really sorry, but I never noticed that he had a camera shooting this whole fiasco, that he was going to open the show with it. It looked like a tornado had struck.

Well, of course, all this was a big hit. David just shook his head at me and said, "Oh, Jack, Jack . . . ," like can't you ever just come up here and be normal? Dave, of course, had to ride the camel and almost knocked his head on one of the studio spotlights, but otherwise the show went great.

When it was time for us to leave, the maintenance people had already fixed a few panels and three or four lights. I'm sure they didn't consider that we had to get the camels back downstairs again. Our dromedaries knocked out those lights and panels the same way they did coming in. Now the building guy was doubly mad. Since then, they put us in a maintenance room instead of the dressing room. But that's fine with us, as long as we're able to mop up all the mess.

In another wild *Letterman* experience, I was bitten by an animal on camera. A friend of mine, Leslie Whitt, director of the Alexandria Zoo in Louisiana, flew in a young twenty-pound beaver that I hadn't handled previously. All went well while I held the beaver on my lap. Then I demonstrated how she could swim by placing her in a glass tank in front of Dave's desk.

The beaver was still okay as I lifted her from the tank—with dripping water drenching me and the stage floor. As I got up to take the beaver off during the commercial break, she started to slide out of my hands. I grasped the base of her tail with my right hand, and she chomped down on the space between my left thumb and index finger; I slid on the wet floor, went down on one knee, scrambled up, and hung on to the beaver until an assistant repossessed her. And all this on camera. Not one of my most graceful exits.

In the two minutes allotted to the commercial break, I wrapped paper towels around my bleeding hand and slipped on a flesh-colored rubber glove (that I had on hand to hold my electric eels) just as we went back on the air. Sometimes the show must go on. We finished the segment, which included electric eels, a Chinese crested dog, and a yak. The glove on my left hand was rapidly filling with blood, so I was very anxious for the segment to end—especially before Dave had a chance to make some comment about my beaver bite.

Immediately after the segment, Suzi Rapp, one of the handlers on that trip, turned to me and said, "Jack, how are you going to get an ambulance at five thirty in New York City, especially at Christmastime?"

Simple. "I'll just run."

After several blocks I reached Roosevelt Hospital. Once there, people thought I was a shooting victim with blood spattered all over my clothes. Of course, the first question was, "What happened?" I didn't want to tell them that a beaver bit me on the David Letterman show, so I improvised.

"My beaver bit me." Strange looks were exchanged. "My beaver bit me in Central Park." I'm not sure they ever believed me, but they patched me up just the same.

The next time I was on the show, Letterman said to me, "Jack, I hope you learned your lesson."

"What's that, Dave?"

"You never mess around with another man's beaver!"

After that, I began bearing the brunt of David Letterman's jokes on a regular basis. I don't mind; I really don't. I know Dave loves the animals. He treats them better than he does most of his guests. And I'm always amazed at his knack for coming up with the lines.

"Have these guys been eating onions, Jack?"—when I brought out the twin gorillas.

"Is this your idea of a good time in Columbus?"—when I showed him how a chinchilla takes a dust bath.

"Jack, you're 100 percent sure this is a female, right?"—when I had him milk a goat.

Of course, sometimes I step into it. Like when he's asking me how far a particular bird can fly, and I'll say, "Oh, they'll fly real far, Dave." He'll just look at me without saying anything for a few seconds, the audience will laugh, and I'll think, *Uh-oh . . . here it comes.* "You're not a zoo director, are you, Jack?" he'll say. "There is no zoo in Columbus, is there?"

On *Letterman*, the punch lines continue even after I'm long gone. They'll sometimes have a special emergency bulletin that comes up after I leave that says something like, "Attention viewers: Please be on the lookout for large mountain lion. Last seen leaving the Ed Sullivan Theater. If you spot it, please be sure to contact Jack Hanna at the Columbus Zoo." You wouldn't believe the calls we get!

Since the eighties, I've continued to visit *Good Morning America* about once a month and *David Letterman* about three times a year. In the meantime, I began making my rounds on *Larry King Live, Ellen, Maury*, the FOX News network, CNN programs, and many others. I have lots of fun on the shows and really enjoy the interaction with the hosts and the audience, but because I rarely watch TV, I don't always recognize some of the other celebrities I run into.

When doing *Letterman* a few years ago, I was in the green room with this nice, blonde young lady. To be friendly, I asked, "So, do you sing or something?"

She smiled. "Yeah."

"Hi, I'm Jack Hanna." I held out my hand.

"Britney," she replied, shaking my hand. She came out to see the animals, and one of my handlers later explained that she was pretty popular.

On another trip, Suzi Rapp and I were heading to *Letterman*, and this oddly tall guy started running toward me from across the street. "Mr. Hanna! I love you!" he boomed when he caught up. *Um, okay,* I'm thinking. He looked like a nice guy I had met on Hollywood Squares. I thanked him, and we went on our way. Afterward, Suzi told me he was on some show about a guy named Raymond.

Once my wife, Suzi, and I were sitting in the green room at a television station, and Suzi was grooming one of our long-haired Angora rabbits, trying to get rid of its tangled fur balls. Rabbit hair was flying everywhere. There were a few other people around, and noting one lady's country-western style of dress, I said to her, "So what do you do?"

"I'm a country music singer," she answered with a familiar twang.

"Oh, really?" I continued. "What's your name?"

"Reba McIntyre." Now, I do listen to country music, and that was one name I did know. I was so embarrassed that I was afraid to ask the other girl's name.

Kate Hudson and Drew Barrymore have been on *The Late Show* the same nights as me, and the producers ask them if they would want to sit in on my segment. Despite the chaos that always ends up happening, they really seem to appreciate the animals.

It doesn't hurt my feelings if people are clueless who I am. I don't consider myself a celebrity. Actually, I don't really even like the word. Yeah, people know my face from seeing me on television, but who am I kidding? I know who they're watching, and it sure isn't me. It's that cute little baby barn owl, a cuddly cub, or Fluffy, the largest snake in captivity. Next to that, how could a person like me expect to rise to celebrity status?

I think the closest I've gotten was in 1996, when *People* magazine named me one of its 50 Most Beautiful People. I had never really read the magazine, but one day somebody called me from New York and said that I'd been chosen for their most beautiful people issue. *What? Was this some sort of joke?* Once they convinced me it was, in fact, not a joke, they told me that they wanted to come take my picture. I told them, "Oh no, I've got plenty of pictures. I'll send you one." Still they insisted on a photo shoot.

"I've worked with people in local news who've had way bigger egos than he does. People need to see him on TV. Jack's just a guy who enjoys life—a good role model. More people should be like him."

—Glenn Nickerson, Director, Cameraman, and Editor

When the issue came out, I couldn't believe it. "Devastatingly sexy," Helen Gurley Brown was quoted as saying. Sheesh. And even my friends

Betty White and Bo Derek were in on it, offering quotes for the magazine. Boy, did I get ribbed after that! Charlie Gibson called the office and very politely asked, "May I speak to the world's most beautiful person?" I was flattered, but I don't think I'll ever live that one down.

On the flip side, I've also, out of habit, forced my "celebrity" on poor, unsuspecting victims. While filming in New Orleans, Dan Devaney, our sound guy, and I plopped down on a park bench, and this guy came by and held out a piece of paper. I was probably thinking about everything but that piece of paper. Automatically, I took it out of his hand, signed it, and handed it back with a smile and a nod. "Oh . . . ," he began, a little stunned, "I just wanted directions." Golly day, was that humbling!

When we go into truck stops, most of the time no one recognizes me until I open my mouth. They'll say, "That's amazing! You sound just like Jack Hanna!"

And I'll say, "Yeah, people tell me that all the time."

"Everyone needs a little privacy, so I've tried to convince Jack to wear jeans and a T-shirt on occasion so he would be harder to recognize in public. However, I don't think he even owns a pair! Jack's safari outfit isn't his 'costume'; it is truly a part of his identity."

—KATE OLIPHINT, PERSONAL ASSISTANT

For the most part, we do try to be low-key when we're traveling. It's quicker and easier to unload the animals if there's not a crowd around. Kate, my assistant, faces a unique challenge when it comes to booking a place to stay. Most places don't allow pets, much less zoo animals. It's gotten tough enough just to get them in—most people know what's up when Jack Hanna checks in—and most of them have to be exercised, cleaned, watered, and fed too. We've made a few friends in the hotel business and have learned where we're welcome and where we most certainly are not.

Before we learned the ropes, we made the mistake of taking a sarus crane for a walk in the lobby of the Rihga Royal, not the kind of hotel where birds were typically allowed. Still, we figured the marble floor would be easy to clean. After prancing around for a while, the birds started cawing and scratching on the marble floor and startling some of the other guests. Before we knew it, we were doing some swift talking with the manger, the birds ended up in his office, and we weren't allowed to stay there anymore.

For a while, we did find a nice home at the Mayflower. We've stayed there for years and are sad to see it—and its welcoming owners—go. Our rooms were a mini zoo, with monkeys dangling from the luggage rack and penguins in the bathtub. There was a bar downstairs, so you always had people double-checking the number of drinks they'd had when they saw a big cat walk by.

"Jack, Suzi, and I were supposed to go to dinner, so I called to see where they were. 'Suzi's out in Central Park milking the goats,' Jack answered matter-of-factly. 'She's doing what? Where?!' I couldn't believe it. Jack said, 'Well, what do you want her to do, milk them in the hotel room?'"

—PATTY NEGER, COORDINATING PRODUCER, *Good Morning America*

One of the most challenging aspects of cohabitating with animals is the constant lack of sleep. Many of the animals are nocturnal: an owl will hoot, a cat will pace, an alligator in the bathtub will thrash and splash around all night. After three or four days of this, you can turn into a zombie. But I've never heard anyone complain, and the animals seem to enjoy the change of scenery.

Without my handlers in the promotions department, there would be no *Good Morning America* or *Letterman* or *Ellen* or *Larry King Live* for Jack Hanna—no television shows of any kind, for that matter. In fact, I probably couldn't give a speech at a grade school without somebody to help me with the animals.

I do about forty to fifty live shows a year, too, in which the handlers are indispensable. I mostly just do the talking, speaking to the audience about the animals, trying to tell them things they can relate to. The handlers continue to have the animals entering and exiting the stage, pointing out details on the animal as I speak. We'll show them the quills of a porcupine or explain that a binturong smells like buttered popcorn—fun facts that will help the audience walk away remembering information about that animal.

Before and after the shows, I autograph postcards for everyone who wants one. I see everyone from toddlers to senior citizens, animal lovers all. After the shows, the handlers bring out some of the animals for a little show-and-tell. Everyone seems to love that.

Be it television or a live theater show, I have three or four handlers stationed off-stage, ready to take care of any situation that might arise. They know when or when not to come on, when to keep an animal from going into the audience. They're a very dedicated group of people.

The keepers feel fortunate to go on national TV; they also get to travel, and they play a part in our various public relations programs. They receive credit for their hard work back at the zoo that they might not ordinarily receive if the Columbus Zoo weren't in the spotlight. I try to give everyone the opportunity to participate, and I'm grateful that they do it with so much enthusiasm. I could never do it without them.

Naturally, I consider television and live shows important educational tools for the benefit of wildlife. However, taking animals on national television has been a bone of contention among my critics in the zoo world and animal rights activists. They've said that I'm showboating, that I'm misrepresenting wildlife, that the alien conditions cause the animals undue stress and that these trips generally serve little purpose. I couldn't disagree more. Although the regulations are getting tougher and the list of acceptable outreach animals is shrinking, I'll continue to do everything I can to bring these animals to the public as a means of promoting animal conservation and awareness.

Entertainment-oriented shows reach large audiences, audiences that might not be in tune with the worldwide wildlife situation. If we can capture the attention of the millions of young people who watch the *Letterman* show, we can gain new recruits to the role of conservation. The national exposure of well-known television personalities endorsing our zoos and supporting endangered wildlife is invaluable, and the live animals that appear on the tube are our best salesmen.

CHAPTER 14

Into the Wild

I didn't know it at the time, but from that very first appearance in front of the local TV camera to the national exposure on Good Morning America and Letterman, I was being prepared for yet another lifetime adventure. From the start, I've jumped at every chance to film animals in the wild. But I never dreamed I'd be able to build a career hosting my very own animal television series doing just that.

Okay, maybe I had dreamed it. When I was young—heck, even now that I'm old—Marlin Perkins was my hero. As a kid, I would sit mesmerized as the host of Wild Kingdom explored worlds that made my family's farm look like an anthill. And the animals he encountered made my animal collection seem as exotic as, well, ants. To even glimpse, in person, the worlds I had visited only vicariously through Marlin Perkins was more than I could fathom.

Yet I've learned there's a power much greater than ours that sets our dreams in motion long before we dream them. Now, looking back, I see that everything I had

Meeting Marlin Perkins, my childhood hero, was one of the greatest thrills in the world. (Jack Hanna)

learned, every difficulty I had overcome, was just preparing me to live out my dreams and beyond. Those wheels were set in motion long before I realized it. And now those wheels . . . and wings . . . and waters have carried me around the globe—doing what I love most—several times over.

"[Presenting Jack with the Marlin Perkins Award] was long overdue.
He's been a marvelous and exceptional leader in the zoo and aquarium world.
His service to the association and to the profession are unparalleled."

—TED BEATTIE, PRESIDENT AND CEO, SHEDD AQUARIUM

On one of my first trips to East Africa, I met a fantastic person, Anna Merz, who had dedicated her life to the preservation of the black rhino. She does not like publicity and doesn't talk about what she does. But I found out, from mutual friends David and Delia Craig, that she had spent the last of her savings to put up a four-hundred-thousand-dollar electrified fence on sixty thousand acres that had been donated for a rhino sanctuary called Lewa Downs. Poachers had broken through the sanctuary fence more than once to try to attack her animals, so you can imagine what they would do in the wild.

On the sanctuary, Anna Merz spent her days caring for and observing her twelve rhinos. Rhinos are very solitary animals, and getting them to breed is next to impossible. In small numbers, free-ranging males just can't find the females at the right time. In an effort to educate on rhino behavior, Anna eventually published her findings in *Rhino: At the Brink of Extinction.*

Suzi, Glenn Nickerson, Dan Devaney, and I meeting a young rhino being cared for at Lewa Downs. (Rick A. Prebeg)

172

Anna was very leery of me at first, just as she is of all strangers. She had six African guards to protect sixty thousand acres—each was assigned to two rhinos—and her goal was to raise awareness of her beloved rhinos in hopes of receiving donations for their protection. She was a listener, not a talker, which might have helped us in the long run, since I'm just the opposite.

Since some of my wildlife trips were geared to one-hour TV specials for WCMH in Columbus, I thought, why not do a special just on the rhino? Anna agreed to participate when she realized that I wanted to do this to help people become aware of the rhino's plight, and for no other reason. From then on, we became good friends.

We filmed that special, "The Last Rhino," in 1985—half of it tracking the efforts of anti-poaching units in Kenya's parks and the other half following Anna Merz in her rhino reserve. It was a very powerful documentary, and it resulted in the development of Rhino Rescue, Inc., a program to help fund her ranch.

While we were there filming the special, Anna had a six-month-old rhino named Samia that she'd hand-raised on a bottle. The baby had been abandoned by its mother and had become totally dependent on Anna, to the point of following her everywhere, even trying to get in bed with her.

Pope John Paul II was about to visit Africa at the time, and the Kenyan government wanted Anna to bring a young rhino for him to bless, as a representative of all wildlife. She didn't want to do it, for fear that the trip—they would have to travel by plane to the Masai Mara—might

Another endangered black rhino at the Chipangali Wildlife Orphanage in Zimbabwe. "Thunder" was just nineteen days old. (Rick A. Prebeg)

harm Samia. She was adamantly against it and told me so. She said it was unfair to put that stress on the animal.

Even though the health of the animal is always the priority, my PR wheels were turning about a mile a minute. What better way to publicize a species' struggle for survival than to have it blessed by one of the most powerful men in the world? I talked to her about it for half an hour, telling her that I understood her fears for the animal's health, but also that she had to balance the potential harm to Samia against all the good that would come from people all over the world learning about the rhino. She saw my point and agreed to do it.

On the big day, they flew Samia to see the Pope. When it was her turn, the pope must have moved wrong or something because Samia took off. The pope did get within a few feet of her, blessed her, and said a few words about how this beautiful animal is virtually extinct and how the entire world must share the burden of God's endangered creatures. Probably due in part to Samia's shyness, this made worldwide headlines, accomplishing our goal of generating awareness of the black rhino's fight for survival.

Ten years later, we returned to follow up on Anna and the rhino sanctuary. By this time, Samia had long outgrown following her surrogate mother around and was roaming the sixty thousand acres as an independent adult. Our film crew rode through the fields with Anna to try to catch a glimpse of one of the several black rhinos that lived there. When we finally spotted one—it was the most amazing thing—the rhino immediately recognized Anna, and this two-to-three-thousand-pound, almost prehistoric-looking animal skips over to her like a puppy. It was Samia, rushing to greet Anna, her dear old friend.

Thanks to Anna's initiative, Lewa Downs now has a remarkably successful breeding program involving fifty-five black rhinos. Charitable organizations have been established around the world—including the United States, United Kingdom, Austria, Asia, Switzerland, and Canada—to offer financial support to Lewa. The conservation focus has also broadened to include the Grevy's zebra, sitatunga (an aquatic antelope), elephants, and other area birds and mammals. Anna Merz is a shining example of how one person can initiate remarkable change within the animal world.

At another rhino sanctuary in Kenya, we were greeted by a fascinating woman, Kat, who relayed the story of her husband, Simon Combes, the founder of the Rhino Rescue Trust. She was from the States and met Simon, a world-renowned wildlife artist and adventurer, at her gallery opening in Colorado. They married and moved to Kenya, Simon's homeland. On the afternoon of December 12, 2004, they took a hike on a mountain to enjoy a holiday. Cautiously Simon always scanned the grassy area for wild animals and saw nothing. As they were walking passed a bush, an enormous male Cape Buffalo that had been lying down charged them, goring Simon several times with his horns. Kat and a friend who was with them tried to beat him off by throwing rocks and other objects, but nothing would deter the animal. A solitary male Cape Buffalo can be extremely aggressive, and they are responsible for many human deaths per year. Tragically, Simon did not survive the attack by the rogue Cape Buffalo, but his legacy lives through his rhino sanctuary and his beautiful paintings of African wildlife.

I once witnessed for myself how dangerous a Cape Buffalo can be. While on safari in 1986, I was walking back from dinner from our campsite in East Africa, when a Cape Buffalo suddenly came out of nowhere and charged. Jumping back against a tree, I barely avoided his deadly horns, and I bet I stayed behind that tree for a half hour, just to be safe! Escaping danger, I felt fortunate to have made it through that one alive.

A heartwarming story about a different type of sanctuary was filmed in Florida and involved an elderly English couple, Peter and Mary Gregory. Scraping together their finances they started The Retirement Home for Horses, a sanctuary for abused horses and other animals that would not have otherwise survived. Many of the horses are terribly crippled, blind, or toothless. They handle these animals with tender loving care and provide a pastoral place where they can peacefully live out their lives.

Two of the horses were rescued from the Everglades, where people had tied them to the trees to be devoured by the alligators. Sometimes this is done because people think they have no other way to dispose of their horse and often do not have the financial means to take care of them. By doing this, a criminal offense is avoided because there is no way to trace the horse back to the owner. If caught, such an act would clearly be considered cruelty to an animal under the Animal Welfare Act.

Peter and Mary are now in their seventies and work hard every day to ensure the welfare of these animals, knowing them all by name. Because their hearts are so big, they also have fourteen rescue dogs living in their home. With all that unconditional love from the animals, they will never be lonely.

I had done features for local stations, like the first one on Anna Merz, and even the local series, Hanna's Ark. But when I was approached to do a nationally syndicated show, *Zoo Life*, I thought, *Hey, this stuff could get serious. Zoo Life* was the real deal. But after we had taped about forty episodes, financial problems arose, and that deal soon ended.

"I've been all over the world, and I've never been around a man who's had his pants rip as much as Jack! There have been so many times when we've been out shooting, and Suzi's back at the camp stitching his shorts."

—Larry Elliston, Producer, *Animal Adventures*

My next big project was *Jack Hanna's Animal Adventures*, which was—can you believe it?—the number one syndicated wildlife show in America. It reached about 95 percent of U.S. households and was viewed in more than forty countries.

My daughter, Kathaleen, served as a co-host with me on many of the *Animal Adventures* filming trips. Even though Kathaleen lives in England, before she had children, she was able to meet me in Africa, South America, Thailand, or wherever to film the show. She has an uncanny sense of humor and is so much fun to be around, but sometimes her practical jokes really get me—like tickling me with a strand of grass and yelling, "Snake!" Of course the crew gets in on it, too, filming the whole thing.

When it comes to adventure, Kathaleen is all for it! One time we were in Brazil, and she was lowered three hundred feet on a cable into a cave. I was glad she volunteered to do that shoot!

Traveling over the years with the film crews has brought so many wild and unforgettable experiences. But some experiences, like the first segment openers I recorded for *Animal Adventures*, I wish I *could* forget!

Just one of the many seam-splitting moments my pants have endured, this time in Israel. (Rick A. Prebeg)

We had decided to open and close each *Animal Adventures* episode from my "base camp" at Busch Gardens in Tampa Bay, Florida. I would stand in my base camp, which sort of looked like an African home, holding some animals to give the introductions and closings of each show. The rest of the footage would be from filming on location in the wild.

To generate buzz about the new series, everyone had been invited to get a behind-the-scenes look at the filming from my base camp. Anheuser-Busch had all these top people come in; there were major advertisers, media, the president of *Animal Adventures*. You name it, they were there.

In fact, for the fourteen years that they sponsored *Animal Adventures*, Busch Gardens was always very supportive. That is one organization that practices what they preach when it comes to conservation. Without Anheuser-Busch, Busch Gardens, and Sea World, *Animal Adventures* would have never gotten off to such an amazing start, much less been as successful as it ended up being.

But in the very beginning, on this particular sunny September day in Tampa, the filming conditions were less than ideal. We started filming at eight o'clock, and before lunch, the temperature had already gotten up to around a hundred degrees. There was no shade where we were positioned, except for the noisy Sky Ride that would come over and halt filming about every three minutes.

Reading teleprompters, holding up animals, and trying to look energetic, I was just flat-out nervous as I introduced each show. But by noon, I started feeling weak and dizzy, so I suggested we stop and eat.

We headed over to a restaurant in the park that served hearty meals, like beef, mashed potatoes, fried chicken, salad, and apple pie. I was starving; I ate everything I could get my hands on. With a full stomach and regained composure, I headed back out to finish filming.

"We thought, It's our first day shooting with Jack Hanna, and we've killed him!"

—LARRY ELLISTON, PRODUCER, *Animal Adventures*

At the set, I was happy to see that most of the media had left, and there was just a fraction of the people who were there before. Thirty minutes later, I started feeling dizzy again, but I didn't want to say anything. Then the cold sweats started. "I've gotta sit down." Someone helped me to get out of the spectators' view, then I just went down for the count.

I remember looking up and seeing a nurse floating around amidst everything else circling in the air. She said something about heat exhaustion. Somebody called 911 and told them to bring the ambulance in the back gate to avoid the onlookers and media, if there happened to be any left.

We weren't in the ambulance long before I started losing my lunch. I must've filled up a whole bucket, because I heard the guy yell, "Give me another bucket!"

At the hospital, I remember the nurses standing over me with a little notepad, trying to use the trick question tactic. "Where do you live?" she asked.

Easy. My good friend John P. McConnell had offered to let Suzi and me rent his old house near the zoo, and we had just moved. But at the moment, the exact address had slipped my mind. I'm not sure how "Hogback Road" could ever slip a person's mind, but it did.

"I don't know where I live."

This was met with a raised eyebrow. "Don't be funny."

"No, really, I forgot the address."

Then a look of concern. "What city?"

"Columbus, no, I mean, Dublin, Ohio. . . . I live at the zoo."

"You live where?"

"At the zoo."

"Okay. You live at the zoo."

She walked out, and five minutes later, a neurologist walked in. He asked me a lot of questions and explained that a heatstroke can affect your brain. But all I wanted to know was when I was getting out of there.

When they told me they were going to keep me overnight, I told them I wasn't staying. I had to film my show. I tried to convince the Busch people to let me come back and film that afternoon, but they wouldn't agree to that. So I asked if we could start at six thirty the next morning. And we did. Fortunately, the rest of that session was filmed without incident . . . and with lots of water.

However, another close call would come soon after in the Kalahari Desert in Africa. Suzi, Kathaleen, Julie, the film crew, a few other friends, and I were stationed at a remote horse camp, where we stayed in tents. During the day, we rode the camp's horses to go out and view wildlife. We had been filming like crazy, out riding the horses among the elephants and other wild-life. My guard was up as we were filming, especially since I had noticed lion-claw scars on one of the horse's flanks.

Plus, the Kalahari Desert is one of the hottest, flattest places on earth, and I had learned from the whole Busch Gardens thing to drink a lot of water, so I was hydrating nonstop. About six o'clock that night, I started to feel a little queasy. I went to sit outside by myself. Soon my heart starting pounding, and I couldn't get my breath. I felt for my pulse, and it was racing like a hummingbird's. I couldn't believe it. Alarmed, I called to my friend

Dan Devany, our sound guy (he had been a medic in Vietnam) and asked him to check my heart rate. I didn't have any pain, but I felt really weak.

"Holy mackerel!" Dan shouted. "It's 140 and rising!"

"Jack isn't just somebody we work with; he's a best friend."

—Guy Nickerson, President, Spectrum Productions,
Partner & Producer of *Jack Hanna's Into the Wild*

That was it. I just knew I was having a heart attack, and the anxiety over that didn't help my condition at all. Typically, the film crew would have been filming all of this for a good laugh later, but this time they really thought I was a goner. Soon people from the horse camp came over to see what was wrong. Once they understood my symptoms, they exclaimed, "Oh, it's heat exhaustion!"

"No way," I said. I learned my lesson with that. "I drank a lot of water today."

Still, they decided my body needed liquids, fast. Their basic first-aid kit had few medical supplies . . . for humans. What they did have was an IV for a horse.

"Okay, put it in," I said. I wasn't going to just sit there and die. They came at me with this pencil-sized needle and a bag of fluid and got the IV going into my arm. I still wasn't getting any better.

The camp radioed out to get help, but there was a terrible storm, and the helicopter couldn't fly in it. Luckily my good friend, and longtime financial advisor, Ted Altenburg was there. He said, "Jack, you've got two choices. You can sit here and think you're okay, or we can get the hell in the jeep and take off!"

Before heading out, Kathaleen and Julie bid me a heartbroken farewell, thinking they were seeing me alive for the last time. A guide, Suzi, and I got into one jeep, and a guide and Ted got into another. Then we set off on a four-hour trip to the nearest town.

"As we're getting in the car, Jack pulls me aside. He's not worried about himself. He's worried about his family and—in a way that only a person like Jack Hanna would— starts telling me how to take care of Suzi and the girls and the people at the zoo who are so special to him because they've been working with him for years. It was amazing."

—TED ALTENBURG, FINANCIAL ADVISOR AND LONGTIME FRIEND

Those few hours seemed like days. The flooded roads were treacherous, a series of rough, muddy ruts. Amazingly, the jeeps kept plowing through the torrential rainfall. But I caused even further delays with our frequent stops for me to relieve myself.

Finally, we arrived at the Maun Airport where they had an emergency medical plane waiting. They helped me get into the plane and started two IVs, one in each arm, before they went back out to clear customs. Well, about that time, I had to pee again. Picking up my IV bags, I walked off the plane into the pouring rain and did my thing. When the medics returned, there was quite a scramble trying to find their AWOL patient.

It was close to three o'clock in the morning when we landed at the hospital in Johannesburg. The doctor arrived around six o'clock and started talking. "So, you're from Columbus? I was just there for a conference." Immediately, I felt at home and he reassured me that I wasn't going to die.

When the diagnosis was finally made, boy, did I feel goofy. I had *water intoxication.* That's right. While filming in the hot sun, I drank *too much* water and flushed out all of my electrolytes. I just couldn't get it right. A tell-tale sign was the constant urination, due to the lack of electrolytes, along with the increased heart rate. "The next time you're on safari," the doctor told me, "make Gatorade your best friend."

My doctor did say I could go home after about two more hours of IVs . . . if I promised to rest in the hotel for a few days. Needless to say, I agreed to rest. However, I flew back to the crew, and we were filming again by eleven o'clock the next day.

We had been staying at a place in Botswana called Jack's Camp, where my daughter Julie had a close call. Bending over by some bushes, she was observing a large green chameleon. She noticed it was partially gray, had a puncture mark, and was not moving steadily. Then, for some reason, she turned her head, and she looked right into the black eyes of a venomous green mamba about two feet away. The mamba had bitten the chameleon and was waiting to consume it, which he eventually did. I don't even want to think about what would have happened if Julie had reached down to pick up the mamba's dinner! Julie truly felt that there was an angel on her shoulder that day.

I've seen many fearful animal adventures, but I've learned that fear certainly shouldn't prevent you from experiencing the adventure. The death of my good friend, Earl Wells, made me realize that you're just as likely to be harmed in the comfort of your home as you are in the unforgiving African desert.

Earl was the director of the Fort Wayne Zoo, one of the nearest zoos to Columbus. He had traveled all over the world, adventuring into the wild with the best of us. Despite his years of adventures, his time came at home on a ladder outside his home doing some everyday repair work. In a moment, he lost his balance and fell into a nest of bees. They swarmed him, and he was unable to be saved. Although Earl was taken unexpectedly, all of the hard work he did to protect our wildlife will live on forever. And for what it's worth, he's made a more fervent adventurer out of me.

My filming adventures haven't all been horrible brushes with death; they've really been a blast. Even the trip to the Kalahari—minus the medical interlude—was loads of fun, and it ended on an especially high note.

While filming all over the area for a couple of weeks, Kathaleen and I especially had fun riding on four-wheelers across the salt flats at Jack's Camp. In the distance, we saw these long tables decorated with flowers, with white tablecloths blowing in the breeze and bottles of champagne set out for us. I thought I was seeing a mirage! We got to spend our last night of the trip together celebrating and recounting all we'd experienced there.

In a later trip to Thailand, our crew was greeted by royalty. After we had been filming a few days, the princess of Thailand invited us to a very nice, very long meal at the palace. If you know anything about me, you know that when it comes to food, I always scarf it down and run, and this meal was about four hours long. The film crew and I were all on our best behavior, tasting the different Thai delicacies and trying our best to mimic the Thai dining customs.

What a relief it was, when at the end of the meal, the princess got up and threw all the formalities out the window. She grabbed a mike, asked the band to play some rock 'n' roll, and started dancing and singing along in sort of an eighties-rock-karaoke show. We couldn't believe our eyes . . . or ears! I don't think she stopped dancing for two hours!

Besides our personal concert at the palace, we saw numerous other unbelievable sights in Thailand, like the biggest crocodile ever on a croc farm there. We filmed a pig playing surrogate mother to some baby tigers. We also went to an elephant training camp, where the elephants are trained to perform helpful tasks, like logging, for the Thai people. When one elephant gave me a ride across a river, not only did he take a bath, he gave me one too!

Elephants are truly one of the most fascinating creatures on earth. We've only begun to discover what we *don't* know about them. I've seen an elephant trainer come back after fifteen years and say the elephant's name, and the elephant perks up. If another elephant dies, other elephants in the group will kick sand on it and won't leave it. Their social skills are highly developed.

I wouldn't say an elephant is an animal to fear, but you certainly have to have a healthy respect for their sheer power.

We are always on the move, following all of the amazing wildlife, while filming on safari in Africa. (Rick A. Prebeg)

Once on the Serengeti, we'd noticed elephants hanging around near the camp. I was told that because of the early rains, there was a certain fruit growing there that affected them like a narcotic.

Two Burger King franchise owners, Charlie Parton and Dick Daugherty, had bedded down and were almost asleep when they heard some noise alongside their tent. Their scene was like something out of Laurel and Hardy:

"Hey, Dick. Would you please quit scratching the tent?"

"I'm not scratching the tent."

"Well, who's making that noise?"

In the next moment, their tent was all but wiped out by a bull tusker rooting around for a piece of fruit the guys had left in there. (This is a no-no. Elephants don't see very well, but their sense of smell is phenomenal and can reach up to five miles with the right wind.)

Dick and Charlie crawled out from under the crushed canvas while guides chased the elephant off with torches. Everybody was all right, but it was a close call—they could have been stepped on. Naturally, these guys took their fair share of ribbing for the remainder of the trip.

Another frightening moment call was on our 1987 safari when we were out on a lake in Rwanda looking at hippos. There was an enormous herd of hippos swimming out there, and we were all having a good time watching their antics. Our boat was a rickety old thing that looked like the *African Queen*, but we all laughed it off.

Just before we headed back toward shore, we veered over to have a closer look at a mother and her baby—mostly to get some better pictures. (That's where you get in trouble; whenever you want a better picture, there's usually a risk factor to either animal or human.) When the mother disappeared underwater, I knew there was something wrong. Suddenly, the mother hippo came up under the boat and lifted the whole thing up on one side, about five feet into the air.

People went flying every which way, and one woman hanging over the edge taking pictures almost went overboard. She was halfway in the water when a couple of guys pulled her up. When the hippo came and rammed a second time, we were braced for the impact, so we were all okay. Still, I figured we'd better call it a day.

One time, we were filming in Louisiana at a zoo swamp habitat and didn't see any alligators. I was standing on a very narrow ledge that looked like a replica of Tom Sawyer's raft. When I started to lean over to dip my hand in the water (bad idea), my sore back stopped me. Grabbing a broom instead, I splashed the muddy water around, and out flew a huge gator! If he'd ever gotten a hold of my arm, I would've been a goner. I still have nightmares about that one!

Sometimes when traveling abroad, just getting there is the adventure! Years ago, having a group of fourteen on safari in Zimbabwe, formerly Rhodesia, we were headed to the Victoria Falls Airport. When we arrived, I asked for our seat assignment to Dar es Salaam, Tanzania. The counter clerk gave me a puzzled look when I continued to request ten nonsmoking and four smoking seats.

At this point the clerk started to laugh and said, "We haven't had a plane fly to Dar es Salaam in years." To make a long story short, there are two airports that service Victoria Falls. We were at the wrong airport in the wrong country. We were supposed to be at the Livingstone Airport in Zambia that also services Victoria Falls, instead of the Victoria Falls Airport in Zimbabwe. The plane that we were to take only departed once a week, and it was waiting for us just on the other side of the falls. To make matters worse, the border between the two countries closed every Friday at noon and did not reopen until Monday morning. Of course it had to be Friday at 12:15 p.m. Instead of relaxing on the coast in Dar es Salaam, we were stuck in 100 degree weather in Zimbabwe, and my guests were not happy.

My doctor and close friend, Joe Cross, casually looked at me and said, "Well Jack, that's just typical A.T."

I asked, "What does that mean, Joe?"

He grinned and said, "Africa Travel."

For better or worse, it's always an adventure.

On one filming adventure for a story on bats, I felt like we were playing a role in a horror movie rather than a wildlife show. We shot at two different locations, the first being a jungle in Puerto Rico. After hiking through the jungle, we finally came to the opening of a remote cave. Everyone put on gas masks to protect them from the accumulated foul gases created by the bat defecation. As our guide, the film crew, and I started walking into the cave, the smell of guano was an awful stench, even through the masks.

Snakes were clinging to the walls, and I spotted one curled up on the floor just as I was about to step on it. After going about fifty yards in total darkness, except for the narrow streams of light from our headlamps, we witnessed one of the most amazing things in nature—a "moving carpet." There were thousands of bats overhead slowly moving like a gray fur rug, making a quiet screeching sound. As we stood there to film, the stench was getting worse as the crew and I could feel the droppings of the bats landing on our heads. Needless to say, it was a hair-raising experience.

Our guide told us that we needed to come back at seven o'clock that evening because that's when the action really happens. Arriving at 6:30 p.m., we saw nothing but calm and quiet, and I was beginning to be skeptical of the cave inhabitants' ability to tell time. To my surprise, just before seven o' clock, clusters of these very endangered Puerto Rican boa constrictors crawled out of the forest and were hanging on branches right in front of the cave entrance. Then like clockwork, the big exodus took place at seven o'clock. Swarms of bats started flying out, hundreds at a time. My hair was blowing straight back as if I were standing in a wind tunnel. The snakes had been waiting for the bats too, and in midair they nabbed the creatures for dinner as they flew out of the cave. I would not have believed it if I hadn't witnessed it myself.

Down in Florida I crawled into another bat cave with the film crew. This time I had to wade in water that at one point was as high as my neck, while my head was brushing the top of the cave. Knowing this was completely nuts, especially if there had been a flash flood, I was trying to remember if I had a living will! Finally we came to this huge opening about the size of a large gymnasium, with a thirty-foot-tall ceiling, again covered with a "moving carpet." When I crawled out of that cave, I was covered from head to toe in a tar-like bat guano. It was terrible!

A much more highly recommended means of viewing wildlife is by hot-air balloon, particularly in Africa. It's not cheap, but it's worth every penny. Before sunrise, in the still morning air, the colorful balloons are inflated to a towering four-story height and then launched just as the sun is rising over the Serengeti Plain. They'll take the balloons up to a thousand feet or so and back down over roaming herds of wildebeest, antelopes, elephants, dik-diks, giraffes, lions—they're all there early in the morning.

For two hours, you soar over these animals, seeing them in large numbers, sometimes making a kill and sometimes just resting in the grass. The serenity up there is something else. Except for the intermittent hiss of the hot-air generator,

As if on cue, this lion approached while we filmed a segment of dialogue about lions. (Rick A. Prebeg)

the quiet flight and sense of peaceful solitude is completely undisturbed. Upon landing, a short walk through the tall grass leads you to a champagne breakfast, which is enjoyed under the shade of the acacia trees. There may be a better way to spend your money, but I can't think of any.

I could fill volumes with all of the unbelievable journeys we've had. I've felt the mist on my skin as I've flown over Victoria Falls in an ultralight aircraft (and kissed the ground when I landed!), and we've watched a pride of lions surround us while our vehicle was stuck in the mud. To have the privilege of visiting those animals on their own turf, untouched and uninhibited, there just aren't words to express the wonder of it all.

The ultimate thrill was a flight over Victoria Falls in an ultralight. We dedicated the show to the pilot who tragically died just three weeks later in an ultralight accident. (Rick A. Prebeg)

Just as fascinating as the animals of the world are the people who inhabit it. There's nothing like meeting people from the many cultures of the world, seeing how they live, and being a part of their day-to-day activities. It's not just about filming these people—although I do want to educate the world about their culture—but I want to know them. I want to learn about what makes their culture unique, and then I want to try it for myself.

"He has a genuine love of animals, but that's not what he's the best at. He's really best at people. He's never treated his fans badly. In Kenya, three girls from Ohio walked up, and in the middle of shooting, Jack dropped everything and talked to them."

—Glenn Nickerson, Director, Cameraman, and Editor

In Namibia, we were fortunate to meet a ranger named Chris, a big guy who reminded me of a Viking with his flared out, reddish-blonde hair. Driving is tough in those parts by the skeleton coast and inland—lots of rocks and sand, and more sand! Getting stuck was always a big possibility. Often, we would drive up a precarious dry river bed, and we had to watch out for the deceiving quick sand.

Chris was very adept at the tricky driving, but what made it more amazing was he did it with one hand. His left hand and part of his arm were taken off by a crocodile. Consequently, Chris would shift the jeep with the end of his left arm.

When he was a ranger in Kruger National Park, the temperature was boiling hot, and he decided to take a dip in a muddy pond inhabited by a big croc. Chris saw the croc was sunning himself on the bank and told the other two rangers to watch the "big boy." As he waded in, another huge crocodile lunged out of the murky water and grabbed his right arm and shoulder. He knew he would drown if he were pulled into the croc pool, so he kept his stance trying to fight off the croc, while his left arm was flailing around.

In all the commotion, no one was keeping a vigilant eye on the "big guy" lying on the bank, who slithered into the water hole. Suddenly, this crocodile leaped out of the pond, grabbed Chris's left arm, and yanked it off. At this point, he still had a croc attached to his right shoulder.

He eventually was able to pry himself from the croc on his right, but it was too late for the left arm. It is just a miracle he didn't lose both arms.

Upon hearing the story, Suzi said to Chris, "At least the croc got your left arm and not your right."

Chris responded, "Yeah, that would have been great if I had been right-handed." Amazingly, he still seems to manage with little noticeable disability.

While filming in the outback of Australia, I met one of the most wonderful families, Dave, Cathy, and two of their children, Hilton and Lara. Another daughter, Stormy, was away at college. They were originally from Zimbabwe, Africa, and had owned a beautiful resort there. But their brother-in-law had been killed because of a corrupt government, and Dave discovered he was the next on their hit list. Suddenly fleeing their homeland with three children, they escaped to Australia, leaving everything behind.

Dave found a job working on a large preserve trying to promote tourism, while Cathy homeschooled their children. Cathy's dad, a tour operator in Africa had been killed several years ago by an elephant. Her remarkable mom stayed back in Zimbabwe to take care of their animal sanctuary.

During our visit, Dave was going to take us out on a waterway to view wildlife, but one of the boat motors didn't work. So what did Dave do? He jumped into the crocodile–infested, murky water to fix the motor! Suzi begged Dave to get out of the water, reminding him that his family needed him and that we could can the boat trip and film something else.

When the film shoot was over, it was hard to leave that incredible, kind family. As we said goodbye, we asked Dave to promise not to wade in any more croc-infested waters to fix boat motors. But he just looked at us and grinned.

We recently filmed in Tasmania with our conservationist friend, Andrew Kelly, at the Trowunna Wildlife Park. It was so interesting and exciting to film how they are trying to save the endangered Tasmanian Devil from extinction, due to a contagious facial cancer. Traveling on to mainland Australia, we visitied with Deb Tabart, seeing the huge strides she has made with conservation efforts for koalas—such a rewarding sight. Then we were fortunate to film again with Wes Mannion (Steve Irwin's best buddy) and to see Terri, Bindi, and Robert at their incredible Australia Zoo.

Encountering a culture for the first time will certainly offer some surprises and sometimes even a few frights. Our recent trip to the Masai Mara was no exception. Suzi had once heard the story of a young boy who had not completely zipped up his tent. When the boy fell asleep, a puff adder crawled through the opening, bit the boy on the head, and killed him. After that, she was always extremely careful to zip the tent all the way.

One night on this particular trip, Suzi had tightly zipped our tent and climbed into bed. When her toes touched the foot of the bed, she felt a very smooth, warm object under her blanket. Jumping out of bed, she flew through the air and skidded across the burlap mats on floor, screaming, "Jack! Jack! There's a big snake in my bed!"

I was horrified myself, but since I was supposed to be the fearless animal handler, I rushed to her rescue to remove the creature and restore our tent to safety. I threw back the covers and there was the culprit: a hot water bottle to warm her feet. What we had believed to be a deadly predator was a luxury the camp had provided for the cool Serengeti nights.

While we were filming in Costa Rica, our six crew members and Suzi were served a creamy side dish with their breakfast. Suzi, of course, said it was the best yogurt she had ever tasted. No one else agreed; they pushed each of their six bowls down to Suzi, and she ate every one. Later in the meal, Suzi complimented the server and asked if the restaurant made their own yogurt. "Yogurt? That's not yogurt," he said. "It's sour cream." Suddenly the yogurt didn't seem so yummy, and all seven bowls of sour cream made their way back up. Suzi now tends to clarify with the server before indulging in unidentified foods.

Even the most common everyday practice for another culture can be a new experience for us, and we appreciate all they have taught us. Most of the time we're just inviting ourselves into their home country, so we always treat the land and the people with respect. People seem to pick up on and appreciate that, and as a result, I think they're genuinely sad to see us go.

"What the viewers don't know about Jack is how incredibly generous he is to the people we would do stories on. In Africa and places around the world, Jack was taking school supplies, writing checks—not just exploiting someone for a story."

—LARRY ELLISTON, PRODUCER, *Animal Adventures*

In April 2005, we filmed the last *Animal Adventures* show. Leaving the series was a very difficult decision for me. It's like a baseball coach leaving a World Series team. But I had gotten to the point where I really wanted more say-so in my own series. I wanted the show to be what Jack Hanna would say and do and cover. I wanted to feature people who were dedicating their lives to conservation. I wanted my family—my wife, kids, grandkids—to be able to go and be involved. I want it to be more realistic, more spontaneous, more natural, where everyone just goes out and experiences the animals and has fun.

"I told him, 'Jack, if the new show is going to be yours, we've got to show conservation, philanthropy, family, and fun. It's who you are, and I want to build that into the show.'"

—GUY NICKERSON, PRESIDENT, SPECTRUM PRODUCTIONS,
PARTNER & PRODUCER OF *Jack Hanna's Into the Wild*

Of course, there is always a risk in pursuing a new venture like *Into the Wild*, but it was something I needed to try. You pursue your dreams, even if they're far out, right? Knowing this would probably be my last series, my family and I were just enjoying being together while filming amazing animals in amazing places. And I was just praying the show wasn't a complete flop. Then, in the summer of 2008, the risk of following that dream paid off more than I could have ever imagined. After our very first season, *Jack Hanna's Into the Wild* won an Emmy—an *Emmy!*—for Outstanding Children's Series. Continuing to travel the world, with my family by my side, sharing it with the audiences back home, *and* getting professional recognition—I just don't know how it could get better than that.

Since 1995, the crews of Jack Hanna's *Animal Adventures* and now *Jack Hanna's Into the Wild* have traveled the seven continents, exploring what the animal world has to offer and bringing it back to viewers. I just hope that some of those viewers are cross-legged kids, unable to take their eyes off of the amazing creatures that exist—that beckon—in a world beyond their own. I would be honored if by presenting a person with a glimpse of the wonders of the animal world, I have carried on the legacy of inspiring a dreamer—a budding conservationist, an animal enthusiast, a TV adventurer—as Marlin Perkins did in me.

CHAPTER 15

Land of a Thousand Hills

The country of Rwanda, located in central Africa, is known as the Land of a Thousand Hills. It's gorgeous, like a little Switzerland—yet it has suffered a much more tumultuous past. When most people hear about Rwanda, they immediately relate it to the Rwandan genocide of the 1990s and the book or film *Hotel Rwanda*. While these tragic events are an inescapable part of its history, Rwanda is a country very much living in the present and looking toward the future. Under the leadership of President Paul Kagame (ka-GAH-me), the people of Rwanda have begun to heal and embrace its natural resources as a means of rising from the ashes. As a result, the entire world will benefit. Rwanda has so much to offer us.

One of Rwanda's most invaluable resources is the endangered species that inhabits the Virunga Mountains to the north: the critically endangered mountain gorilla. Poachers, disease, and destruction of habitat have put these incredible creatures high on the endangered list. With the people of Rwanda struggling, they've had to turn to the only resources they have to survive. It has taught us that in order to save the animals, you have to save the people who live there first. With worldwide conservation efforts—for both the people and the animals of Rwanda—we've begun to see some progress in the reversal of that effect.

If you have seen the film *Gorillas in the Mist* (the movie based on Dian

Fossey's book about her eighteen years living with the mountain gorillas), you've seen a remarkably close approximation of the experience of watching the gorillas in the wild. Fossey was very anti-tourist because tourism helped the gorillas acclimate to humans, including poachers. Yet she came to recognize that tourism has helped make the survival of the mountain gorillas a worldwide concern.

My first visit to the Virunga range in 1984, in hopes of witnessing a mountain gorilla in the mist, was one of my biggest disappointments ever. I had read all the books and waited two years for the permits. I'd been to Africa a half-dozen times already, but seeing the mountain gorillas was an excursion I'd been looking forward to all my life.

With all of our planning, everything was in place. We had arranged for a permit for each of the fourteen people in our group. The tours allowed six people per group, and there were three groups. Yet on the day we were to see the gorillas, the guides told us that only two groups would be able to go because one of the gorilla families had wandered into the Congo. Twelve people would be able to go; two people would have to wait at the base of the mountain. The people in our group insisted that I go—because I was the tour director and all that—and the rest would draw straws or something. But we wouldn't even discuss it; Suzi and I would not go, and that was it. In our despair, Suzi and I sat there waiting for the others to return. I promised her not to worry—we'd be back!

Returning the very next year, we had permits for two days to make sure we'd get a trek to visit the gorillas. Because of the disappointment of the previous year, our anticipation was off the charts. On the first day, it was miserably hot, and to reach the gorillas we had to hike a long way through many stinging nettles. Although we were wearing gloves to protect against them, people were still getting stung, causing a discomfort that lasts for about thirty minutes. Finally we were rewarded with a remarkably clear viewing of a big silverback lying on a thick jungle bed in an open area, as he enjoyed his afternoon siesta. We were totally mesmerized. Here was the real king of the jungle, just resting on the grass, watching his family romp around the jungle.

The time limit for viewing was one hour, which felt like just a few minutes—such a brief stay for such a magnificent sight.

The next day was even better. After about an hour's hike under a beautiful, clear, blue sky, we reached a gorilla family of about a dozen members playing in a bamboo thicket. This was what I had always dreamed of—gorillas of all ages swinging in the trees above us.

We all remained very quiet and still. I'll never forget the lady next to me. She had all this camera equipment, but she was too enthralled to take a picture. She just couldn't do it. There was a gorilla overhead that relieved himself all over her, but she didn't move. I remember thinking, *Lady, you don't have to sit there while this gorilla pees all over you*, but she didn't care. This was the most fascinating experience she'd ever had, as it was for all of us.

The gorillas were having a blast. We had caught them when they were playing, especially the youngsters, who were within two or three feet of us. Every so often the big male would look at us very sternly, and we would look away, the way we were supposed to, so that there'd be no confrontation. Then he'd go back and sit down with an unmistakable air of authority. The experience was beyond anything I had ever imagined. And it's kept me coming back ever since.

My trips to Africa now number in the fifties, and with every visit it seems to offer another fascinating experience, not only with the animals, but with the people as well. In Rwanda, the stories of resilience and rebuilding are unbelievable. Our first exposure to this was through a woman named Rosamond Carr.

Rosamond was an American woman who had moved to Africa with her husband in the late 1940s. After their divorce, she moved to Rwanda and supported herself selling cut flowers that flourished in the volcanic soil on her farm. In 1994, Ros hid refugees from the genocide on her farm to save their lives. Then later, when the people responsible for the genocide found out, she received word that they were sending people to "kill the old woman." For her safety, Ros came back to the United States for a while, then returned to Rwanda to find her home destroyed and the staff members killed.

Soon after, Charlene Jendry, one of the founding members of the Columbus Zoo's Partners In Conservation (PIC), received a letter from Ros saying that she was starting an orphanage for the surviving children of the genocide. She was eighty-two years old at the time—*eighty-two* and setting out on a new courageous, selfless venture.

Suzi and I, along with some other close friends, enjoyed a visit with Rosamond Carr and the kids at the Imbabazi Orphanage in Rwanda. (Rick A. Prebeg)

Charlene brought me the letter, and I didn't hesitate: "Tell her we'll cover her operating expenses."

Charlene just looked at me. "How?"

"I don't know." But how could I tell this woman no? She was over there risking her life and sacrificing her home for children who had just survived one of the worst tragedies in history. The least we could do was find a way to come up with a few bucks.

About a month later PIC received another letter from a man in charge of the mountain gorilla veterinary clinic in Rwanda, saying they didn't have the money to hire the staff they needed. She brought me the letter, and again I said we would cover it. But we still had to find the money. In September of that year, PIC had its first fundraiser for those two causes. Now, more than fourteen years later, we've raised more than $1.5 million for both humanitarian and conservation projects in Rwanda and the Democratic Republic of the Congo.

Rosamond Carr passed away in September 2006 at the age of ninety-four, but the Imbabazi Orphanage continues to give refuge to over one hundred orphans in Rwanda. Now, in addition to helping support the hundred-plus children there, PIC also helps to fund tuition for secondary and college students. When I was in Rwanda last summer, I visited the orphanage, and it was amazing to see the young lives still being changed because of this one woman's determination to make a difference.

"If it had not been for Jack, who had the courage to say we could do it, those things wouldn't have happened. At every stage, he has been totally influential in making sure that the lives of animals and the people in their habitat countries are taken care of."

—CHARLENE JENDRY, FOUNDING MEMBER, PIC

As a result of our involvement with the orphanage, we met another incredible individual, Frederick. During the genocide, fifteen-year-old Frederick had been on a bus that was stopped by the Hutu regime. Being a Hutu himself, Frederick typically would have been considered an ally to the Hutu men. But everyone else on the bus was Tutsi, which in the eyes of these Hutu men meant an inescapable death sentence.

The group of Hutus had everyone step off the bus. They then turned to Frederick and said, "If you kill them, you will live."

The unbelievably brave teenager answered, "My God won't let me do that."

As punishment, the Hutu men tied Frederick up and made him watch unmentionable atrocities before they killed every last person on the bus but him. Leaving no person unscathed, they cut off Frederick's arms about three inches below his elbows and left him for dead in his intended grave on the side of the road.

But in their violent fury, the men had made one life-saving mistake: they had bound Frederick so tightly that the ropes acted as a tourniquet and kept him from bleeding to death. Frederick was found the next day, clinging to life, and was taken to a hospital where he spent the next year recovering.

The amazing Frederick, despite the loss of his hands, makes painting seem almost effortless. (Charlene Jendry)

Finally, the Red Cross took him to the Imbabazi Orphanage. Frederick's mother and two siblings had survived the genocide, but his mother was unable to care for a child with no arms.

After meeting him, Charlene recounted his story to me, and I called my friend Dr. Nick Baird to see what we could do about prosthetics. He talked to Hanger Prosthetics & Orthotics East, Inc., here in Columbus, and they offered to provide state-of-the-art prosthetics for Frederick at no charge. PIC paid for his airfare, and he stayed for about two months until doctors and physical therapists had helped him to adjust to using the new devices. Frederick was so grateful. He said, "They gave me the opportunity to be independent again." He was especially excited to be able to tie his own shoes.

It's an amazing story of survival—but that was really just the beginning.

Charlene told me that Frederick later asked her, "Why do you think I didn't die?"

She responded, "Why do you think you didn't die?"

"Because I think God has something else for me to do," he answered. "I think he wants me to help kids just like me." And he began to explain how he and another guy from the orphanage, Zackary, wanted to open a school for disabled children.

In the meantime, he taught himself to paint, and we sold the paintings at the zoo. When he and Zackary had earned enough money, they rented two small rooms and opened the UBUMWE (meaning "unity") Community Center in an abandoned building that barely had a floor.

I was blown away when he opened that center. Here was a guy who had witnessed the unthinkable, lost both of his hands and part of his arms, and thus his ability to function in everyday life, and was separated from his family. I would imagine many people would sit and wallow in self-pity for a while, but not Frederick. He immediately found the positive aspect of it and just took off.

When Frederick came back to have his prosthetics adjusted in 2006, I talked to him in detail about the center's needs. Dr. Baird presented the situation to the zoo board, and then and there, the board voted to fund the building of a new facility for the center. With PIC continuing

Frederick and Zackary, who together founded the Ubumwe Community Center. (Jack Hanna)

to assume the cost of the operating budget, Frederick and Zackary are left to worry about the important things—teaching survival skills to the disabled and beggar children in their community.

The new UBUMWE Community Center now serves about eighty adults and children who attend daily. At the center, they learn sewing and other crafts to help them to become financially independent despite their physical challenges. It is also here where many of them receive their only meal of the day. Right now it costs about thirty dollars each day to feed the eighty children and adults a hot lunch.

There is not massive starvation in Rwanda, but there is widespread poverty. Suzi and I always bring a suitcase full of clothing and other items for our Rwandan neighbors. We've done other things that seemed rudimentary and inexpensive coming from a country like the United States. But to them, it was pivotal.

"Probably one of the neatest things about Jack and Suzi Hanna is that they truly want to make this world a better place to live."

—TED ALTENBURG, FINANCIAL ADVISOR AND LONGTIME FRIEND

Suzi and I with President Kagame and his family, along with our dear friend Rosette (director of ORTPN). (Jack Hanna)

Once a few of us bought charcoal stoves and enough charcoal to fuel a small village for a year or more. The cost was minimal in U.S. dollars, but for them, it meant having fuel at hand, eliminating the need to go out and destroy their precious forests in order to cook a meal for their families. In the past, they have not destroyed gorilla habitats out of pure negligence; they've done it mostly out of necessity. Eliminating that need preserves the habitats of the people and the animals who share the fragile ecosystem of the Rwandan mountains.

Over the years, we've searched for other small ways in which to serve the people of Rwanda. Using the new series as an outlet for conservation efforts, we've already filmed a couple of *Jack Hanna's Into the Wild* episodes there. We filmed a segment on beekeeping and together with PIC presented the bee-keepers with twenty-first-century beekeeping equipment. Their traditional method, which involved calming the bees with smoking bowls of dung, was the source of many forest fires. But since PIC started supplying the new equipment, there have not been forest fires in years, they're able to produce 50 percent more honey for income, and the beekeepers also help to keep poachers at bay while they're working. One simple change can have such a huge ripple effect for an entire community.

"The president is a very quiet man, but he and Jack were just talking and laughing. I believe it was at that moment when that bond was forged."

—CHARLENE JENDRY, FOUNDING MEMBER, PIC

As I spent more and more time there, I came to know and admire President Kagame. Some have called him a dictator, but what he has done for that country in just over a decade is remarkable. After the genocide, he had eight million people with nothing—no water, no electricity, no education, no infrastructure. And today, it's likely one of the safest, cleanest places in the world—they've even outlawed plastic bags! Democracy just seems to be flourishing under his honest leadership and stable government.

When President Kagame approached me about being on the Presidential Advisory Council for Rwanda, I was completely honored. It was already something I'd set my heart on, but discussing it with him made it official. The feelings were reminiscent of my early days at the Columbus Zoo where I saw both great need and great potential, and I knew that in some way, I could help to do my part. At that point I knew I wanted to continue to build that momentum of change in Rwanda, so we began to explore other ways I could help to make a difference.

"After President Kagame asked him to be an ambassador for Rwanda,
he really came home changed—absolutely changed. For a man who already
had such dignity and caring for people, it just took it to another level."

—CHARLENE JENDRY, FOUNDING MEMBER, PIC

President Kagame understands true progress. He isn't looking for handouts; he's looking for businesses to come there, for people to be employed and educated. Within a free-enterprise system, you have to believe you can build your wealth to whatever you want it to be, whatever you've dreamed about. But right now, the most they can dream about is having food, staying warm, and not having to walk six miles for water.

Seeing my daughter Suzanne take off her fleece pullover and give it to a shivering child, I realized the dire need for just the basics in an entire village. You want to help everybody; it's frustrating and overwhelming when you can only make a dent. But you just have to start somewhere.

One day Ted Altenburg and I sat down with one of President Kagame's cabinet members to have dinner and discuss options, one of which was for me to build a home in Rwanda. We discussed some possibilities and went to look at property along the lake. Then we decided to check out the land close to the gorillas. I was certainly considering the house option, but to ensure against making a rash decision, I first wanted to consult with Ted.

He said, "You know, Jack, you've always wanted to do something to help out here, and what better way to do it? I don't care if you make money or lose money, if you wanna build a house here, let's do it." That's what makes Ted a great advisor. He knows about the money, but he also knows it's not all about the money.

Excited to have Ted's stamp of approval, we started the ball rolling immediately. First there was the paperwork. We had to get a United States attorney working with a Rwandan attorney to get all of the details in place, and I thought that was never going to end. But finally, when it was all settled, Suzi and I sketched out what we had in mind, and construction began.

Our home built as a symbol of our support for the beautiful country of Rwanda. (Jack Hanna)

Once Suzi and I received word the house was finished, we hopped on a plane to Rwanda to see our new home for the very first time. As we drove up—I will never forget it—Suzi and I were completely overcome with emotion by the reception. All of the workers and their families had shown up, and all of the children were wearing white in honor of the special occasion. There were native dancers and music, and when they saw us, everyone ran to greet Suzi and me, waving and embracing us as the newest members of their village.

Suzi and I could not believe it; they had worked so hard. The house was beautiful, and the whole village had taken time out to organize a spectacular welcome for us. Suzi and I just watched in disbelief, tears running down our cheeks.

One of the most emotional moments of my life was walking with President Kagame to greet about twenty-five thousand people at the annual gorilla-naming ceremony in Rwanda. (Rebecca Rose)

The people of Rwanda had truly made us feel like a part of their community. More recently at a gorilla-naming ceremony, President Kagame affirmed that feeling. In Rwanda, naming the gorillas each year is a huge event, but I had no idea how huge. All kinds of people were there—and not only Rwandans.

The president of Animal Planet was there, as well as Steve Irwin's producer John Stainton, the chairman of the board of Macy's, John Dick (consulate to Rwanda), and many other visitors. Waiting for the procession to start from our home, I was standing off to the side when Rosette Rugamba, Rwanda's director general of tourism, came over and said, "The president wants you to walk over the hill with him."

A few others and I were helped into traditional ceremonial dress, and we stood in procession to walk with the president. When we crossed over that hill, it took my breath away. There were about twenty-five thousand people all waiting below to celebrate the naming of the gorillas. And during the festivities Rosette introduced me as: "Jack Hanna, who is a part of our Rwandan family." Again, they had me in tears; it was truly an honor.

Because of my involvement with Rwanda, I was recently asked by my pastor, Steve Norden, to be one of the hosts for a prayer breakfast in Columbus. It was there that I had the absolute honor of introducing Immaculée Iligabiza. Now living in the United States, she is the author of *Left to Tell,* the unbeliev-ably harrowing story of her struggle to survive the Rwandan genocide of 1994. For ninety-one days, Immaculée hid in a three-by-four-foot bathroom—with seven other women—that served as her salvation from the brutal Hutu regime. Her family, and close to a million other Rwandan people, were not so fortunate.

Surprisingly, though, as I read her story, the ominous horror of her experience was lifted by Immaculée's unceasing prayer and belief in an omnipotent God. And in the end, amazingly, she had no hatred for those who murdered her family. In

Meeting Immaculée Iligabiza at a prayer breakfast. She's truly one of the most amazing people I've ever met. (Jack Hanna)

fact, she went so far as to visit her family's killers in prison and offer her forgiveness. As she explained, "By harboring hatred and anger, you become the victim or prisoner. Forgiveness sets you free." Immaculée is such an inspirational example of unconditional love and the true power of forgiveness. It is character such as this that has helped the Rwandan people to survive and recover from such an inexplicable tragedy.

At a welcome dinner for our film crew with Rwanda's president, Paul Kagame. (Rick A. Prebeg)

After just a few years, it's become obvious that such a small thing as building a house has done more for the people than any of us ever anticipated. For what I put into it—building there is relatively inexpensive—the returns for Rwanda have been phenomenal. First, the simple fact that I have built a home in Rwanda helps to send the message that it's a safe, beautiful country. Then when guests visit, if they stay in my house, all of the proceeds go directly back into the country. And if they don't stay in my house, they are still contributing to the country's economy. Finally, after experiencing the country firsthand, visitors fall in love with it as I did and feel compelled to support to local organizations. One of the most prominent examples is Bill Gates, who had lunch at the house in Rwanda after trekking to visit the mountain gorillas. His foundation has magnanimously contributed to helping the Rwandans, especially in the medical field.

But in the end—make no mistake—it is *I* who am indebted to them. The country of Rwanda has given me experiences and inspiration that no amount of money could ever buy. The Rwandan's love, kindness, and forgiving nature are beautiful examples for all of us to follow. There is no greater joy in life than giving back to people and wildlife in need. In the years to come, I am excited to watch Rwanda live up to its name, a name derived from a word that means "to grow." And my family will be there as much as possible, in our true home away from home, doing all we can to facilitate that mission.

CHAPTER 16

Montana Hanna's

In October 1987, I was invited out West to do a fundraiser by a young, enthusiastic zoo director, Jim Duncan. Visiting Montana for the first time, I fell in love with the state, the people, the mountains, all the Big Sky country. Almost right away, I decided to purchase a lot and build a cabin on some land adjoining Absarokee-Beartooth Wilderness. At first, I only planned to make it a vacation retreat for my family and me, but after a few trips out there, I thought, *This is where I have to live.*

I became just as excited about seeing native wildlife in Montana as I had in Africa—in a way, more so, since we have so little of it left. Within a few visits, I had already seen a mountain lion, a black bear, loads of bighorn sheep, moose, elk, golden eagles, grouse, beavers, otters, and a host of other animals, large and small.

The land was on a large ranch that had been subdivided for private ownership. At an elevation of five thousand feet, it lay at the base of Cathedral Mountain and overlooked the Stillwater Valley. From my porch, the idyllic view over the Stillwater River seemed hardly changed from what it must have been like 150 years ago. Only the bison and Native Americans were missing. As much as I loved that cabin, and Montana in general, I just could not get out there as often as I had anticipated.

Then while I was covering some northern Montana fires as a news correspondent for ABC, I came upon Flathead Lake right outside of Glacier

National Park. This incredible lake is the largest natural lake in the western United States and is one of the cleanest lakes in the world. When the sun comes up in the morning and hits the mist rising off the lake, the ethereal atmosphere makes you think you're in heaven.

Having a home on that lake someday was a huge dream, because at the time, I couldn't even afford a tree out there. Then we found about five acres on the side of an extremely steep hill that nobody wanted; it had been for sale for years. We put a ridiculous bid on it, and we ended up with land right on Flathead Lake!

Over the years we saved our money to build, and in the spring of 1997, Suzi and I flew out to Montana and went for a walk on our property. I told her I had a surprise, and as we came up the hill, there stood the treehouse cabin I had secretly hired Randy Baker (aka Handy Randy) to build while we were in Columbus. Elated beyond belief, Suzi and I spent our next two summers in that little cabin.

Since then we have built what we now call the "main house" and two other guest cabins. We use them for the rare occasions when the whole family gathers, and Suzi and I still spend the summers on the lake, bringing our daughters and grandchildren when they're able to get away.

The grandkids love Montana. Every June through September, I rent animals from a local farmer. I know it sounds sort of crazy to rent animals, but I can only take care of them in the summer while I'm there. The farmer makes a little money, and we have loads of fun. The grandkids love going down to the chicken house; decorated with an old wooden sign "the Egg Factory," where they check the chickens' nests for eggs every day. The chickens do not always understand the conflict that can arise when each grandchild doesn't get his or her own egg, so Suzi is always prepared with a few store-bought cartons of brown eggs just in case. We also have goats and cows that roam around, and we have a garden that the kids help take care of and then reap the benefits of the harvest during the summer. Raspberries and cherries are their favorite treats. The outdoor activities in Montana offer endless entertainment and adventure, even if you are chased by a bear! That's a real adrenaline rush—you just pray the pepper spray works! Once Suzi and I were hiking with a group of friends and ended up lost on a twenty-mile hike bushwhacking through the wilderness trying to find a pristine lake.

We regularly go fly-fishing, camping, boating, and hiking. I don't really fish. I just follow Suzi around and carry her rod for her. But the hiking, now that I can handle. Our friend Claire Wilson had done all but four of the day hikes in Glacier National Park and would tell us everything about them. Because of her love of the mountains, she was just a wealth of information and got us hooked on exploring the mountains by foot. There is nothing better than being immersed in God's almost-untouched creation and experiencing it for yourself.

Our friends and camping buddies Keith and Becky Palmquist once took us canoeing and fly-fishing on the beautiful North Fork River of the Flathead. Thinking this would be a relaxing day, Suzi and I settled into a canoe for the first time in our lives, ready for the serene wildlife viewing. Boy, were we in for a surprise!

After paddling through roaring white water, our canoe was speeding like a torpedo toward a huge bank with protruding branches in the bend of the river. We were unable to turn away, and before we knew it, everything was upside down, floating down the river—fishing rods, food, paddles, even our poor, battered bodies.

The rest of the day was no less exciting. Black flies attacked us, the drenched car keys didn't work (except to set off the alarm), and we had to hitch a ride to the nearest phone—which was in the middle of nowhere—to call a tow truck. Despite our surroundings, there was no serenity to be found on that trip!

On another camping trip, we headed to Canada to go hiking and looking for wildlife. My wife is a fruitaholic, and our camper was teeming with crates of peaches, plums, nectarines, cherries, blueberries, watermelon—you name it. When we were stopped at the border, the border patrol asked if we had any fruit, to which we replied, "A whole orchard full!" The officer then informed us that because of the pits, it all had to be left at the border. But when Suzi heard that, she wouldn't allow it. She stood there in front of the officer and, crate by crate, removed every last pit from the fruit. The officer just shook his head, saying, "This is a first!"

One Saturday morning back in Montana, while we were still working on the main house, I was sitting outside when an old 1970s truck with a big crane pulled up. In the back there were two huge rocks, probably thousands of pounds each. I had asked the builder if we could arrange to have some big rocks put out front by the bridge.

I walked out there and said to the driver, "Hey, how ya doing?"

"I'm just delivering your rocks," he called.

"Okay, thanks. I'm Jack Hanna."

He said, "Stefan von Trapp."

And with that, I went back in the house and started eating my typical Special-K-with-bananas breakfast. After a few minutes, I shook my head and said to the bowl of cereal, "That's amazing! I can't believe that guy's name is von Trapp. The only von Trapp I know is that Sound of Music guy."

"What did you say, Jack?" Suzi called from the kitchen.

"Sue, the guy in the driveway says his name is von Trapp."

"Jack, I wish you wouldn't do that. You're always making things up. Besides, the von Trapps live in Vermont; they don't live here."

After I finished my breakfast, I went back out, and I couldn't help but mention it. "You know, I was telling my wife the only von Trapp I know is from *The Sound of Music*. You must be his long-lost cousin or something." About that time, these four little heads peeked up out of the truck. There was one little boy, maybe four years old, and three little girls, probably all under ten.

He looked over at them. "Those are my kids."

"That's amazing."

He smiled. "Yes, and that was my grandfather."

"The colonel or the captain or whatever?" I asked. "That was your grandfather?"

He nodded and went back to work.

I burst back into the house. "Sue! Sue, you're not going to believe this! He's the von Trapp's grandson!"

She just looked at me. "Jack, you're crazy."

"Okay, come out there," I insisted. "I'll show you."

With our friends, the von Trapp family, after Neal McCoy's concert in Texas. (Jack Hanna)

I practically dragged her up to Stefan and said, "Tell her who you are. She doesn't believe me."

He confirmed my crazy story, and Suzi freaked out too. We couldn't believe these people were sitting here in my driveway.

Stefan's kids now travel all over the world, singing in the von Trapp family tradition. But when they are in Montana, they're our favorite hiking buddies. They love to hike as much as we do, and sometimes as they trek along the Glacier National Park trails, they'll just start singing a capella: "The hills are alive. . . ." I'll get chills just listening to them.

Not only are they remarkably talented, they are the kindest Christian family and are so generous with their time, always willing to sing to the sick or disabled. My brother-in-law Jack is a quadriplegic as a result of progressive multiple sclerosis. Every summer our friend Larry Wilson flies Jack and his caregiver, Felix, out to Montana to be with us along with the help of Suzi's other brother, Dave. Often, the von Trapps will call and ask, "Can we sing for Jack today?" Their willingness to share their amazing talent brings tremendous joy, especially to someone whose quality of life has been jeopardized.

I've done fundraisers with them, and they always leave the audience misty-eyed. One that we did together was for country singer Neal McCoy's East Texas Angel Network. This project helps families with disabled children who can no longer pay their bills. The sense of hope that is generated is electrifying, and with Neal McCoy and the von Trapps, the audience gets an awesome show in return.

Once I was told that you can be happy anywhere if you have friends. We make it a point to surround ourselves with all kinds of great friends in the mountains of Montana. If we haven't already brought a bunch with us—and even if we have—we invite another bunch to dinner. It's not really a planned thing. We'll just meet somebody, be it the von Trapps, two pilots out hiking, a young couple at the local grocery store, and the next thing we know, we've got twenty-three people coming for dinner. Suzi sometimes shows up forty-five minutes after everyone else because she's still out shopping for groceries. But she never complains. She enjoys it as much as I do. Often we entertain around a campfire up at the farm and just to be safe our friend Doug Averill will drive over his firetruck. Of course all the kids love that!

"There is never a day in Montana when his house isn't full of visitors."

—NICK BAIRD, FAMILY DOCTOR AND LONGTIME FRIEND

One time our close friend, Robert Ludlum, author of the Bourne series, came over for dinner. Sitting down on our low benches on the porch, he completely went over backward and did a somersault. We thought he had broken every bone in his body. When I asked him if he was hurt, Robert said, "The only thing I hurt was my pride!"

Another group of friends I can't wait to see in Montana are the Dirt Bags. Years ago John Creamer moved here from Georgia and extended the invitation for a men's Bible study on Friday mornings in the casual setting of a local bar. There were no labels or prerequisites—Christians, Jews, atheists were all welcome. The Dirt Bags—including such well-known participants as Jeff Foxworthy and Maury Povich—have gathered for years to study the Bible and listen to tremendous speakers. After three meetings you even get an official Dirt Bag hat! When the group first gathered, there were about six guys. Now the group has grown to three hundred men at six o'clock in the morning and four hundred men at eight o'clock! That's a lot of Dirt Bags!

At one typical last-minute party, we had invited about sixty people to a potluck dinner. The problem was, the temperature had gotten close to a hundred degrees that day, and we had no air-conditioning. Our friends Paul and Mary Ann Milhous suggested we have the party at their home where it would be cool, and we didn't protest. So all of our friends came to the Milhous' home with their special dish. But they had to give us a little ribbing throughout the night. "Boy, the Hannas know how to throw a party," they'd say. "They have it at someone else's house, and everyone brings the food!"

Most of the year, though, our cabins are empty. During those times, we'll offer a week's stay in the cabins at fundraiser auctions for zoos, Rwandan projects, cancer centers, and the like. At the last Zoofari fundraiser for the Niabi Zoo, a five-day stay brought thirty-nine thousand dollars. Obviously, someone just had thirty-nine thousand dollars they wanted to give to the zoo, but the stay in Montana offered a little something in return. Those cabins have proven to be a priceless investment both for my family and for those charities in need of support.

"They just genuinely love and care for people, and people respond to that."

—KATHALEEN STEPHENSON, DAUGHTER

Another Montana real estate investment I had made years earlier in 1990, however, had everyone questioning my sanity. When I told Suzi I was buying the town of Dean, Montana, well, she was less than thrilled. But here was this quaint little block-long ghost town in the middle of nowhere with amazing potential, and before you knew it, I signed on the dotted line. It would become Montana Hanna's.

Within the Montana Hanna's complex, we built a gift shop, the Stillwater Saloon, and the Trout Hole Restaurant—all with the Beartooth Mountains towering in the distance. I wanted to create a place where families could get together when they visited Montana. My intention was to establish a sense of community. So my brother Bush and I worked on filling out this complex and set a date for the grand opening.

The night we opened, probably a dozen people showed up. Those dozen people helped to put a lasting mark on Montana Hanna's, quite literally. After a few hours of celebrating, someone thought it would be a great idea to brand the building. So we rounded up branding irons from area ranchers, and we all stood around the fire, heating our branding irons. When they'd turned red-hot, we'd walk over and press them into the old barn wood on the wooden building. There's no telling how many brands we put in the side of that building, and they're still there today. It's just one of the many signs of the community that came together to make Montana Hanna's a success.

"We all thought he was out of his mind. I mean, this is in the middle of nowhere. There's no population. There's no anything. It is remote. But as only he can do, he just takes off on this project and launches it and does a fabulous job."

—ROBIN HOLDERMAN, COLUMBUS ZOO BOARD MEMBER AND LONGTIME FRIEND

Before long, we decided we needed some city officials, so we had an election. Bar and restaurant patrons could nominate and vote on the mayor, vice mayor, and sheriff. Then we would burn their names into wooden signs and hang them in the saloon. Everyone loved the elections so much, it became a yearly tradition.

Our longstanding sheriff was a little person named Dennis. He was no more than three feet tall. Patrons would pick him up to place him on his bar stool. I even had a pay phone installed about two feet off the floor so that it would be easily accessible to our favorite sheriff. Everyone loved Dennis. Even though our mayor and vice mayor would change, Dennis remained sheriff year after year.

Over the years, other events—like our New Year's, Fourth of July, and Halloween parties—grew to be community traditions. For our first New Year's

Party, I hired the biggest guy in the area to be a bouncer. He was about 6'8", and the "SECURITY" shirt I had made for him barely covered his stomach. Boy, I was glad I had him. When two guys got in a fight, he threw one out and was holding one up off the ground. It was like a real-life cowboy movie.

For the Fourth of July, we went all out. There was nowhere in the area that you could go to see fireworks, and we wanted the real deal. Bush learned about pyrotechnics, and let's just say we bought enough fireworks to light up the big Montana sky.

"We had a sign made that said, 'This is America.' And it was."

—Robin Holderman, Columbus Zoo Board Member and Longtime Friend

---

We put up fliers announcing our big Fourth of July bash, but had no idea how many people to expect. Then on the big day, families started rolling in with their lawn chairs until we had probably five hundred people or more. That's saying a lot for a town with a population of zero! Of course, with any first-time event, we had our glitches—like embers from the fireworks falling on the crowd—but we became pretty efficient at it over the years.

There was also an annual Halloween party at Montana Hanna's. People would dress up in outlandish costumes with sparkles and really get into it. But everything we tried to do was family driven. We'd have games for kids, like horseshoes, and there was always the wooden cowboy-looking playground to let them enjoy their Montana cowboy-town experience to the fullest.

Joan Lunden and Charlie Gibson even brought the Good Morning America crew out in the mid-nineties to film around Montana Hanna's and southern Montana. For part of the filming, the whole crew set out to go horseback riding through the Beartooth Mountains. Having been born and raised in New York City, some of the crew had never been on a horse before in their lives, and they were terrified. There were about twenty of us going through the steep mountain trails that were sometimes only a couple of feet wide. Even Joan, an avid horse-back rider, looked a little nervous when the terrain got the most treacherous.

But when we made it to the top, all of the anxiety melted as they panned around for their first breathtaking, birds-eye view of Montana. Endless blue sky above, mountain streams below, and snow-capped mountaintops for as far as the eye could see—that was the Montana I had fallen in love with, and I hoped that for a moment, all of America would stop their morning routines to fall in love with it too.

"That was the only saving grace; you knew the horse didn't want to slip off the trail and die."

—JOAN LUNDEN

After a refreshing picnic, we successfully made our way back down the mountain without losing anyone. Although exhausted physically, the group returned mentally refreshed and newly enamored with the bountiful beauty that surrounded us. To end the day in true Montana Hanna style, we moseyed back to the saloon, sat around the campfire, and recounted the day's adventures.

In 2003, after over a decade of good old-fashioned family fun, I made a bittersweet decision to sell Montana Hanna's. As much as we loved bringing the families of neighboring communities together, we just didn't have the time or energy to dedicate to the management of the complex. But the tradition carries on without us. Montana Hanna's still stands on the outskirts of the picturesque Beartooth Mountains welcoming local families and weary travelers alike.

Although the buildings named Montana Hanna's are no longer mine, the mind-set still is. The breathtaking mountains and crystal waters of Montana will always be the place where I go to slow down and get a little closer to nature, my family, and even myself. If you're ever out in the mountains of Montana, discovering it for yourself, keep your pepper spray handy and your eyes open. You never can tell what kind of characters you'll encounter there.

CHAPTER 17

My Girls

If you were to take away the zoo, the TV shows, the African safaris, and the Montana mountains, I'd still have more than any man could wish for because I have my girls. Those adventures wouldn't have been half the joy without those four beaming faces to come home to. But no matter where they were, Suzi, Kathaleen, Suzanne, and Julie have always been my lighthouse on the shore, my North Star, heck, my GPS navigator that keeps me coming home.

"Sue is the den mother, always taking care of everybody. If you could have an ounce of the goodness she has, it would change you immensely."

—GLENN NICKERSON, DIRECTOR, CAMERAMAN, AND EDITOR

Since college, Suzi has been the one constant in my life who has kept me going through it all. She's never let me doubt for a second that we're in this thing together, and she has always been my biggest fan. Having been almost everywhere on my filming trips, she has helped our crew a great deal. When we're riding around trying to get shots in the wild, she's out talking to the people; she is our lead PR person in the field. When I'm on the road without her, I'm always calling and she encourages to keep going, telling me that my work is making a difference. There's no doubt I wouldn't be where I am today without her.

"With Suzi, everything is the best she's ever had. In Mexico,
we had guacamole every single morning. And every morning she'd say,
'This is the best guacamole I've ever had.'"

—GLENN NICKERSON, DIRECTOR, CAMERAMAN, AND EDITOR

My wife is just an incredible human being. I've never seen Suzi wake up and have a bad day; every day and everybody is beautiful to her. Her faith in God is boundless, and she's the most giving person you'll ever meet. Drugs, alcohol, or cigarettes have never been her thing. She's into blueberries, watermelon, and organic food. In Montana during the summer she is always going to Loon Lake Farm to buy fresh produce and homemade goat cheese. She makes me eat cookies with flaxseed in them and gets upset when she catches me hording chocolate chip cookies. Suzi's pure heart and her willingness to listen, I would say, are the bedrock of our marriage. We've now celebrated forty unbelievable years of marriage, a rare feat that we recently commemorated with another rare feat—a breathtaking twenty-four-mile hike through the Grand Canyon! On top of it all, she has also raised three

Our growing family: Kathaleen and Suzanne in front, and in back, me and Suzi, with Julie, just a few days from her debut. (Jack Hanna)

Kathaleen, 3 (Jack Hanna)

Wildlife was really just the norm in the Hanna household.

Suzanne, 2 (Jack Hanna)

All three girls grew to have a loving respect toward the creatures of the wild.

Julie, 10 (Jack Hanna)

beautiful daughters, which is beyond a job in itself.

After Suzi and I got married, we welcomed girl, after girl, after girl into this world. Even when *they* had children, it was girl, after girl after . . . But I'm getting ahead of myself.

Kathaleen and Suzanne were born in Knoxville, Tennessee, and Julie was born in Winter Park, Florida—in that order. They each took their respective roles in a house full of wild animals. To them, it was nothing for a lion cub to be in the crib with them, a monkey to be hanging from the stair rail, or a llama to follow them around in the backyard.

When they were in school, they always had an advantage when it came to projects involving animals. Suzanne once did a report on elephants, and instead of bringing a poster for a visual aid, she brought a live baby elephant! Then, when they studied India, Suzanne took Taj, the white tiger we were raising at home, for show-and-tell. Of course, you could never do that today. In fact, my granddaughter Caroline just did a project on elephants, and she said, "Can we call J. J. to bring an elephant?" But Suzanne had to explain that J. J.—that's what they call me—couldn't bring elephants to school anymore.

As the girls grew to be teenagers, our house was often the meeting place for their youth groups. Where else could the kids have Bible study in a homemade zoo, with baby ducks in the bathtub, baby wallabies hanging from the doorknobs in make-shift mothers' pouches, and a tiger curled up by the couch?

Admittedly, my line of work also had its drawbacks when it came to family life. I worked seven days a week—a true workaholic. Suzi always made it to the girls' functions, but often I wasn't able to because of some kind of meeting at work. However, every Sunday was our precious family time together. We went to church, stopped by Kentucky Fried Chicken, then went to the zoo for our picnics. After lunch, we would ride around on the golf cart and pick up trash on the zoo grounds. It became a game, oddly enough, to see who could find the most garbage. I appreciated having a job where I could bring my family along with me. Those Sunday afternoons will always be special to me.

One of the saddest times in our family's life was in 1987 when I received a call at six in the morning from our dear friends, Kaye and Jim Callard. Their beautiful daughter Katy had died in a tragic car crash. Katy and her older sister, Brittany (Kathaleen's best friend), were like members of our family. At the celebration of Katy's life, our minister, Reverend Steve Norden, eloquently spoke about the incredible impact this fourteen-year-old had made. We had also been asked to share some ways in which she had touched our lives. Her smile was bigger than life, especially when she saw the animals which she dearly loved at the zoo or in our home. It was the first time our family had experienced a precious young life being taken so close to home. Katy reminded us that every day is a special gift, and the strength you receive from your faith in God is invaluable.

When the girls were in high school, I started traveling to many different countries. It was difficult to leave my family at home. I always looked forward to Suzi coming with me for two or three weeks on safari each year. Even though Suzi's parents were often at home with the girls, we always had an uneasiness about traveling to Africa. If something terrible should happen, parents never want to consider their children being raised without them, but it was an ever-present thought when we were traveling without our girls.

"When they would go on their African trips, as a kid that was obviously hard, but now as an adult, I can see how that made me into a secure individual because I knew that their marriage came first and how strong of a relationship they had."

—SUZANNE SOUTHERLAND, DAUGHTER

While in China discussing the breeding loan of the giant panda, Suzi and I took a day off to see one of the greatest wonders of the world, the Great Wall. (Jack Hanna)

Our family trips were so anticipated, typically a trip to somewhere in the Caribbean. One trip to Jamaica was especially memorable—although some of those memories aren't so positive. For one, the curvy roads caused Julie to become carsick, and she lost her lunch before even arriving at the hotel. Then, after settling in, our first swim in the ocean proved disastrous as well. Suzanne was stung by a jellyfish, leaving a painful, burnlike injury that lasted for days. After that incident, no one took a dip in the beautiful turquoise waters the rest of the week!

One of the happier moments of our trip to Jamaica. (Jack Hanna)

Things finally turned positive when we went to explore Dunn's Falls. Climbing over the rocks and through the falling waters was a refreshing adventure. Whether the memories were wonderful or horrible, though, I now treasure every single moment we were able to capture as the girls were growing up. It may be cliché, but it does happen so fast.

Suzanne was my first daughter to get married, and boy, did I have a hard time with that. Her boyfriend, Billy Southerland, was the a nice guy, but I didn't even want to give him a chance.

Suzanne was impressed with his fun-loving and laidback personality; however, when the big day came, I just wasn't ready for Suzanne to leave home. In my heart she was still my little girl. I thought they were too young because they were in their early twenties, but looking back I think Suzi's parents and mine thought the same thing when we were married in college. Billy and Suzanne's wedding reception was at the Columbus Zoo alongside the river—with camels and all.

Billy is allergic to animals, and of all people, he chose to marry a zoo director's daughter. For ten years, he wasn't able to stay in our home when he and Suzanne would visit because of the animals. Once at the zoo we had just left the tigers when his chest tightened up, and he had difficulty talking and breathing. We rushed him to First Aid, and they brought him around. I guess any man who continually risks his life to be a part of the family deserves a chance, right?

Together Billy and Suzanne have given us four of the greatest gifts in the world: Brittany, Blake, Alison, and Caroline. But when we found out Suzanne was expecting Brittany, the name "Grandpa" just didn't seem to fit. We then decided that I would be called "J. J.," short for Jungle Jack, and Suzi would be "Nana Hanna." We thought they would eventually shorten Suzi's name to "Nana," but they've instead shortened it to "Hanna." We sometimes get odd looks when people hear them calling their grandmother by her last name, but that's just the way it happened.

Working all the time, I've always regretted not spending more time with my girls as they were growing up, so I'm determined not to make that mistake with my grandchildren. Ever since Brittany was two years old and in preschool, I've been taking animals to her school, doing little animal education programs for them. That tradition continues to this day, although now I visit Brittany in her middle school and Blake, Ali, and Caroline in their elementary school. Together they have a blast helping me handle and show the animals to all of their friends.

Ten-year-old Blake with his number-one football fan! (Jack Hanna)

With Blake, I go to the football games; I had always missed seeing my daughters cheer when they were growing up. Watching Blake play elementary football, for me, is like watching the Super Bowl. I try to set my whole schedule around those games. He once told me, "J. J., if I ever make it to the pros, I'm gonna make sure you have a seat in the front row every time." Man, I thought I was going to cry when I heard those words. That little guy has a great heart and is already a little conservationist. Every night, Suzanne tells me, he prays for all of the endangered animals. When there's a spider or an ant invading the house, no one is allowed to kill it. He says, "If God didn't have a reason to be making that spider, he wouldn't have made it."

Brittany is a thoughtful, self-reliant, beautiful young woman and is already a brilliant writer. She enjoys sports and adores being around animals. Ali, Blake's twin sister, plays soccer, basketball, and the piano beautifully. She truly has a sweet heart, plus she's quick-witted and fun. Ali's often in the kitchen cooking up someone's favorite dish. Every morning she wakes up, greeting you with a big smile on her face. And Caroline (named after my mom), my little C. C., is the youngest of the four and is as independent as they come. She's always standing on a chair to serenade us with the latest song she has learned. I cannot wait to see what the future holds for these precious grandchildren, but I plan to be cheering them on, whatever it may be.

With Blake and my little namesake, Jack, who will no doubt create a rugby fan out of me someday! (Cheeky Monkey Photography)

A little over a year after Suzanne and Billy married, Kathaleen and Julian Stephenson were walking down the aisle. Kathaleen and her best friend, Brittany, had gone to England to study and both ended up marrying best friends. One night at a pub, Julian came over to Kathaleen and used the pickup line: "You're blonde; you must be an American." They had dated for several months when they came home for Suzanne and Billy's wedding. On the way back to England, Kathaleen was deported. It was decision time! I knew she was in love, and separation was difficult. I wasn't surprised at all when Julian called me to ask for her hand in marriage.

Suzi and I traveled a little further for that wedding—all the way to Surrey, England. We hardly knew anyone there except for the bride and her sisters. Suzi even met a couple on the bus and invited them to the wedding, saying, "You'll be the only friends I know there!" Our close friends, the McConnell's traveled all the way over so their three children, John, Jessica, and Porter, could be in the wedding party. After the wedding at an eleventh-century church in England—with me wearing a top hat, tails, and the whole nine yards—we had another reception back here in Columbus at the zoo with the rest of our family and friends. But, to my dismay, Kathaleen and Julian's stay here was only for the reception. Kathaleen and Julian returned to the United Kingdom to make their permanent home. They now reside in a little village called Haslemere, which looks like it just popped out of a storybook.

Kathaleen and Julian waited over ten years before bringing little Gabriella into our lives. That little British version of Kathaleen has stolen our hearts. It's amazing to hear her already speaking with an English accent, saying "Mummy" and "where are my wellies (boots)?" Two years later, Kathaleen and Julian had a baby boy. We had rushed over to see Gabriella's birth, only to be scared to death by her complicated birth, so we decided to wait the second one out. When we called to check on the little guy, I thought I was hearing things when Kathaleen said, "Baby Jack is doing just fine." Baby Jack! I couldn't believe it. That was one of the greatest gifts of my life, to have a little namesake. Until baby Jack was born, the only thing named after me was Jack the rabbit!

I'm still learning to fit in over there in Kathaleen's new home. Tea and scones just aren't my thing! In 2007, when invited by my good friend John Dick to speak at a fundraising gala that Princess Anne would be attending, I told him, "John, no one knows me over there." But he relieved my doubts, and I thought, *Hey, it'll be a good time to visit the grandkids.* But boy, I didn't realize what a big deal it would be. I spent a lot of time preparing my speech because not many people over there had even heard of me. I wanted to make a good impression for my friend; plus, I didn't want to embarrass Kathaleen.

When I went to speak at Whitehall Palace, I was equipped only with my safari suit, although I was to be speaking at a black-tie event. Suzi looked beautiful in a dressy blouse and long, black skirt that Kathaleen had given her to wear. But when we arrived, they asked us, "At what time would you like to change?"

Suzi and I looked at each other. "We are changed," she answered politely.

Once we made it into the dining hall, Suzi looked around and, noting the table décor, commented, "Wow, that's really interesting. I've never seen potato chips used to decorate a table before." At that, the event facilitator turned to us and said, "Those aren't potato chips. They are rose petals." Strike two.

Soon they took me back to review my program with me and to let me know the time allotted for my presentation. They heavily stressed to me the importance of strictly following my schedule. However, once I got on stage, time just seemed to fly, and before I knew it, the director was telling me to wrap it up. I hadn't even shown my video; I didn't know what to do! From the stage, I called out, "Do we still have time for my video?" Silence. "Can I show my video?" Still no answer. So I looked directly at Princess Anne. "Do you care if I show my video?" I detected a faint smile. "Aw, screw it! I'm going to show it anyway!" Finally a response: the crowd burst into laughter.

In spite of my fashion faux pas and running a little over on time, the crowd seemed to enjoy the speech, and Princess Anne was even gracious enough to personally thank me for my time. Most importantly, John was pleased, and Kathaleen just seemed to be proud to have me there addressing the princess. Until I can convince Kathaleen to move her family over here, I'll be crossing the Atlantic Ocean as often as I can.

As for my youngest little girl, Julie, I treasure every single second that I am privileged to be with her. She truly taught us the fragility of life when she was only two years old, having been diagnosed with and surviving leukemia. Then, when she was finishing her sophomore year in college, she went to visit Kathaleen in England and seemed to have a stomach virus while she was there. After she returned home, I heard her vomiting and immediately told her to go to the doctor. I knew something wasn't right.

Julie went to her oncologist, Dr. Fred Ruyman, who had been treating her since the age of two, and he did a CAT scan. When we came home that evening, the phone was ringing, and I answered it. As the doctor told me the news, I think I turned totally white. For about thirty seconds, I was in a complete state of panic. "Julie has a very large brain tumor!" I cried. "What are we going to do?" Out of necessity, Suzi and I pulled ourselves together so that we could be strong for Julie.

She went from being fine on Friday to having brain surgery the following Monday. That was, without a doubt, the longest day of my life. We had a small gathering the night before to spend time with friends, including our minister Steve Norden, to lift her spirits as much as possible. And honestly, we just didn't know if she would make it through the surgery. She had already escaped death once when she beat leukemia. What were the odds she could do that again?

With Julie, now happy and healthy, and two other family members, Brass and Ben.
(Jack Hanna)

Monday morning Suzi and I did the most difficult thing ever: we said good-bye to our precious daughter and watched the surgically shrouded nurses roll her back to the operating room. Then we waited. I don't remember a time when we relied on our faith more than that one day.

Fortunately, the neurosurgeon, Dr. Ed Kosnik, allowed our dear family friend, Dr. Nick Baird, to go into the operating room with her. After nine hours, Nick came out of the operating room, and I wasn't sure I really wanted to hear what he had to say, until he said it. "Guys, everything's going to be okay." With that, he lifted the weight of the whole world off of my heart and mind. They had removed Julie's tumor, and it looked to be benign. We couldn't have been more grateful. When she came out of surgery, she wrote us a note: "I love you. Love, Moo Cow," using her nickname given to her by her sisters.

Most people probably take life for granted until they are faced with a life-threatening situation. Because of my experience, I appreciate each and every day with my wonderful family and friends, and I realize that it's not the material things in life that are important, but the love and care that surrounds you.

—JULIE HANNA, DAUGHTER

After her recovery, as difficult as it was, Julie went back to college for her junior year. Due to the brain surgery and the cranial radiation she received as a two-year-old, the processing of information was very difficult for her. Still, she continued working part-time at the zoo while going to school and graduated the next year. Today, she continues her work in the Promotions Department at the zoo. She's an inspiration to people everywhere, lending her time to St. Jude Children's Research Hospital and other fundraising efforts for children with cancer.

Golly day, it has been a wild life so far, and I never could have survived it without my girls—my four precious, loving, amazing girls. I often wonder what kind of toll my career has had on my family, but who can argue with these results? Our geatest joy has been watching our girls grow into amazing women, and now we get to see it all over again as they raise families of their own.

CHAPTER 18

Zoos—The Last Hope?

On a recent visit to a local college, I offered zoo passes to one of the professors. He promptly replied, "I don't believe in zoos." Some people share his opinion, many who do not appreciate the invaluable service offered by zoos around the world. Ideally, yes, maybe animals should forever roam freely in the wild, but the truth is that most animals do not have a wild to go back to. And if they did, many of the species would not survive there.

Since the early 1900s, animal habitats have been rapidly disappearing all over the world. It is common knowledge that man's progress poses the greatest threat to the animal world, which is now losing species at a very alarming rate. Some researchers estimate that as much as fifty percent of the world's animals and plants will be on the path to extinction within a hundred years. Zoos, which fifty years ago represented a very small part of the problem by taking animals from the wild, have today become part of the solution. Many zoos, including Columbus, have programs to release certain animals back into the wild whenever possible.

In nearby Cumberland, Ohio, The Wilds is really the epitome of conservation and is an organization in which I am quite proud to have had a hand in developing. The Wilds got off to a very slow, rough start, but when the Central Ohio Coal Company donated over nine thousand acres for a site, we knew we could make it happen. Five zoos got together—Akron, Cleveland, Pittsburg,

Toledo, and Columbus—and created, as a separate entity from the zoos, the largest animal conservation center in this country. The Wilds is now under the umbrella of the Columbus Zoo. Drs. Nick Baird and Evan Blumer were extremely instrumental in The Wilds's development and success, and if it hadn't been for their dedication and devotion, this first-class remarkable conservation center would not be here today.

The habitats there are amazing—the closest thing I've seen to natural habitats anywhere in the world. Even flying over The Wilds in a helicopter, you think you're flying over the wilds of Africa. And the best part, for the general public, is that you can ride across the landscape in an open-air bus and see some of the rarest animals in the world. We're very lucky to have here in Ohio—or even here in the United States—a center like The Wilds that is on the cutting edge of animal conservation.

Thanks to zoological advances, animals in zoos today increasingly enjoy natural habitats where they can develop and flourish. Zoos continue to improve and to meet the particular needs of diverse groups of animals, with the ultimate hope that they may breed and further their species. Captive breeding programs, such as the one at The Wilds, have saved such species as Asiatic wild horse, Arabian oryx, Père David's deer, American bison, Hawaiian goose, black rhino, Asian rhino, giraffe, and Grery's zebra, and we are hopeful about many others.

Propagating the species was not the primary purpose of the old zoos. Sure, if an animal could breed, that was fine. But the main objective was to obtain as many species as possible to exhibit to the general public. Don't worry about the conditions, just show the animal. For example, if a zoo director had a male spotted hyena, rather than acquire a female to allow breeding, he might be more concerned with getting a striped hyena. That way he could say he now had a spotted *and* a striped hyena. He could have an Asian *and* an African lion, a Siberian *and* a Bengal tiger, etc.

When I arrived in Columbus, *cage* had pretty much become a nasty word in the zoo world. Yet at the same time, Columbus still had North American cougars displayed next to primates in the gorilla house. That's an example of what I call the "menagerie effect"—accumulate all the animals you can and put them behind bars. Well, I'd had enough of that, and desperately wanted animals in natural habitats. Besides, people do not want to see animals behind bars. One of the great benefits of having animals outdoors is that it serves as a reminder of our rich wildlife heritage in the world today and how we are in danger of losing it.

One of the first things I did in Columbus was to take inventory and decide which animals would have to go, through either donations or sales to other zoos. I'm sure I surprised some people, but the purpose was to relieve overcrowding, to give our other animals more room. You have to look at the overall picture.

It's a mixed blessing for me to have had the experience of being the director of a very old zoo in Florida, along with being a board member of an equally old zoo in Knoxville, before coming to Columbus. My main job at both places was to raise money and raise awareness so that they could continue to exist. That experience provided a clear perspective of the complete spectrum of the way things used to be in the zoo world versus how they are today. We've come a long way.

The dawn of each day at the zoo presents new adventures, new challenges. Many of these challenges turn out to be medical in nature, and our veterinarians must often be highly creative in meeting them. Did you know, for example, that it is almost impossible to determine the sex of a hyena? That human birth-control pills work on a gorilla? That Preparation H may help in reducing a growth on a snake? Exotic veterinary medicine is still a relatively new field; our doctors constantly exchange information with other zoos. We are also fortunate to have the services of The Ohio State University School of Veterinary Medicine. Still, sometimes they must break new ground because no research or precedent exists. And where endangered animals are concerned, the benefits of successful treatment far outweigh the risks.

One such risk that ended up a huge success involved a male snow leopard named Sacha. This little three-week-old cub had a caved in chest, pushing his heart against his lungs. After explaining that Sacha's chances for a normal life were slim and conveying genetic risks involved for future generations, the veterinarian determined that the only option was to euthanize the cub.

My daughter Julie, however, had a different prognosis. At first glance, she had fallen in love with that little snow leopard. With tears in her eyes, she pleaded with me to let her try to save Sacha. This same daughter had just beaten the odds in surviving a brain tumor—how could I tell her I wouldn't allow this cub the same chance?

That week, Julie just happened to have an appointment for her first annual checkup since her brain surgery with her neurosurgeon, Dr. Kosnick. During her appointment, he asked what she was doing that summer, and she relayed the story of Sacha. Right away, Dr. Kosnick made a call to a pediatric surgeon, Dr. Teich, who agreed to examine Sacha at Children's Hospital. The diagnosis was pectus excavatum (caved-in chest), and he felt Sacha would probably outgrow the condition. Well, that was all the hope we needed. Julie took it upon herself to raise Sacha, and the two of them grew to have an almost inseparable bond. Sacha did have a difficult time breathing and eating, but Julie cared for him relentlessly, day and night, determined to help him thrive. And Sacha returned the favor. He just happened to arrive when Julie was still in treatment after her brain tumor was removed, and by helping this little guy to make it, Julie was healed in many ways as well.

In the end, Sacha beat the odds, just as Julie had. He responded beautifully, and within six months, his chest filled out. He grew into a magnificent, adult snow leopard and has sired many cubs, none of which have shown any genetic disorders. While Sacha has moved on to Wichita, Kansas, one of his offspring, Rocky, came to stay with us at the Columbus Zoo.

A little hope and determination was all it took to save that

Julie shares an inseparable bond with her beloved snow leopard cub, just one of the many animals she has taken under her wing. (Jack Hanna)

one animal on the verge of extinction. And even more than that, his invaluable bloodline continues in the cubs he has sired. Every critically endangered animal that you save—and every one that you help to reproduce—could be the very last one of that species. In that alone, there's no way to put a value on the services that zoos perform.

Over the years, I've watched the zoos become more and more specialized, and the Columbus Zoo is no exception. We know what our strengths are—the great apes, manatee, cheetahs, and elephant husbandry, among others—and we stick with them. Some zoos are known for their penguin collections, some for their giant tortoises. I think the movement to go with your strengths is a good one, and the animals are the winners in the long run.

Most everyone has been supportive of ideas to create centers of excellence for our animals, but there was one project—bringing in manatees—in which everyone was a little hesitant to jump on board. At the time, there were very few manatees in zoos outside of Florida, so why in the world would Columbus, Ohio, be the perfect spot for a rehabilitation center? *Well,* I thought, *why not?*

"He literally strong-armed that one through both federally and locally,
and before we knew it, we were building a
$13 million manatee exhibit, and they were in a truck on their way."

—ROBIN HOLDERMAN, COLUMBUS ZOO BOARD MEMBER AND LONGTIME FRIEND

In 1997, as a result of tons of community support, the Columbus Zoo opened Manatee Coast, where zoo patrons can stand in awe of the almost 200,000-gallon manatee world and watch these amazing creatures swim and roll among the familiar fish of their natural habitats. It was the first manatee exhibit outside of Florida to partner with the U.S. Fish and Wildlife Service's Manatee Rescue and Rehabilitation Program. The purpose of the program is not to hold manatees captive for the public's viewing pleasure, but to rehabilitate manatees that are sick, injured, orphaned, or otherwise in need of human intervention. It is a tragedy that these gentle mammals are often injured or killed by motorboats. And the ultimate goal, which is sometimes realized, is to release these endangered mammals back into the wild.

The conservation benefit of the manatee exhibit has been twofold. Not only are the manatees provided with a safe, nurturing home in which to recover, but people are also knocking down the zoo doors to see them. The additional interest generates additional revenue to support the zoo's conservation efforts, and the visitors go home having gained knowledge of and an appreciation for a species in danger. Who can argue that the result has been anything but a tremendously positive impact on the animal world?

There have been many other smaller evolutions in the zoo world over the years. Just the feeding of animals alone has changed in many ways. I mentioned earlier the outstanding diet that our gorillas enjoy—diets go a long way toward ensuring breeding success. But it's also what the animals don't eat at the zoo that can be very important.

In the old days, people were encouraged to feed the animals. This led to a great deal of abuse. Today, zoos go to great lengths to stop public feeding. When I was little, back in the 1950s, you took bread to feed the ducks, bananas and raisins for the monkeys, peanuts for the elephants. It was fun, but it was wrong.

For many reasons, feeding animals in zoos today is generally not permitted. Indiscriminate feeding can give the animals improper nutrition and unnatural behaviors. Having bears sit up on their back legs to beg for marshmallows is neither natural nor educational and certainly not healthy. In the old days another sad result of public feeding was all the nonorganic items we pulled from animals' stomachs—plastic bags, all sorts of coins, glass bottles, etc. Sometimes instances were fatal. At the Columbus Zoo we have a display with an assortment of the items we used to find inside animals (after autopsies) that we call "the museum of human stupidity." One look at it is self-explanatory.

On a more positive note, we, like many other zoos, have established a successful "Adopt an Animal" program, which allows the public to share in the cost of feeding animals. Individuals, schools, or even corporate or civic groups can sponsor any single animal at the zoo to help offset our annual food costs, which are over $650,000 a year.

"Jack puts his money where his mouth is in supporting wildlife organizations throughout the world."

—LARRY ELLISTON, PRODUCER, *Animal Adventures*

Programs have also been established within the Columbus Zoo that reach out in conservation efforts around the world. Through programs such as Partners In Conservation (PIC), the Columbus Zoo and its supporters are able to impact the animals in the wild by helping to conserve their habitats, offering medical support for the animals, and supporting those who provide animal sanctuaries to endangered species. PIC many times supports humanitarian efforts in these areas as well, realizing that the needs of the people must be met before the natural resources can be preserved. In my early years at the zoo, such programs were unheard of or, at the most, an extremely lofty goal, but now that goal has been met and exceeded, with conservation programs now being a natural extension of today's zoos.

It is truly said best in a quote by Baba Diom, the Sengalese conservationist, "In the end, we will conserve only what we love, we will love only what we know, and we will know only what we are taught." This quote may be overused in the zoo world, but that's because it so clearly defines part of what zoos today are all about.

Why even have zoos at all? The question comes up often enough, and I don't resent it. There are many reasons for the existence of zoos, but in my mind, five important points stand out: conservation, education, rehabilitation, research, and recreation.

More than 150 million people will visit zoos and aquariums every year. Most of these people are simply seeking a recreational experience that can't be found anywhere else. Zoos afford them the opportunity to experience animals firsthand. People can read great books or watch well-made wildlife television specials, but nothing replaces the direct impact of seeing a living, breathing creature that one would not ordinarily see.

Today, zoos are focused on conservation. We breed animals, both to propagate species that are often endangered and to provide animals for our own and other zoos—again, we rarely capture them in the wild anymore. Returning animals to the wild is an altruistic and utopian concept that, in our lifetimes, can realistically happen in only a few instances. But still, we give it our best attempt when possible.

Having animals in zoos has helped us to learn much about their health and their reproductive and environmental needs. With the gene pool so limited in many instances, zoological research has enabled us to make great advances in areas such as embryo transfers that will help save nearly extinct species. With apes, thousands of hours of just plain watching qualifies as valid research toward learning more about their social habits, which, in turn, will further their species.

The educational side to zoos is a never-ending process, particularly with regard to children, who learn not only about the habits and ways of animals they're seeing for the first time but also about endangered and threatened species. What they're gaining is an awareness we hope they'll carry with them for the rest of their lives.

Here at the Columbus Zoo, we strive to offer the highest quality education programs for the community. We have designed preschool programs, merit badge opportunities for Scouts, camp-ins (where groups can actually spend the night at the zoo!), Breakfast with the Animals, Zooper Saturdays, and lots more—all attempts to reach out and increase the awareness and appreciation of wildlife in our community and throughout the world. We even have classes for high school students to spend time at the zoo and earn credits toward their diploma.

As simple as it may seem, good signage and graphics also play a vital role in zoo education. Habitat signage can tell you were the animals are from, what they eat, how many remain, their migrations, all kinds of information. When I visit a zoo, I often look at the graphics before I even look at the animal.

In Columbus, we have over three hundred docents, volunteers who form the backbone of our educational program. These volunteers all have to take a series of classes, after which they become certified for their many areas of work. Docents donate thousands of hours to the zoo, teaching, answering visitors' questions, leading tours for the disabled, protecting animals, watching for births, and organizing events, just to name a few of their activities. If we had to pay them even the minimum wage, the work they do would add up to hundreds of thousands of dollars annually.

Everyone in some way takes part in conserving our wildlife resources. Ignorance, not malice, is often the greatest threat to animals. Education alone plays a great part in creating awareness and halting endangering practices. By removing the demand for exotic animal products, we can all help eliminate the incentives for poaching, illegal trade, and the loss of wildlife. By volunteering our time, becoming members of the local zoo, educating our children about conservation, we can all do our part in protecting and enhancing the lives of these magnificent creatures.

We may be able to survive in a world where the giant panda, the beautiful snow leopard, and manatees exist only as pictures in a book. But do we *want* to? The choice is ours.

Before I Go . . .

*To laugh often and much, to win the respect of intelligent people and affection of children,
to earn the appreciation of honest critics and endure the betrayal of false friends,
to appreciate beauty, to find the best in others, to leave the world a bit better
whether by a healthy child, a garden patch, or a redeemed social condition, to know
even one life has breathed easier because you have lived. This is to have succeeded.*

—RALPH WALDO EMERSON

How do you measure success, in a life, in a career? Not a day goes by that I
don't ask myself: Is this the right way to go? Am I doing the right thing? Not
just in the routine decision making of life, but with the overall picture in
mind.

Back when I was selling real estate in Knoxville or trying to promote a
wilderness movie, I knew it wasn't the right direction for me. When I first
arrived in Columbus, it was like the weight of not knowing what to do was
lifted right off my shoulders. My life opened up again; it took on a purpose.
And as my work in the animal world began to expand—through national
television appearances, through my television series, and most recently
through our work in Rwanda—I knew that I was doing exactly what I was
put on this earth to do. There isn't a more satisfying feeling than that.

"I am always in awe of anyone who is so lucky to have been able to find a passion to that degree in his life and make it his vocation, and then inspire that same kind of passion in everybody around him."

—JOAN LUNDEN

But what of the future? I know that animals will always be an important part of my life, whether in the Columbus Zoo, the mountains of Rwanda, or my backyard in Montana. But to answer the often-asked question of when I'll retire, well, I just don't know. Right now, I'm the Director Emeritus of the Columbus Zoo, filming for *Jack Hanna's Into the Wild* a representative of Busch Gardens, authoring a children's book series, regularly appearing on national television shows, doing about fifty theater speeches a year, and making regular appearances for nonprofits. Wearing that many hats, I wouldn't even know where to start in handing them off. I guess as long as I'm having fun and making a difference, I'm going to continue doing the best I can. Only God has the answer to the questions of my future.

I do know this: I'm eventually going to take my last breath, and when I do, the television appearances, the money, the notoriety will all be gone. But one legacy I'll be immensely proud to leave behind besides my family is the Columbus Zoo. I have the greatest feeling in the world walking through that vacant zoo at night and seeing how it has changed over the last thirty years. Just knowing I've had some part in that makes me feel like the most successful man on this planet. Long after I'm gone, I know that this zoo will continue to be a wonderful resource for our community and visitors—a place where people come to have fun and learn about the world's amazing creatures. Our new director, Jeff Swanagan, is a hands-on visionary, and the zoo will continue to grow and flourish under his guidance and leadership. The Columbus Zoo is and will continue to be one of the finest zoological parks in the world, working tirelessly to preserve our animals and the environment for future generations.

Being fortunate enough to have seen the world, I only wish everyone could visit these amazing places. And now when I travel, I think, this may be my last time to go to Botswana, the Grand Canyon, Tasmania, the last time I talk to Larry King, Ellen DeGeneres, or David Letterman. I no longer take things for granted; I think about things a lot differently. When you're young, life is limitless, but as you get older, you know it's coming. Your body can only do so much. And there's one word: *time*. A friend of mine, Mike Thomas, was recently diagnosed with a life-threatening condition and he said, "You can have all the money or fame in the world, but it makes no difference because you can't buy time."

Yes, I have goals, and I still feel like I have a lot to accomplish. I want to spend more time with my grandkids. I'd like to be a better Christian. I'd like to see Rwanda—its people and its animals—thrive. But when I look back and see my life played back before me, I wonder, *Who would have thought that some regular guy from Tennessee would've had the opportunity to do all that?* I've been very lucky—no, not just lucky. I've been blessed. Who could ask for anything more than that?

If you had told me when I was a teenager that I would one day be director over a phenomenal, prospering zoo, I would have been thrilled. If you had told me that I would also be traveling the country, making appearances on national television and in theaters with my animals, I would have been flat-out amazed. And if you had then told me that I would someday travel the world, seeing animals in their natural habitats, filming my own television series with my wonderful family, and meeting the people around the world, well, I just wouldn't have believed you. It's been a wild life so far, and in it I've already lived the dreams of a thousand lifetimes.

Acknowledgments

An enormous thank-you to my loving and supportive wife, Suzi, who has been with me every step of the way. She is truly one of the kindest and sincerest people in the world, and her encouragement, guidance, and support have been a gift from God. Together, we are so thankful for our three daughters Kathaleen, Suzanne, and Julie. Suzi and I are very proud of the wonderful women they've become. We are also thankful for our sons-in-law and cherish the time with our grandchildren who continually challenge us in new ways!

A very special thank-you to the Columbus Zoo and Aquarium Trustees, staff, volunteers, and visitors. Your support over the years has meant so much to me.

I'd also like to thank the team that helps me hold my life together while I'm on the road traveling from TV appearances to filming trips to speaking engagements. Kate Oliphint manages my schedule and all of our relationships. She tells me when, where, and what! Rick Prebeg has been with me for more than twenty-five years and always has his camera in hand. He plans and accompanies me on all the TV filming shoots. Without him we'd have no pictures to document our life! Nancy Rose has been a trusted friend and attorney for twenty years. I frequently rely on her expertise and advice.

One of my favorite parts of this job is taking animals to the people—lectures, picnics, churches, theaters. I wouldn't be able to do this without my wonderful group of animal handlers. First, I'd like to thank Suzi Rapp who has trained and coordinated animals for me for more than twenty-five years. I couldn't do it without her and her department at the Columbus Zoo. There are so many other indispensible people who help with our appearances: David and Anita Jackson, Tom Stalf (Niabi Zoo), DeWayne Connolly, Grant and Jamie Kemmerer, Grey Stafford (Wildlife World Zoo), Susan and David Kleven, David and Deania Hitzig, Jarod Miller, Dan Breeding, Joe Fortunato, and Joel Slaven, to name a few.

Thanks to the Thomas Nelson team, especially Amy Parker for spending time away from her family to get to know mine better—from traveling in a van full of animals between speaking engagements to attending a family dinner with my grandkids in Cincinnati! Frank Breeden of Premiere Authors made the initial connection with Thomas Nelson, and I'm grateful for his help in navigating the ins and outs of the publishing world. A special thanks to David Gernert for believing in these crazy stories and to John Stravinsky for originally writing many of them.

A big thanks to Guy Nickerson, Elaine Pugliese, and the team at Spectrum for embracing some of my wild ideas over the years. They've been a blast to work with—traveling the globe in search of fascinating animal stories and cultures.

Thank you to Busch Entertainment (SeaWorld and Busch Gardens) for believing in me and supporting *Animal Adventures*—one of the longest running animal TV series in history!

And thank you to my friends and colleagues who were interviewed for this project: Bill Wolfe, Blaine Sickles, Charlene Jendry, Dan Devaney, Dan Hunt, Don Winstel, Ernie Levine, Glenn Nickerson, Guy Nickerson, Jack Pidgeon, Jerry Borin, Joan Lunden, Larry Elliston, Matt Roberts, Nick Baird, Patty Neger, Rick Prebeg, Robin Holderman, Sally South, Steve Taylor, Suzi Rapp, Ted Altenburg, and Tom Stalf.

Finally, I'd like to thank **you** for picking up this book. I hope you enjoy reading about my WILD life and in the process you learn more about the fascinating animals that we are lucky to share a planet with. I've loved animals since I was a little boy, and they still captivate and amaze me to this day. I hope they do the same for you.